CORICANCHA

CORICANCHA

(GARDEN OF GOLD)

Discovery of Peru and
Conquest of the Inca Empire

by
A. F. Tschiffely

London Hodder & Stoughton Limited

THIS EDITION FIRST PUBLISHED, MAY, 1943
THIRD IMPRESSION · · FEBRUARY, 1949

Made and Printed in Great Britain by C. Tinling & Co., Ltd.,
Liverpool, London, and Prescot.

AUTHOR'S NOTE

DURING my extensive travels through Great Britain and the United States of America, I have been astonished by the general public's ignorance of South America, the people who live there, and of the continent's fascinating history. Although many books have been written about the conquest of Peru, I fear that most of these are much too long and involved to appeal to the average person who has neither time nor inclination to make a profound and exhaustive study of history. The story of Atahualpa's execution and of certain aspects of the fall of the *Inca* empire are known to most people, but, unfortunately, certain popular historians and writers, full of national or religious prejudice, have influenced their readers to believe that all *conquistadores* were merely gold-greedy cut-throats, and some authors have laboured under the illusion that the subjects of the *Incas* lived in an earthly paradise, and under a perfect and blissful social system which the Spaniards maliciously destroyed.

The fact that Indians were robbed and on occasions ruthlessly massacred, is not sufficient reason to point at the *conquistadores* with a finger of accusation, horror and scorn. Had it not been for deep religious conviction, and the firm belief that they had a holy mission to fulfil, these amazing men could never have accomplished what they did. Even the richest treasures taken to Spain by them, are insignificant and puny when one takes into consideration what, alone materially, they gave to the New World. Among many cereals, fruits, vegetables, shrubs, trees and plants imported into the Americas by the Spaniards, are wheat, oats, barley, oranges, lemons, grapes, figs, melons, bananas, pears, apricots, quinces, cherries, nuts, almonds, sugar cane, lettuce, spinach, certain beans, lentils, asparagus, rice, flax, clover, roses, carnations and numerous other flowers, oil-producing plants and trees. Until they introduced cows and goats, Indian babies consumed only milk of the human variety, no domestic milk-giving animals having been available. Besides the llama, the only domestic animal kept

5

by the Peruvian Indians was a bird of the duck species. Thanks to the Spaniards' vision, and thought for the future, Europe and the rest of the world benefited greatly by the discovery of the new lands across the ocean, maize, potatoes, the tomato, cacao (chocolate), many varieties of flowers, vegetables and medicines being exported from there.

Spain has always been a singular contradiction, but instead of attempting to explain this, many writers have found it much easier and more convenient to invent dark legends against this fascinating land. In connection with this I categorically state that the object of this book is not to vindicate the Spaniards, but to present an often badly distorted phase of history in its true light.

Among the writers and historians of whose works I have freely made use, are Herrera, Zaraté, Gomara, Montesinos, Garcilaso de la Vega, Sarmiento, Quintana and many others. I have mentioned only the names of the outstanding characters, in so doing endeavouring to avoid confusing the reader, and I have refrained from interrupting the narrative by moralizing or by psycho-analyzing the chief actors in this unique drama ; for surely their actions speak for themselves. If I have succeeded in giving a simple, yet vivid, scrupulously accurate and clear picture of the conquest of Peru and what led to it, and have produced a book both young and old people—no matter of what creed or nationality—can read with equal interest, my aim will have been achieved.

A. F. Tschiffely.

London, January, 1943.

I

AFTER a crusade that had lasted for well over seven and a half centuries, the last of the Moors and Jews had been driven out of the Iberian peninsula. Enthusiasm and religious fervour rose to fever pitch, for at last Spain was re-united in the Holy Catholic faith. Another reason for jubilation lay in the fact that, almost at the same time, Columbus returned home from his first voyage of discovery. True, he had set out in search of a short sea route to the Spice Islands which Marco Polo had described as forming the eastern extremity of India, and, at the time, no one knew that, instead, Columbus had discovered a new continent. This was in 1492, when spices were worth their weight in gold in Europe where such were in great demand to make the one-sided meat menu more palatable and digestive.

Not only Spain, but the whole of Europe gasped ; for so, after all, the few scholars—who, despite the vigorous opposition of the Church, had maintained that the world was round, and not just a disk with Jerusalem as its centre—were right : the world was round.

Seven years after Columbus' first voyage of discovery, Amerigo Vespucci, the Florentine navigator, reached the mainland of America, the continent being so named after him.*

At intervals, as subsequent expeditions returned to their home ports with glamorous tales of new discoveries, excitement and enthusiasm grew more and more, especially so when some of the ships brought new wonders hitherto

* The origin of the name " America " has been disputed on the following grounds : Vespuccio's Christian name was neither Amerigo nor Americo, but Albericus (Latin) or Alberico (Italian) ; Albert in English. Prior to 1506, all his documents are signed Albericus. In 1499, when Alonso de Ojeda discovered Central America, the Indians of Cumara, pointing at the land, called it " Amerriqua," meaning " Land of Wind." Among other Indian tribes the name for the mountains dividing Lake Nicaragua from the Mosquito coast was also " Amerriqua." Between the years 1510 and 1515 the name Amerriqua was already popular in Europe.

unknown in Europe. Greedy eyes gleamed, and the news spread like wildfire when, most sensational of all, some of the daring explorers brought ornaments and articles of . . . GOLD. The more material minded of the Spaniards who were not interested in the conversion of heathen to the Christian faith, saw attractive prospects beckoning them from across the sea. Here, indeed, were chances for men thirsting for adventure, fame and wealth.

From all parts of Spain they flocked towards different ports from which expeditions sailed to the Promised Land. Quite naturally, these were motley recruits, consisting of well-seasoned soldiers, hardened in different campaigns in Europe, down-and-outs, men disappointed with their homeland for various reasons, and in some cases criminals, for if such sailed across the seas for sufficient periods, their sentences were remitted. On the other hand, a number of Dons came forward, gallant soldiers and sailors, priests, humanitarian and otherwise, and even scholars who later wrote invaluable records, some of which have fortunately been preserved to be handed down to posterity.

From the earliest days Spaniards had despised commerce as a calling fit only for servile people ; a proud attitude which was greatly encouraged by the discovery of gold, or be it a direct way of attaining wealth.

The story of the first attempts to settle along the northern coast of South America and along the Atlantic coast of Central America is one of great daring, courage, untold sufferings and death through disease, shipwreck and bloody encounters with the natives. And it is a tale, too, of massacres, looting and of rivalry among leaders of expeditions ; ambitious men who struggled for supremacy and authority over the newly discovered lands.

In those days sea voyages involved great discomforts and hardships, and not infrequently dangers. In the tiny wooden vessels space was so limited that men were packed together in their quarters below the decks like so many sardines. Bunks there were none, neither light nor ventilation, and the sleeping quarters were so low that a person could not stand erect in them. On the decks it was impossible to walk about, for everywhere and in every direction were ropes, pulleys and a mass of other things which made movement as good as impossible. Sanitary arrangements were most primitive, and food was served out very sparingly, and usually was of such poor quality and badly cooked that modern bill-sticker's paste would have been eaten in preference. Mice, rats and insects, big and small, swarmed everywhere, and not infrequently the larger species of rodent were hunted and eaten as delicacies. The very limited and all-important supplies of fresh water soon became stagnant and stank. In addition to these discomforts there lurked the ever present danger of disease and sickness, the most common and dreaded among them being scurvy, which often decimated the crews, leaving these veritable " hell ships " badly undermanned.

In one such vessel a tall, strong young man managed to stow away. Very little is known about his early youth, except that his parents were poor *hidalgos**—of whom there was a fair sprinkling in Spain at the time. When old enough he became a sailor, and later settled in the West Indies where, assisted by Indians, he cultivated land granted to him by the Government. Full of debts, and anxious to escape from his creditors, he made up his mind to disappear and try his luck as a soldier of fortune, an occupation which promised to be more exciting and lucrative than farming. Being a debtor, he was not allowed to leave the West Indies, hence he sneaked on board a ship which carried a medley of soldiers and adventurers. When the stowaway was discovered, the vessel was already on the high seas, and the captain was so incensed that he threatened to put him ashore on the first island they might reach.

The young adventurer—whose name was Vasco Nuñez de Balboa—was, indeed, fortunate that the captain changed his mind, and forgave him ; for in those days expeditions

---

Hidalgo is derived from *hijo de algo*, meaning " son of someone."
In Portuguese : *fidalgo*.
Latin : *filius alicus*.

frequently took with them criminals and other malefactors, to be put ashore on islands where unknown Indians lived. If, at a later date, these human guinea pigs were found to be still alive, it meant that a landing could be made with relative safety, and if the criminals had been among the Indians long enough to learn their language, that interpreters would be available. On the other hand, if the poor wretches thus landed had disappeared, it was assumed that they had been killed, and the explorers knew that they had to proceed with caution if they ventured ashore. Several Spaniards used for this purpose were fortunate, falling among Indians who treated them as semi-divine beings ; but what happened to most of the others can easily be imagined. If a man thus landed was lucky enough to survive, it was customary to grant him a pardon.

The stowaway, Balboa, soon proved to be a great asset to the expedition, for in addition to being brave and intelligent, he knew how to earn everybody's respect and admiration. Thanks to these qualities and to his ambitious character, within a few years he became one of Spain's most famous captains.

It was during an eventful exploration along the shores of the Gulf of Darien that Balboa began to have a special regard for an adventurer-soldier who—like himself—was born in Estremadura, in Spain, a part which produced some of the most outstanding men who took part in the great drama of the conquest of the Americas. This man was Francisco Pizarro, whose name, for unlimited physical courage, tenacity and almost incredible achievements in the fields of exploration and conquest, was destined to become immortal.

At the time, he is thought to have been over forty years of age. Although controversy exists regarding the year of his birth, it can with a fair degree of accuracy be stated that he was born about the year 1470, and that he was an illegitimate child of Colonel Pizarro—who had served with some distinction in various European campaigns—and of Francisca Gonzales, a woman of poor and humble origin.

Born in the town of Trujillo, the baby Pizarro is said to have been abandoned by both parents, and according to some stories his mother dumped her offspring at the door of a church. Such was the predicament of the hapless infant, according to one tale, that, had it not been for a sow which suckled it, it would have perished miserably. Circumstances certainly did not improve for the foundling as he grew to be a boy, for young Pizarro had no one to look after his welfare, and it is believed that he never enjoyed the benefits of even the most elementary education. Having lived like a starving stray mongrel for some years, according to one account, his father eventually employed him as his swineherd. One day, due to accident or design, the pigs in his care escaped and were lost. Feeling guilty of neglect, and not daring to return home without his charges, Pizarro joined some tramps, and in their company made his way to Seville from where, together with other adventurers, he sailed for Santo Domingo (Haiti), trusting that Fortune would be kinder to him there.

Whatever truth there may or may not be in these legends of his early life, it is certain that he had no reason to feel homesick, or to shed tears of sorrow when the last view of his native land slowly faded out of sight after his ship had left the mouth of the River Guadalquivir, on its way towards the west, across the Atlantic Ocean.

Little or nothing is known about his activities in the next few years, but we hear about him again in about 1510, when already well over thirty years of age, as a trusted captain he took part in the expedition of which Balboa also was a member.

Alonso de Ojeda, the commander of this expedition, proved to be one of the most unfortunate men in the whole history of exploration, misfortunes and disasters constantly besetting his path. It was under him that both Pizarro and Balboa first rose to command men.

After hostile Indians had forced Ojeda to retreat from Northern Colombia, he decided to set sail and seek the mouth of the River Darien (also called Atrato) where, according to rumours, gold was said to abound. Having failed to find what he was seeking, but still determined to go on with his quest, he founded a colony in the region. Soon, however, provisions ran short, and, to make things even worse, Indians constantly attacked the white men with their dreaded poisoned arrows, giving them not a moment's rest. By degrees hunger and exhaustion so weakened the Spaniards that their only hope of salvation lay in the arrival of an expected but delayed relief ship. At last, when mutiny threatened to break out, Ojeda decided to sail back to Haiti in search of relief.

Having put Pizarro in charge of the sixty men who were to remain in the colony, he left after having promised to return within fifty days. Losing his way, however, Ojeda's long series of misfortunes came to an end when, upon landing in Cuba, he was killed by Indians.

In the meantime, ignorant of this disaster, Pizarro and the fever-stricken and starving men under his command waited anxiously. Intolerable damp heat, terrific rain storms and clouds of mosquitoes and gnats tormented the men who began to die, one by one. Fifty agonizing days passed, and still no sign of relief. At last Pizarro decided that the only salvation lay in returning to the coastal regions of Colombia where, though the natives had been hostile on the occasion of the expedition's previous visit, the climate was not so bad, and food fairly abundant.

The problem which now confronted Pizarro was how to cross the Gulf of Darien in the only two boats that were available, both being too small to hold sixty men. After some deliberation he came to the conclusion that the only way to overcome this difficulty was to wait until death should reduce their numbers sufficiently to make embarkation possible. In due time, when this had occurred, and the miserable little band of sick and starved Spaniards reached the open sea, terrific storms battered them mercilessly, tossing the boats about like peas in a pod. Eventually, shortly after they had managed to take refuge in the port which now is Cartagena, two vessels were sighted at the horizon. As it turned out, these were the relief ships hapless Ojeda had gone in search of.

Their commander, Fernandez de Enciso, having learned what had happened, took over the command of Pizarro and his men, and, despite their protests, insisted on returning to the abandoned colony near the River Darien.

As bad luck would have it, the two ships—in which were brought one hundred and fifty new men, a number of horses, arms and a good supply of provisions—ran into a severe storm during which the larger was wrecked, but although almost its entire cargo was lost, the men managed to save themselves. Upon reaching the abandoned colony it was found that houses and everything that had been left there had been destroyed by the Indians who lost no time in again harassing the Spaniards, who were given no rest, day or night.

When even the most valiant soldiers began to despair, one of their number stepped forward and told his companions that, some years previously, he had been to a region, not far along that coast, where the Indians did not use poison on their arrows, and where food was plentiful. The man who spoke was Balboa.

His listeners, who had given up all hope of salvation, took new courage, and after a weary peregrination the expedition reached the place to which Balboa had referred, and there founded a new settlement. Many of the men who looked upon him as their saviour, and greatly admired his bravery, initiative and other qualities, were so discontented with Enciso that they revolted against him, and appointed Balboa as their new leader. Though Enciso still had a fair following, his supporters were in a minority, a state of affairs which led to discontent and disputes.

Though a considerable quantity of gold had been obtained from the Indians, and this was shared out fairly among the Spaniards, quarrels among them continued until, one day, gun-fire was heard in the direction of the gulf where two ships were then discovered. Smoke signals having been exchanged, the vessels made for the shore where the new arrivals told a long and sad story about their recent adventures and misfortunes. At their head was Diego de Nicuesa, whom the Spanish Government had appointed to act as Governor to all the newly discovered regions along the Atlantic coast of Panama and the Gulf of Darien. Originally he had set out from Haiti with five ships and eight hundred well armed men, but accidents, disease, fights with Indians and many other calamities had reduced this number to a mere handful.

Considering that Balboa and his men had suffered untold hardships, and had fought many fierce and bloody battles against Indians to gain a solid foothold where they were, it is not surprising that they resented the appointment of a Governor who, to make things even worse, happened to be a tyrant.

Balboa, now supported by Enciso and his partisans, cut short all arguments with Nicuesa, and, despite his protests that his appointment as Governor was legitimate, put him on board a small vessel and told him to report at the Court. The last seen of the ship and the skeleton crew of eighteen men who manned it, was when it disappeared at the horizon.

After further disagreements and quarrels with Enciso, Balboa also expelled him from the colony.

On his own once more, he made a number of minor explorations, and during one of these, along the Atlantic side of the Isthmus of Panama, he and his party were astonished to meet two Spaniards who were living among the Indians, naked, their bodies painted green with a vegetable dye. The two men informed Balboa that, a year previously, they had been put ashore for crimes they had committed, and that they had had the good fortune to fall among friendly Indians whose Chief had presented them with land and even wives. Among other things they informed him that in the region he had reached, gold was common, and that there was an abundance of food which he and his party badly needed at the time.

Shortly after these events, Balboa and his men were the

guests of a very friendly Indian Chief who presented his
white visitors with seventy slaves, and, what pleased them
much more, with a considerable amount of gold, chiefly in
the shape of ornaments. Many of these were immediately
smelted down, and later the ingots were distributed among
the officers and men, one fifth being put aside for the King
of Spain, according to the law.

During the share-out, a dispute arose among the Spaniards,
tempers became hot, and it seemed as if the loudly shouted
words of threat were about to lead to bloodshed. The
Indian Chief, who was standing near, attentively watching,
suddenly realized that gold was the cause of the trouble
among his white guests. Stepping forward, he overthrew
the improvised balance on which the metal was being
weighed out. Then, placing himself between the quarrelling
parties, he spoke to them through one of the two Spanish
renegades who now acted as interpreter.

" Why," he asked, " fight for so little ? If it is gold that
made you leave your homeland to disturb other people,
I will tell you of a land where your desires will be fulfilled. But, if you proceed there, you must be stronger in
number, for you will have to fight against powerful kings
who will vigorously defend their domains. First, you will
meet a Chief who is very rich in gold, a Chief who lives at a
distance of six suns from here. Later you will come to a sea
which lies in this direction." Here the speaker pointed
towards the south, before continuing, " You will find
people there who sail in ships not much smaller than yours.
These people are so rich that they eat and drink out of
plates and vessels made of the metal you would seem to
covet so much."

To this speech the Spaniards listened with open mouths
and staring eyes, for what they heard surpassed the wildest
dreams that had made them leave their homes. All were
convinced that they were at the very gate of India and that
wealth and glory would soon be theirs. Balboa could see
himself returning to Spain in triumph, having discovered
the short route to the Land of Spices which Columbus and

others had been unable to find. And, in addition, with gold . . . much gold.

With the least possible delay, a messenger was sent to the West Indies to ask for reinforcements. In order to gain favour, and to speed up matters, Balboa remitted a considerable amount of gold to the king, as well as a number of presents in the shape of golden ornaments, to be given to the Governor of the West Indies, and to some of his friends. Unhappily, however, the ship in which the messenger travelled, was wrecked, and both he and the treasure were lost.

Time passed, and still no news nor reinforcements arrived. At last Balboa thought of making the voyage to the West Indies himself, and from there to proceed to Spain, in order to report to the king the discoveries he had made so far, and thus gain favour with him. However, the officers and soldiers refused to lose so excellent and well-liked a leader, and therefore begged him not to leave them.

At this critical stage two ships laden with provisions and men arrived, and to everybody's joy with the welcome news that the authorities in the West Indies had appointed Balboa Governor of the regions he had discovered. In a letter written by a friend, he was informed that his old rival, Enciso, whom he had ousted from the colony in the Darien, had returned to Spain where he was busy accusing him of all sorts of villainies, including usurpation against the Crown.

This information only served to stimulate Balboa's desire and urge to make new and even greater discoveries. Despite the fact that he badly needed more soldiers, he then and there decided to seek the ocean and the rich land he had heard about. If he succeeded in his enterprise, the king's gratitude would be his, and whatever accusations Enciso made against him, they would be of no avail.

Accompanied by one hundred and ninety soldiers--most of them clad in cumbersome suits of armour—and a thousand native porters, put at his disposal by a friendly Indian chief, Balboa set out into the dense Panamanian jungle. Only here and there beams of sunlight penetrated through the forest, rendered twilight by a mass of lianas and parasitical plants, engaged in the silent though deadly struggle for light. Cursing as they hacked their way through this labyrinth, the soldiers slowly advanced, followed by the naked savages who groaned under the weight of their loads. Some days the expedition barely progressed two miles through this dripping and steaming inferno, a great part of which consisted of malarial swamps. Torrential rains, oppressive damp heat, wild beasts, deadly snakes, clouds of tantalizing mosquitoes : in fact, nature itself seemed to have conspired to repulse the expedition. Yet, despite the incredible hardships and dangers, the white men forged ahead into the unknown.

A number of wild rushing rivers and numerous streams with their harmless-looking though treacherous bottoms, consisting of deep layers of soft mud of decayed tropical vegetation, were crossed on roughly improvised rafts, or by means of dangerously swaying foot-bridges, constructed for the purpose. Along the banks of these streams and on the edges of swamps, basked alligators and crocodiles, motionless, like so many mud-covered trunks of trees ; but waiting to snatch up any member of the expedition who might be unfortunate enough to fall into the water. During the night, sleepers were often startled by the ugly gurgling snarls of prowling jaguars and panthers in search of prey. On such occasions, for a while, the silence of the jungle was broken by an infernal concert made on the roof of the forest, by monkeys, parrots and many other animals and birds whose slumbers had been disturbed. Then again, all was silent, but occasionally a terrific crash could be heard as an ancient giant of the forest fell to the ground, pulled down under the weight of lianas and masses of creepers. Occasionally, also, a long spell of silence would be broken by the harsh cry of a nocturnal bird of prey, or by a long whistling hiss as an alligator in a nearby swamp rose to the surface of the water to expel its foul-smelling breath from its lungs.

Every day the expedition pushed steadily ahead until a mountain range was reached. Nearing its summit, Balboa called a halt, and went ahead, alone, to survey the lay of the land.

Below, the roof of the jungle appeared like a billowing sea, but when the solitary man looked to the south, he beheld a sight in the distance, which made him fall on his knees, and with extended arms give thanks to his God. Arising, he called and beckoned to his companions below to come to his side. Upon reaching their leader, and having seen the wonder he indicated, there were wild scenes of rejoicing which mystified the naked Indian porters who looked on from below.

This happened on the 25th of September, 1513, when Balboa had the first glimpse of the sea the friendly Indian chief had mentioned. The first part of his information had proved to be correct, and now none of the Spaniards doubted that the final goal, India, could not be far off.

The first scenes of jubilation over, Balboa assembled his men, and, having named the newly discovered ocean the " Great South Sea " (to-day known as Pacific Ocean) he addressed them in words befitting so momentous an occasion. The bearded, lean and grimy warriors, their armour rusted by steam and tropical rains, must have been a strange sight on that mountain top, with the deep-blue glimmering surface of the ocean in the distance.

Presently the joyful Spaniards cut down a tree, and having shaped it into a cross, erected it on a pile of rocks. This done, Balboa called Pizarro to his side, and ordered him and two soldiers to go ahead and reconnoitre the forests in the direction of the sea.

A few days later this tiny advance guard reached the coast where one of its members, a soldier named Alonso Martin, seeing an Indian canoe that happened to be tied near the place where he stood, jumped into it. After a while the rising tide reached the canoe, so that thence-forward Martin was able to boast that he was the first Spaniard to have been afloat on the newly discovered ocean.

Soon after this, Balboa and a number of his men came out of the forest, and descended towards the beach where all sat down to rest while waiting for the tide to rise still further.

Presently Balboa, clad in full armour, in one hand holding his drawn sword, and in the other a Spanish flag on which was painted the image of the Virgin, waded out into the waters and in a loud voice proclaimed : " Long live the mighty and powerful kings of Castile. In their name I take possession of these seas and regions ; and if any prince, be he Christian or infidel, claims any right to these, I am ready to contradict him, and to defend them."

For the next few days Balboa reconnoitred the surrounding land, but not without a number of brisk fights with different Indian tribes. The Spaniards always struck quickly and fiercely, and therefore none of these encounters lasted long, superior arms making resistance impossible. On several occasions, when a volley was fired, the terrified natives immediately fled into the forest.

Balboa proved to be as good a diplomatist as he was a soldier, for, after having defeated his enemies, he always extended a hand of reconciliation and friendship to them, and invariably the chieftains were only too glad to accept it. Here and there—through the medium of interpreters—the Spaniards again heard further tales about a rich land in the south, and in one place the Indians even described strange animals which they said were used as beasts of burden by the people in that land. In order to make their description more realistic, the natives drew the shapes of these animals in the sand, and the eagerly watching Spaniards took these drawings to represent a kind of deer. In point of fact the Indians' stories and descriptions were true, and their drawings more or less correct, for the animals they had in mind were llamas which had never yet been seen by white men.

What naturally most delighted the Spaniards was when Indians presented them with much gold. It had not taken the natives long to realize that the acquisition of this metal was the white men's greatest desire. When, in one place along the coast, a chieftain presented Balboa with many fine pearls, he immediately asked where these came from.

Pointing to some islands, the chief said that masses of even finer specimens were to be found there. When Balboa expressed his desire to visit the islands, the chief warned him that the season was not propitious for venturing to sea in canoes ; but eventually, when Balboa insisted, a number of canoes set out. A terrific storm and furious seas nearly cost the reckless Spaniards their lives. However, their luck held out once more, and all managed to save themselves, though they returned to the mainland completely exhausted, and without their clothes and armour.

Four and a half months after having marched into the Panamanian jungle to discover the " Great South Sea," Balboa returned to the colony in the Darien where he was given a triumphant reception. The sight of so much gold and so many pearls made hopes for the future soar high, and no one doubted that, at last, the gates of India had been reached.

Laden with much treasure, many interesting trophies and a few Indians, a ship was sent to Spain in charge of two especially appointed men who were to give a detailed account at the Court of what had been accomplished and discovered.

Upon landing in Spain, the two messengers were informed that Balboa's old rival, Enciso, had made so many accusations against their leader that the king had decided to send a Governor to take charge of the colony in the Darien, together with a number of newly appointed officials, among them Enciso.

When Balboa's two messengers appeared before the king, and he and his courtiers heard the tales about the new discoveries, and saw the dazzling treasures from Panama, everybody present became wild with enthusiasm. Whatever evil stories had been believed about Balboa were at once forgotten, and he was given the title of *adelantado*, that is, Governor of the sea he had discovered, as well as of any lands he might discover in the future, and the king at once ordered fifteen ships and two thousand men to be equipped and sent to the Darien.

News about the recent discoveries spread through Spain like wildfire, and according to one story, gold was said to be picked up in nets in Panama, which was named " Golden Castile." No wonder then that noblemen down on their luck, and adventurers of every description and rank struggled to become members of the expedition which was making ready to sail.

Sixty-nine days after the armada had set out from Spain, the destination was safely reached. The new Governor—a thoroughly unpleasant aged Don named Pedrarias—had a bit of a shock when he met Balboa, whom he expected to be living in luxury and pomp, surrounded by a veritable court, and attended to by many slaves. Instead, he found him very simply dressed, quietly giving instructions to a few Indians who were busy putting a palm leaf roof on his modest house.

The new Governor had only been in Panama a short time when, suspecting that Balboa refused to reveal where all the gold was to be found, began a series of intrigues against him.

The noblemen and soldiers who had crossed the Atlantic Ocean with visions of soon becoming wealthy men, now realized that where they had landed gold was not to be gathered in nets, as some had believed on sailing from Spain. Old settlers in the colony laughed, and sarcastically told the newcomers that the nets were hard work, fatigue and danger. In the wake of disillusionment came dissatisfaction and when fever and sickness began to take their toll, despondency was cast over the men who now cursed themselves for having left their homes. Then supplies began to run short, and, to hasten the inevitable, the main storehouse caught fire, most of its contents being destroyed by the flames. Starving noblemen and soldiers, their clothes in rags and tatters, trudged from hut to hut, begging for bits of maize biscuit, or any morsel the more fortunate early settlers might be willing to part with. Seven hundred men died in one month, but a number managed to find accommodation in a ship which sailed back to Spain, whilst others, terrified of the fever, " which turned victims as yellow as the gold they had dreamt of," sought refuge on a nearby island. A number of desperate soldiers invaded Indian territory where they looted, and in doing so antagonized the natives who, in retaliation, attacked the colony.

Taking advantage of the Indians' hostility, Pedrarias accused Balboa of having instigated this new trouble. An astute priest, who on former occasions had intervened on Balboa's behalf, succeeded in reconciling the two parties, and he even managed to bring about the marriage between one of the Governor's daughters and him. This feat of diplomacy accomplished, it looked as if old quarrels and hates would soon be forgotten.

At about this time a ship arrived from Spain, with orders from the king to help Balboa with further explorations. These glad tidings once more made hopes rise in the colony, and Balboa again crossed the isthmus to the Pacific side where he built two ships to make further explorations. After having surmounted many difficulties in the construction of the vessels, they were successfully launched, and stores were being loaded when a messenger arrived to inform Balboa that the Governor required his presence in the colony. Accordingly he set out, and upon reaching his destination, to his astonishment, he was arrested. and thrown into prison.

Pedrarias, his envious father-in-law, accused him of rebellion and treachery, and after a short one-sided trial had the prisoner declared guilty. Although his many admirers protested, he and four other unfortunate men were beheaded in the public square which was filled with a crowd of indignant and weeping people.

Thus, at the age of forty-two, Balboa, one of Spain's greatest sons, met with fortitude an untimely death.

II

IT seemed as if the death of Balboa had left the colony in the Darien without a man to take his place, and that, no one being willing to risk money in sponsoring costly expeditions, the tales about a rich land in the south would be put aside as mere legends.

The Pacific side of the isthmus being healthier, the city of Panama was founded, and the seat of the government was shifted to the new settlement. By this time most of the Indian tribes were hostile towards the Spaniards, and therefore some severe fighting took place during a few minor expeditions organized by Governor Pedrarias. No one dreamt that among the soldiers there was one who would make even greater discoveries than had been made by Balboa. This tall, quiet and somewhat gloomy looking officer, who had already passed his middle age, was Francisco Pizarro. So far, although he had proved to be brave, daring and trustworthy, he had shown no particular ambition to rise to eminence, nor had he showed any signs that in him smouldered the stuff that makes great soldiers and leaders of men. Perhaps his reticence was due to his lowly birth, for, as a foundling of the streets, he may have found it difficult to come out of his shell, and to attempt to place himself level with noblemen of whom there were a number in Panama.

Pizarro had been in the service of the king for some fourteen years, and all he had received as a reward for the many sufferings and dangers endured, was a small tract of land near Panama, and a few Indians to help him cultivate it. He was biding his time when stories about Cortez' amazing discoveries and conquests in Mexico revived interest in exploration in the colony. In a fair-sized ship, an expedition sailed from the isthmus to investigate the coast towards the south, but, as the leader suffered from ill-health, he soon returned to Panama. From Indians who lived near a wide river, some of the explorers had heard about powerful monarchs who were said to rule over prosperous lands, far away in the south. These tales now rapidly spread through the colony ; but men shrank back when they considered how expensive and dangerous an expedition to that mysterious land would be. If the monarchs about whom the Indians had spoken, had at their disposal the redoubtable armies, the fame of which had spread far beyond the borders of those tempting lands, a very strong and well armed force would have to be assembled before setting out with reasonable hopes of success. This would entail great expense, and as no one appeared to be willing to gamble to such an extent, men in the colony just talked, and it looked as if the matter would be left at that.

When the sensational news of Magellan's circumnavigation of the globe (1519–1522) became known in Panama, settlers there realized that they were not at the gates of India, as hitherto they had thought.

For us, to-day, it is difficult to imagine what effect the homecoming of the survivors of Magellan's party must have had on people in Spain, and Europe in general. So, after all, the world must be round, and not a disk; for this globe had been circumnavigated, and here were the men who had done it, alive and well to tell the amazing stories about their travels and adventures. Men of science nodded, theologians scratched their heads, and people failed to comprehend. If Magellan's ships had been at the " bottom " of the world, why had they not fallen off into space? What land could this be that lay between Europe and India? A continent? If so, where did it begin and end? Surely the Patagonian giants and the savages of Tierra del Fuego about whom the sailors told many hair-raising stories, must be beings of the devil, for they lived in a land at the bottom of the world where trees must grow upside down, and snow and rain fall in the opposite direction. It all must have sounded crazy, but yet, here were the men who had accomplished the seemingly impossible : they had sailed round the world.*

Magellan's voyage no less bewildered the Spaniards in Panama, for, as far as they were concerned, India had

---

* Magellan himself did not complete the voyage. He was killed in a fight with natives in one of the Phillipine Islands. After his death Del Cano took charge of the expedition. Of five ships in which Magellan had originally set out from Spain, only one returned to its home port. The name " Great South Sea," which Balboa had given the ocean he had discovered, Magellan changed to " Pacific Ocean," for whilst he crossed it, the waters were calm, or " pacific."

suddenly moved very far away, and now they were intrigued, more than ever before, about the rumoured existence of a land in the south ; the elusive land where gold was said to abound.

It was then that two men took the initiative, and, having obtained permission from the Governor to explore the south, set to work, planning and organizing an expedition. The two men were Pizarro and Diego de Almagro, old friends who had explored and fought together for a number of years.

Like Pizarro, Almagro was said to have been a foundling. Very little is known about his early youth, but he is thought to have been a few years older than his friend. Long experience, natural aptitude and courage had shaped him into an excellent and gallant soldier, and though he was inclined to be quick tempered, he was well liked by the men under him.

At the time when he and Pizarro made their plans for an expedition to the south, there lived in Panama a somewhat eccentric priest who acted as schoolmaster in the colony. Hernando de Luque, as he was named, had previously indulged in several extravagant schemes which had earned for him the nickname of " *Hernando el Loco* " ; that is, " Mad Hernando." However, like so many who are thought to be mad by their less enterprising and thinking fellow men, Luque proved to be a very astute business man.

Ably assisted by this priest—who acted as treasurer and secretary—one of Balboa's old ships was reconditioned, provisions, arms and equipment were bought, and when preparations were complete, eighty men and four horses sailed towards the unknown. Pizarro and Almagro staked all their possessions in this apparently foolhardy enterprise, but it was " Mad Hernando " who supplied most of the money.

Before Pizarro set out, it was arranged that his partner should follow in another ship, as soon as this could be fitted out and manned ; not easy a matter because but few men were willing to risk their lives in so daring an enterprise. Had the Spaniards possessed what is common knowledge among modern navigators, they would have postponed their departure for a more favourable season, for November is one of the worst months in the year for undertaking sea voyages near Panama. Frequently, terrific gales sweep up from the south, rains are torrential, and at such times the whole of nature appears to be in a wild turmoil. However, in those days of search and discovery, explorers did not know this, and therefore Pizarro and his party were well on their way when the elements unleashed their furies.

Buffeted about by mountainous seas, and guided only by very vague information gathered from members of the expedition which previously had sailed some distance along the coast towards the south, Pizarro managed to reach the mouth of the River Biru.

When the weary men landed to explore the adjacent country, they found that all the Indian huts had been abandoned. Incessant rains poured down on the soldiers whose suits of armour were anything but suited for such a vile climate. Where there was forest or jungle, the vegetation was so dense that they had to hack their way through, as in vain they sought fruit or game to alleviate the pangs of hunger which tormented them, for provisions on board the ship had dwindled to such an extent that rations had been reduced to only a handful of maize per man. The many treacherous streams were overflowing, inundating great stretches of this dismal land, parts of which consisted of pestilent swamps. Not only the Indians, but even the animals, birds and reptiles appeared to have migrated to more hospitable parts for the duration of the rainy season.

Forced by hunger, the Spaniards weighed anchor, and once more set out to sea, hoping that soon they would come to better regions. Every kind of physical discomfort and the constant perils of sailing along an unknown coast where gales and turbulent seas threatened to sink their tiny vessel at any moment, began to make even the bravest men lose heart. When torrential rains ceased to fall for brief spells, and land could be seen, it appeared to be similar to the parts along the banks of the River Biru. In the distance, shrouded in vaporous clouds, mountains could be discerned, but everywhere else anxious eyes surveyed the region, it appeared to be covered with dense jungle or swamps, and deserted by man and beast. Pizarro made valiant efforts to cheer his men, but his promises that soon they would reach a land where their hopes would be fulfilled, and their sufferings rewarded, fell on deaf ears, for the only desire the starvelings now had was to return to Panama ; their only hope of survival.

At a suitable place, another landing was made, but again the country proved to be uninhabited, and completely bare of any kind of food such as the Spaniards needed desperately by this time ; in fact, the outlook for the immediate future was so bad that it was decided to send the ship back to the Pearl Islands, near Panama, in search of provisions. For this Pizarro picked a few sailors whom he put in charge of a man he trusted greatly. The plight of the expedition was such that when the ship set out on its urgent mission, the only food available on board was a dry cowhide, and some bitter inner-leaves of palms that had been cut along the shore. Pizarro and the main body of his small army remained where they were, hoping to be able to keep alive until relief should arrive.

Shelters were improvised, and as no other food could be found, roots of different plants, and the buds of palm leaves were collected by men who were still strong enough to go in search of such, for starvation had so weakened many of the others that they lay down to await death to relieve them of their sufferings. Pizarro was everywhere: seeking food, distributing what he found among the most needy, consoling the dying and sick, and attending to their wants as far as circumstances permitted. Twenty-seven men perished miserably, and most of the others lay in agonies, their bodies horribly swelled up with poisonous roots of plants they had eaten. More than six weeks had passed since the relief ship had sailed, and still there was no sign of it. Seeing a column of smoke in the distance, a few men whose strength still permitted, set out in its direction, soon to be lost from sight in the dense tropical forest. Opening for themselves a track through the dripping green labyrinth, they finally came to a clearing where, to their joy, they saw a number of huts. Upon catching sight of the strange white men, the Indians fled in terror, but two were taken prisoner. Like a pack of hungry wolves the Spaniards then rushed into the huts where they found a fair quantity of maize and other foodstuffs.

Thanks to an Indian interpreter brought from Panama, it was possible to interview the prisoners, who again spoke about a rich land in the south. What with this information, and a fair supply of food robbed from the natives, the Spaniards' spirits rose as they retraced their steps towards the coast. Upon approaching their destination they were met by a messenger who brought the welcome news that the relief ship had arrived, laden with many supplies. Overjoyed, the men hastened to the shore where a lively scene of jubilation ensued, as old friends, saviours and the saved, met.

A sorry sight the little colony of men presented. The sick lay in their roughly improvised shelters, and even the fittest looked like so many skeletons. Their armour and clothes were falling to bits with the constant rains, and most of the poor wretches' bodies were covered with ugly painful sores.

The crew of the relief ship, too, had a long tale of woe and misery to tell, for its members had fared but little better on their voyage to the Pearl Islands than had their comrades on that inhospitable shore.

A few days later, slowly and cautiously, Pizarro's ship once more nosed towards the south along the unknown coast. The humidity of the atmosphere was insufferable, and frequently terrific storms threatened to put an end to the expedition. During landings made here and there, the Spaniards had a number of fierce encounters with natives, and in one settlement that was raided to obtain much needed food, they were horrified to find human hands and feet stewing in a pot. During one of these fights, several soldiers were killed, and Pizarro himself had a narrow escape from death.

Storms, and one misfortune after another, so impeded the expedition's progress that, after weeks, only about one hundred and fifty miles of the coast had been explored. Pizarro's ship had been battered about so severely that it badly needed repairing, and as, furthermore, provisions were again running low, he at last reluctantly decided to return to Panama.

. . . .

In the meantime Almagro had been very active in the colony. According to plan, he had managed to fit out a small vessel, and, after a great deal of trouble and persuasion, some sixty soldiers and sailors were hired. Not aware that Pizarro was on his way back to Panama, Almagro sailed to join forces with him, it having been arranged that his partner should leave signals near the shore, such as heaps of rocks, wooden crosses, blazed trees and the like.

Here and there Almagro found evidence that landings had been made, and when he came to a place where signs were still visible that a serious fight had taken place, everybody was convinced that Pizarro and all his men must have been killed. Accordingly, Almagro sadly sailed back towards Panama, but to his great joy, before reaching his destination, he overtook his friend who had made a landing before reaching the colony. The chief reason for this was because Pizarro hated the idea of returning without having succeeded in his quest of the " Land of Gold," and as the Governor had frequently shown that he did not like him, he had ample reasons for not being anxious to meet his superior. Therefore, it was decided that Almagro should go to Panama alone, whilst Pizarro waited where he was.

The Governor, more surly and disagreeable than ever, argued that Pizarro's folly had already cost many lives the colony could ill afford to lose at the time, and that the search of the " Land of Gold " merely amounted to a wild goose chase, led by an irresponsible upstart. Fortunately the victim of the governor's anger and scorn had been wise enough to keep away, or else, in all probability, his plans and dreams would have come to an end, there and then.

Thanks to Father Luque, the Governor was gradually talked over, and finally he agreed that, provided Almagro was placed on a level with Pizarro, as far as the command of the expedition was concerned, he would give permission for a new attempt to reach the rumoured El Dorado to be made. The foul-tempered Governor insisted on this because he now saw a chance of annoying Pizarro who was held in great esteem by his men, but there being no alternative, Father Luque accepted this spiteful condition. Evidently the unenterprising old man had no faith in the outcome of the proposed expedition to the south, for, on the principle that one bird in the hand is worth two in the bush, he relinquished all claims to profits that might accrue from it, provided that he be paid a thousand gold *pesos*.

A few months after this agreement had been made, the Spanish government sent a new Governor to Panama. Pedrarias still continued to hold a kind of secondary position to his successor, and in this capacity he intrigued and squabbled until, a few years later, to everybody's relief and satisfaction, he died.

Thanks to the indefatigable Luque's efforts, events were moving better and more swiftly now. Pedrarias having been superseded, Pizarro left his place of retreat, and travelled to Panama where much had yet to be done in organizing a new and stronger expeditionary force, with its equipment, stores and other requisites.

The first and most important item was to find the necessary money, for by this time funds were running low, and an expedition on a larger scale was bound to entail heavy expenditure. Again, thanks to Father Luque, a lawyer came forward, and put twenty thousand *pesos* in gold bars into the enterprise. This important point reached, a contract was drawn up, and eventually signed by the priest, Pizarro and Almagro. This memorable document begins as follows : " In the Name of the most Holy Trinity, Father, Son and Holy Ghost, three Persons and only one true God, and of the most Holy Virgin our Lady, we form this company." The three partners pledged themselves equally to divide among themselves any land they might discover, as well as gold, precious stones, jewels or any other valuables.

Fantastic as the facts are, here were two men, about to set out in search of an empire, about the existence of which they had only heard rumours from different savages. This empire, all its people and fabled riches had already been divided on paper, the document and the signatures affixed to it having full validity as far as the Crown of Castile was concerned. Despite the fact that neither Pizarro nor Almagro had the faintest notion how large a land lay in the then unknown south, in drawing up this astonishing contract, the rumoured land was named " Peru ".*

During Pizarro's previous expedition, so many men lost their lives, that now it was necessary to enlist new recruits. The majority of the old campaigners placed such faith in their leader and in his enterprise that most of them were ready to follow him wherever he might go. However, the enlisting of new men was a very different matter, for people in Panama considered the " expedition to Peru " to be the folly of madmen. Fortunately, a number of poor soldiers and adventurers who were stranded in the settlement debated among themselves that, in misery as they lived, it would be just as well for them to make a reckless gamble, for where they were at the time, starvation stared them in the face. Accordingly, they came forward in groups, until

* It is thought that this name originated from the River Biru, situated some distance south of Panama.

According to an anecdote (told by Garcilaso de la Vega) the name " Peru " originated when the Spaniards caught an Indian whom they interviewed by means of signs. Thinking that they wanted to know his name, he said " Beru," and when his captors pointed towards the south where the mouth of a river could be seen, he replied, " Pelu ", meaning " river " in his dialect. It is also said that the name " Peru " took its origin from a small island in this neignbourhood, by the natives called Pelua or Petu.

In speaking and writing, many Spaniards find it difficult to differentiate between the letters " B " and " V ". The writing of Indian names and words was no easy matter, certain sounds having no equivalent in the Spanish language. Hence, " Biru ", " Viru ", " Pelu ", and " Peru ", may quite easily have had the same origin.

Pizarro's force numbered about one hundred and sixty men. Two ships were fitted out, a few horses were purchased, and when these, as well as ammunition and general supplies had been put on board, the expedition set out. Some men in Panama shook their heads, and other stay-at-homes laughed, for even if the stories about the " Land of Gold " were true, what could Pizarro and Almagro do against powerful armies with only a handful of very indifferently armed men ?

III

GUIDED by a skilful navigator who had been with Pizarro on his previous explorations, the two ships sailed towards the south, winds and good weather favouring their progress. Upon reaching a point where the land appeared to be better than in the parts explored during the preceding voyages, it was decided to land near the mouth of a river where the sight of fleeing natives indicated that the region was inhabited. In a settlement the Spaniards were delighted to find a fair quantity of gold and much needed food. Pizarro made up his mind to wait where he was, together with the main force, whilst his navigator, in one ship, should reconnoitre the coast further to the south, and Almagro, in the other, return to Panama to fetch further supplies of men, and as many horses as he could buy with the gold recently found.

Shortly after the two men had sailed on their respective missions, Pizarro set out to explore the land along the banks of the river. In one of the settlements discovered, the reconnoitring party captured a few natives who said that further inland, beyond the mountains, was a country where the climate was good, and food abundant. On the strength of this information, Pizarro and his men set out enthusiastically, soon to find themselves in dense forests where masses of entwined creepers and lianas made progress extremely difficult. Gigantic trees, some of which appeared to tower up to the very clouds, made the Spaniards wonder if what they saw was real, or if it was part of a strange dream. On the roof of the awe-inspiring forests screeched flocks of parrots, parakeets and brightly plumaged macaws. Monkeys swung and leapt from tree to tree, at the same time angrily chattering at the invaders of their domain. The daring explorers had to advance with great caution, lest they were bitten by snakes which abounded in this green hell. Where the rays of the sun penetrated through the mass of foliage, humming birds darted from flower to flower, and large, brightly coloured butterflies, like flaming jewels, fluttered. Masses of tantalizing insects buzzed round the men whose bodies were covered with ticks and other parasites which crawl on the leaves in the thick underbrush, or drop down on their victims, attracted by the smell of blood. To make things even worse, hostile Indians occasionally attacked the fever stricken and starving Spaniards, who but rarely caught even as much as a glimpse of their cunning enemies whose arrows sometimes found a chink or opening in the armour. Despite swarms of deadly cannibal fish the explorers successfully crossed rivers, streams and swamps, and finally reached hilly parts where the chills of night made bodies shiver horribly. Dauntless Pizarro made superhuman efforts to cheer his men ; but promises of a golden future now fell on deaf ears.

At last he gave orders for the return towards the river where his two ships were to meet him. After an agonizing march the coast was reached ; but not a sign of either ship. Even the bravest in the miserable band of starvelings began to despair, when the vessel commanded by the navigator appeared, almost immediately to be followed from the opposite direction by that which had been sent to Panama for supplies and reinforcements.

Whilst the famished men eagerly devoured the food Almagro had brought from the colony, they listened to the encouraging news he had to tell. His arrival in Panama had coincided with that of a batch of soldier-adventurers from Spain, and most of these, upon seeing the gold he had

C

brought with him from the south, immediately offered their services. Thanks to Father Luque's efforts, the new Governor had put no obstacles in the way, and therefore, as soon as stores and a few horses had been purchased, Almagro had once more sailed to join Pizarro, taking with him his new recruits.

Old campaigners and newcomers next listened with bated breath to the navigator's account of his exploits and amazing discoveries made during his cruise along the hitherto unexplored coast further towards the south.

According to his story, he had been at sea for a few days when he discovered a small inhabited island to which he gave the name of " Gallo Island ". Proceeding on his way, he was approaching the equator when, in a bay, he beheld a sight that filled him with curiosity, for what he and his crew gazed at in the distance, proved to them that, at least one important part of the story the friendly Darien Indian chief had told Balboa some years before, must be true. With the passing of time his story that at a distance of six suns was a land whose people were so rich that they only ate and drank out of plates and vessels made of gold, and a people who sailed upon the sea in ships not much smaller than the Spaniards', had been forgotten by most men in Panama, and the few who remembered it, occasionally repeated it as a fanciful Darien Indian legend.

Upon approaching the mysterious craft, Pizarro's navigator discovered that it had two masts which held in place a large square sail. The hull of the vessel was made of strong canes, skilfully fitted together, and on a kind of deck were cabins, covered with a thatched roof, to shelter occupants against the sun and rain.

The amazement and surprise felt by the Spanish sailors was surpassed by the Indians who navigated the mysterious craft, for when Pizarro's navigator approached it, a number of terrified natives leapt overboard and frantically swam towards the shore. Boarding the object of their curiosity, the Spaniards found a number of Indians who had hidden themselves in the cabins. Very wisely, the natives were not interfered with, and therefore they soon recovered from their first fright. Looking round, the Spaniards were struck by the many fine and valuable things they saw in that ship. Most of the Indians wore ornaments made of silver and gold, and some were even studded with emeralds. Unlike all other Indians encountered so far, these men and women were not naked, but dressed in finely woven cloth, made of cotton or wool. Among the cargo was a stack of woven materials, some pieces being dyed in many brilliant hues, or artistically embroidered with figures of birds, fish, flowers and strange animals. Well made pottery, mirrors made of highly polished silver, and a variety of other articles were discovered, but what most astonished and delighted the Spaniards was a small balance for weighing gold.

Thanks to an interpreter, it was learned that these Indians, who were trading along the coast, were subjects of a mighty monarch who ruled over a vast land where temples and palaces were full of gold and precious stones.

Before the natives' *balsa* (as Peruvians called their vessels) was allowed to proceed on its journey, three men were taken on board the Spanish ship where they were treated so well that very soon they enjoyed their new and strange surroundings. Pizarro's navigator continued on his southerly course, and shortly after the equator had been crossed, he swung his ship round in order to report to his chief.

With quickening pulse everybody listened to this amazing account, dejected and disillusioned men once more became enthusiastic, and even the sick and wounded forgot their sufferings, for all they now desired was to reach the land of their dreams.

Without losing time, Pizarro gave orders for embarkation, but the two ships had hardly reached the high seas when they ran into terrific storms. However, thanks to skilful navigation, Gallo Island was reached, and fortunately the Indians showed no signs of hostility during the fortnight the white men took refuge there. Bad weather continued, but when the first favourable opportunity presented itself, the ships continued towards the mainland where they arrived without incident. The Spaniards were delighted to see that there the country looked most inviting, and altogether different from all the regions they had lately explored. Everywhere could be seen cultivations of maize, vegetables and fruit, and though the climate was hot, cool breezes blew from the sea.

Cruising along the coast, still in a southerly direction, it was noticed that villages became more and more numerous, and the country more densely inhabited. The natives, however, proved to be so hostile that some even came out in canoes to threaten the Spaniards. Near a big settlement, Pizarro landed with a party, and it would have gone very badly with him, had it not been for a curious accident. Horses did not exist in the Americas until such were imported from Europe. Naturally, the Indians were amazed and frightened upon seeing such strange animals, with their riders whom they took to be one terrifying monster. When Pizzaro and his party went ashore, he took with him a horse, for surely this would impress the natives who were assembled on the beach in great numbers. No sooner had the Spaniards landed than the Indians prepared to attack them, and it would have gone badly with the white men, had not Pizarro's horse stumbled, in doing so unseating its armour-clad rider. The natives were so taken aback by this sudden partition that they hastily retreated, thus giving the Spaniards time to regain their ships.

The sight of thousands of hostile Indians on the shore produced a very discouraging effect on many of the Spaniards; for how could they hope, with a mere handful or soldiers, to gain a foothold in a land where, according to the interpreters, vast and well organised armies were said to exist?

During a council of war held on board, the assembly agreed that an invasion was impossible, unless considerable reinforcements of men and arms were brought from Panama.

After a heated argument between the two leaders of the expedition, Almagro was persuaded to return to the colony, whilst Pizarro and the main body of men waited on the island of Gallo until more soldiers should arrive. When the men heard about this decision, they became discontented, for none could bear the thought of having to linger on that tiny island, with a very scanty supply of provisions, and nothing wherewith to protect themselves against the elements. Many were sick, and others so weakened by prolonged privation that they could barely walk. When mutiny threatened to break out, the ringleaders and a number of the soldiers who were seriously ill, were told that they might return to Panama with Almagro. A group of malcontents who were not given this chance, cunningly managed to smuggle on board a letter to the Governor. In this message they implored him to save them from certain lingering death, and in general gave a most pathetic picture of their sufferings. A number of the disaffected men signed this letter, the writer of which evidently was a bit of a rhymester, possessed of a peculiar and somewhat sardonic sense of humour, for to the text of the letter he added a four-line doggerel in which he warned the Governor against Almagro, whom he compared with a collector of sheep, whilst Pizarro he called the butcher who waits for further victims.*

Shortly after Almagro had sailed, some of the despondent men became so troublesome that Pizarro decided to send his only remaining ship to be repaired in Panama, and at the same time to give the worst grumblers the opportunity to leave the island. Left with the sorry remains of his expeditionary force, he then settled down to make the best of a dismal situation. Fortunately the Indians had fled to the mainland in their canoes, so at least one danger had disappeared. After the last of the provisions had been consumed, the starving Spaniards combed the beaches for crabs, shell-fish, or anything edible the sea might cast up for them. The weather continued to be wretched, adding

* Pues señor Gobernador,
Mirelo bien por entero
Que allá va el recogedor
Y acá queda el carnicero.

to the distress of the marooned men, whose eyes daily scanned the northern horizon for a mast of salvation. When even the most stalwart began to give up the last hope of being saved, two ships were sighted. Such was the joy of those on the beach that they leaped about and embraced each other.

As the vessels drew nearer, the men on the island were mystified, for surely these were not the ones formerly used by the expedition ? The riddle was soon solved when, anchor having been dropped, a Don came on shore and informed Pizarro that the Governor had sent him with orders to take everybody back to Panama.

Apparently the letter written by the malcontents, and smuggled on board Almagro's ship, had reached the Governor and, together with the dismal tales told by the soldiers who had returned to Panama, had made the authorities decide to put an end to Pizarro's mad enterprise which had already cost so many lives.

Having taken a leaf out of the cunning mutineers' book, Almagro had also managed to smuggle a letter on board one of the Don's two relief ships which were to bring back the men from Gallo Island. In this letter he urged Pizarro at all costs to remain where he was. He warned his partner that, if he returned to Panama, all would be lost, for surely the Governor would put a stop to further exploration, and all the sufferings of the past would have been in vain. Father Luque, as well as Almagro, assured Pizarro that they were doing everything within their power to send ships, men and provisions, and they expressed their conviction that, if he held out in his precarious position for some time longer, all would be well in the end.

The emaciated men on the island eagerly devoured the first real food they had tasted for weeks, and they rejoiced at the thought of starting back to a place of safety ; but whilst they gave vent to their feelings, Pizarro looked on in gloomy silence. Then, though all his hopes seemed to have been dashed to the ground, he showed himself to be a man of iron determination.

Assembling his soldiers, he addressed them : " Go back
to Panama those of you who would go in search of work.
Poverty and disappointment there await you. It grieves me
to think that in so doing you will lose the fruits of so many
heroic fatigues, when the land the Indians announced to you,
awaits to crown you with glory and riches. Go, but never
say that your captain did not lead you in all your fights and
perils. Remember that he always regarded you more than
he did himself."

The jaded men in their tattered garments listened in
silence ; but their leader's words did not move them. For
a brief moment Pizarro looked at the pathetic assembly
before him, and then, drawing his sword from its sheath,
with its point traced a line in the sand, from east to west.
This done, he raised his weapon, and, pointing towards the
south, exclaimed : " This is the way to toil, hunger, naked-
ness, drenching storms, aye, perhaps death, though the
death befitting soldiers of the King of Castile, and of the
Holy Church." Raising his voice more, and still pointing
in the same direction, he continued : " This is the way to
Peru ; the way to glory and riches ! " Then, after a short
dramatic pause, he pointed towards the north, and shouted
with a sneer : " There lies Panama, desertion and poverty.
Choose, each man, which side of this line becomes a good
Castilian ! "

With these words he stepped over the line towards the
south, and then, turning round to face his men, looked at
them to see what effect his appeal had produced. Without
hesitation, thirteen of his old followers crossed the line, among
them his trusted old pilot, whilst all the other men turned
away to slink towards the ships that were to take them back
to Panama.

The Don, who had been sent by the Governor to rescue
the party, looked upon Pizarro's action as one of insubordina-
tion, and therefore much persuasion was needed before he
consented to release five Indians who hitherto had acted as
interpreters to the expedition. As a special concession,
Pizarro's pilot was taken on board, for thus at least one

feeble link would remain between Panama and the little band of heroes who had made up their minds to remain on the island with their leader. A small quantity of maize having been put ashore, the ships weighed anchor, soon to disappear at the northern horizon.

A few days after these memorable events, Pizarro and his few courageous followers came to the conclusion that it would be dangerous to remain on the little island much longer. Natives who had fled to the mainland, now occasionally appeared in canoes, evidently to observe the movements of the marooned men who feared that if these scouts found out how few they were in numbers, an attack would soon follow. During a previous cruise Pizarro had landed on a small island, situated at a distance of some seventy or eighty miles from that of Gallo, and now he thought that it would be wise to transfer to that place of relative safety, for the place of refuge he had in mind was uninhabited, and he remembered that good water was to be found there, as well as small game and birds. Accordingly, the little party got busy, and when the construction of a small boat of sorts was completed, everybody, including the faithful Indian interpreters, set out on a perilous journey. Favoured by a short spell of better weather than they had experienced for a long time, the thirteen white men and their few Indian companions, succeeded in reaching their goal without incident.

The island on which they now found themselves had certain advantages over the one they had just left, for besides game and birds, fish abounded in its surrounding waters. On the other hand, the climate was by far the worst of any yet experienced, for owing to torrential rains and general humidity of the atmosphere, the sun was never visible. The jungle that covered most of the island was dense and of forbidding aspect, and everywhere swarmed mosquitoes, gnats and innumerable other insects, the sting of some being so poisonous, that it caused painful ulcerations and ugly swellings. Realising that succour could not be expected for some time, huts were built, and everybody settled down to a life of waiting and hoping.

Every morning and evening, led by Pizarro, prayers were chanted, and all religious festivals marked on the calendar were devoutly observed. Daily, for hours on end, the hazy horizon was scanned for a sign of a ship, but eventually, after seven long and weary months of disappointment, it was unanimously agreed that the only hope of salvation lay in the building of a boat in which to follow the coast towards distant Panama. This plan was about to be put into execution when a shape was seen to rise out of the vaporous curtain over the waters in the distance. Soon all eyes were strained to see what this might be ; but although the men assembled on the beach had but one hope, no one dare express it in words, lest in doing so another disappointment should be added to many previous ones. At last, however, there was no doubt that what they gazed at was a sail, and soon the whole shape of a vessel became visible. As it approached, Pizarro and his companions abandoned themselves to the rejoicings of men who suddenly find themselves delivered from the clutches of certain death, and of human beings who find themselves rewarded with the fruits of their patience and sufferings.

The navigator who had safely piloted every previous expedition, was in charge of the ship which, though well stocked with supplies, had not brought the reinforcements of men Pizarro had hoped for. The reason for this was soon explained when the pilot related what had happened after his return to Panama. Upon arrival there with the disaffected men they had given the Governor such a dismal account concerning happenings in the south, that the authorities decided to put a stop to all further explorations in search of the fabled land, Peru. The Governor was so indignant when he heard about Pizarro's obstinacy in remaining on Gallo Island against orders, that, for a time, he intended to leave him and his few companions to their fate. Fortunately, however, Pizarro's two partners, Almagro and Father Luque had managed to make the Governor change his mind, and so, after much persuasion, he eventually allowed the navigator to sail in one ship, with only a skeleton crew, sufficient to man it. Father Luque tried every argument to convince the authorities that it would be a great pity to discontinue exploring the south, but the opposition maintained that already Pizarro's obstinacy has cost so many lives that, once and for ever, an end must be put to his folly. At long last, after repeated efforts made by the priest, the Governor gave in to the extent that, before the pilot sailed with his small crew, he told him that after having picked up the marooned men, they had his permission to push the exploration of the coast further to the south. But, whilst making this concession, he threatened that, if the ship failed to return to Panama within six months, the consequences for those responsible would be most serious.

Having heard the pilot's news, Pizarro had to decide what to do next. Besides his five Indian interpreters, only thirteen members of his former force had remained with him for all those weary months, and two of these were so ill that it would have been fatal to move them, and therefore all he could muster now was eleven men. True, in addition to these, now there were a few sailors, but in the event of a landing being made on the mainland, they would have to remain on the ship which otherwise would be exposed to the danger of being boarded by hostile Indians. Here, indeed, was a situation to dishearten any man ; but Pizarro made up his mind to stake everything on a last throw of the dice. The two sick men were given provisions and such comforts as were now available, and two of the Indians who had become very attached to their Spanish masters, were put in charge of the invalids. This done, they were left on the island with the promise that they would be picked up on the ship's return journey. Together with the three Indians who had originally been taken off the first Peruvian sailing vessel that was met, Pizarro and his few companions went on board the ship, soon to sail towards the mainland.

After having hugged the coast in a southerly direction for some three weeks, the Indians on board once more found themselves in waters that were familiar to them, for it was in this neighbourhood (in the bay of Guayaquil) that they had been taken off their *balsa* (boat) by the navigator, who now made use of their knowledge of those parts. Landing on a small uninhabited island in the bay, they showed the Spaniards a place of worship which, they explained, was occasionally used by the inhabitants of the mainland. Among the peculiar offerings these had deposited on a kind of altar, were figures of hands and feet, made of gold and silver. Noticing the keen interest with which Pizarro and his men looked at the gold, the interpreters told them that, if they sailed only a little further, they would find, on the mainland, a big town in which masses of gold were to be seen.

Next day, a number of *balsas* were seen sailing across the bay, and upon approaching them the Spaniards saw that they were full of warriors. All were clad in coloured cloaks, and the interpreters explained that they had come from Tumbez, the town the Spaniards were aiming for, and that these warriors were on their way to make an attack on the island of Puna. Drawing alongside their strange craft, Pizarro asked their occupants to accompany him to Tumbez. The natives' first astonishment over at coming face to face with an amazing ship that carried white and bearded human beings, they swung round their *balsas*, and joyfully led the way towards Tumbez,* on the mainland. The country the Spaniards now gazed at, looked more promising than any other part of the coast they had previously seen or visited. From north to south, a mighty mountain range extended as far as the eye could reach, and everywhere appeared to be cultivations, and many villages.

On the beach, a multitude of Indians had assembled to watch the approach of the strange sailing vessel ; a sight which filled them with awe and wonder. Having dropped anchor, Pizarro told his interpreters to go ashore and tell the chief that he had come to offer him friendship, and to invite him to come on board.

When the interpreters landed, their friends and acquaintances who were assembled on the beach, could hardly believe their eyes, for ever since they had heard about the

* Also called Tumpiz by some early chroniclers.

apparition of a mysterious sailing craft that had taken these three men away, they had given them up for lost. And now, there they were, smilingly telling a mass of eager listeners tales of wonder about many things they had seen and experienced since they had been with the white men.

As soon as the interpreters managed to push their way through the excited crowd which surged around them, they immediately went to see the *Curaca*, or " Big Chief " to whom they gave a full account of their experiences, and to whom they also delivered Pizarro's message of friendship. Having listened with keen attention, the *Curaca* ordered a number of canoes to be laden with fruit and other produce of the country. In addition to this, game, fish and a llama were speedily found, and when all was ready, a minor chief was given orders to deliver these presents to the " visitors from another world," and at the same time to discover as much as possible about them and their intentions.

The messenger's amazement upon stepping on board Pizarro's ship was shared by the Spaniards who immediately realized that their visitor was a personage of some authority and distinction, for he moved and spoke with dignity, and the clothes he wore were made of remarkably fine material. Heavy golden discs, suspended from his ears, had so enormously enlarged their lobes that a witty Spaniard immediately nick-named the visitor "Orejón", that is, "Big Ears", a name by which all Peruvian chiefs later became known, for all had the same deformity of the ears, caused by the peculiar golden emblems of their office. Among the many presents the messenger brought with him, the llama most interested the Spaniards, some of whom remembered the occasion when, long before, in Balboa's time, an Indian had drawn the shape of such an animal in the sand.

Pizarro received the *Curaca's* messenger with courtesy, for it was evident that he came of a people whose culture must be far superior to that of any of the Indians so far seen in the Americas. Through the medium of his interpreters, he held a long conversation with his visitor who informed him that he and his *Curaca* (Chief) represented a mighty monarch to whom he referred as *Inca*. The messenger explained that it would be his *Curaca's* duty to send a detailed report about happenings to the *Inca*, and that, therefore, in the first place, he wished to know what had brought the white men to his land, where they came from, and what were their plans for the future. To these very sensible questions Pizarro replied that he and his men were the vassals of the greatest and most powerful ruler in the world, that they came from a mighty land, far away across the seas, and that they had come to teach the *Inca* and his people the word of the one and only true God.

To all this the messenger listened with keen attention and visible signs of surprise, for, as far as he and his people were concerned, there was no mightier ruler than the *Inca*.

Pizarro then showed the messenger over his ship, and in return for the gifts he had brought, he was given a meal of Spanish food, including some wine which he declared to be much more palatable and refreshing than *chicha*,* his country's alcoholic drink, made from fermented maize. Before he was allowed to depart, he was presented with a few pieces of polished quartz and a bead necklace, but what pleased him most was a hatchet made of iron, a metal which, though known, was not used in Peru. For the *Curaca* (Chief), Pizarro sent two pigs, four hens and a cock. The delighted messenger asked his host to allow some of his men to go ashore with him, so that he might present them to the *Curaca*. Accordingly Pizarro selected one of his soldiers and a negro slave who worked in the ship, for surely this combination of colours would impress the natives whose skins were coppery-brown. This choice certainly had the desired effect, for as soon as the two stepped ashore they were surrounded by a mass of excited and curious people. Men, women and children examined the soldier's beard, and even partially undressed him in order to investigate if the skin under his clothes was white like that of his hands and face. The negro also came in for his full share of attention, for some of the natives who thought that the colour of his skin was

* A similar alcoholic beverage is known as mulli among Peruvian Indians.

due to some dye, tried to wash it off. The women were particularly inquisitive, and by means of signs made the two highly amused victims of their attentions understand that if they stayed with them, they would be presented with attractive wives. In order to prove that this was no false promise, two shy and blushing maidens were pushed forward for the visitors' inspection.

The pigs and chickens—animals the Indians had never seen—also filled the onlookers with lively curiosity, and when the cock flapped his wings and crowed, they inquired what the bird was asking for, and every time the pigs grunted everybody roared with laughter.

That evening, when the Spanish soldier and the negro returned to their ship, and recounted what they had seen ashore, most of their stories sounded so far-fetched that no one believed them. They said that the *Curaca* lived in a veritable palace in which food and drinks were served in plates and vessels made of gold, that the Indians were so civilised that even a kind of police force kept order in streets which were lined with well-built houses, that they had seen a fort, cultivations irrigated by means of artificial canals, and that numerous " little camels "—as the Spaniards called llamas—were kept by the natives in well tended flocks. Most exciting, though quite incredulous, were the stories that the two men had seen many people who wore ornaments made of gold, and that they had visited a temple the walls of which were lined with slabs of solid gold, and that the place was filled with masses of artistically made decorations shaped of the same metal.

Next morning, in order to ascertain how much truth there was in these reports, Pizarro sent ashore a man who was not likely to exaggerate things. For this mission he chose a tall, good-looking soldier whom he ordered to put on his full armour, and to take with him an arquebus, one of those fearsome " thunder sticks " about which the interpreters had already told many hair-raising tales to their kinsmen.

Amazed by the new visitor's glittering armour, the natives treated him with much more respect than they had shown to the pair on the previous day. When asked to make the "thunder stick" speak, he pointed at a stout board which happened to be near, and shattered it with a shot. Terrified by the loud report of the weapon, most of the natives threw themselves flat on the ground, whilst others fled in a wild panic. Next, the soldier visited the *Curaca*, who treated him most courteously, and showed him so many amazing sights that, when he returned to the ship and reported to Pizarro, he fully substantiated all the stories told by the other soldier and the negro who had been ashore on the previous day ; so that, when he finished, no one doubted that the "Land of Gold" had been discovered at last. The one thought which tantalised all the eager listeners was that though the opulence of this land exceeded their wildest dreams, there being so few soldiers available, nothing could be done to acquire some of this enormous wealth.

With the promise that he would return at an early opportunity, Pizarro departed from friendly Tumbez to push his survey of the coast further towards the south where, according to the natives, lay the centre of the Indian Empire.

News concerning the arrival of strange white men had spread far and wide, for the Peruvians' system of communication was amazingly swift. Relays of picked runners had carried messages to the remotest parts of the land, and therefore, when the Spaniards anchored in the little bay of Paita, the natives came out in canoes to present them with fruit and other foods, for news had been received that the "visitors from another world" were harmless. On account of the Spaniards' white skins, and the glittering suits of armour some of them wore, the Indians called them *Viracochas*, meaning "Divine beings risen out of the Sea."

Continuing from Paita, Pizarro encountered two or three severe storms, but on the whole the weather and winds were favourable. Very soon the country changed, for now the Spaniards were coasting along the great Sechura desert behind which, to the east, the same mighty mountain range they had seen for weeks before, extends from north to south. Here and there, where rivers traverse the rolling hot inferno of sand, settlements were found along their banks, or near their mouths. The adjacent land was irrigated by means of cleverly made canals, thanks to which green plantations flourished, contrasting strongly with the sandy desolation beyond. Even along the mountain sides, plainly visible in the distance, the industrious Indians cultivated maize and other plants. With infinite patience and great skill, long terraces* had been built along those steep rocky slopes, and the plantations thus made were irrigated by means of canals hewn out of the solid rock. In many places these wonderful constructions extended for many miles, and to this day fill engineers with admiration.

Wherever Pizarro landed, the Indians gave him the same friendly receptions he had enjoyed since his visit to Tumbez. His fame had preceded him, and therefore the natives came flocking out in canoes to examine and admire the strange white men's ship, their arms, and all the many other marvels. In order to avoid antagonizing the Indians, Pizarro had issued strict orders to his men to treat them with kindness and respect, and, above all, on no account to be tempted to steal, or even to accept gold that might be offered to them as presents. In giving these orders he showed great cunning, for evidently he wished to hide from the natives the chief desire that burnt in every Spaniard's heart.

Having cruised some five hundred miles south from the Bay of Guayaquil, his ship dropped anchor in the mouth of the river Santa, along the banks of which were many neat settlements and plantations that were a delight to the eye. Beyond the cultivations, on either side of the river, were

---

* It is thought that these terraces, or *andenes* gave origin to the name "Andes", but some etymologists favour the theory that the name of the longest mountain range in the world is to be traced to the Peruvian Indian word *anta*, meaning "copper". Be this as it may, from the earliest days of the discovery, the Spaniards referred to that mighty mountain range as "La cordillera de los Andes." It is of interest to remark that the word "*anta*" has various meanings in different South American Indian languages. Therefore the author feels inclined to favour the theory that the name "Andes" took its origin from *andenes*, meaning "terraces."

nothing but sandy deserts, and not far away, running more or less parallel with the arid coast, towered the mighty snow-capped ranges of the Andes. Beyond these, according to the Indians, lay fertile regions, and there was situated the capital of the empire ; a marvellous city with many gorgeous temples and palaces in which lived the *Inca*, surrounded by his courtiers, nobles, and his huge armies. Here and there along the coast, the Spaniards had seen well-constructed forts and other defensive constructions which clearly showed that the Indians knew a great deal about warfare, and some of the buildings, particularly temples, were well constructed, and with considerable architectural skill.

Pizarro had seen and heard enough to convince him of the wealth and power of this empire, and therefore, after a short sojourn among the friendly natives near the river Santa, he started on his return journey to report his astonishing discoveries to the Governor in Panama.

Here and there, at places previously visited on the way south, his ship anchored for a day or two, much to the delight of the Indians, who were so hospitable, and the country so attractive, that one of the sailors deserted, thus putting ideas into his companions' heads.

Pizarro had some difficulty in preventing more desertions, but at two places he touched, he allowed, in one case a soldier, and in the other a sailor, to remain behind. This was done because he considered it would be a great help to future expeditions to find Spaniards who would be acquainted with the country, its people, language and customs.

Upon reaching Tumbez where another friendly reception awaited them, two Indian youths were taken on board, to be trained as interpreters. Having duly baptized the pair, one of them became known as Felipillo, this being the diminutive for the Christian name, Felipe, Philip in English. This youth Felipillo was destined to play a very important part in the drama shortly to unfold itself, for with the discoveries Pizarro had made, ominous clouds were gathering over the *Inca* Empire. Before the Spaniards left Tumbez, the

D

Curaca presented them with a few more llamas, and then the ship sailed towards the islet where the two sick men had been left in charge of two faithful Indians. Upon arriving there, it was found that one of the invalids had died, and so, without losing time, the other, together with the Indians, were taken on board, and the return voyage was resumed.

After an absence of over a year, Pizarro and his little party of heroes arrived in Panama towards the end of 1527. When it became known in the colony that the " Land of Gold " had been discovered, great excitement prevailed, but some of the settlers and officials refused to believe the glowing stories told by Pizarro's men, and the more level-headed members of the community realized that even if all these tales were true, it would be a costly and dangerous enterprise to conquer that rich and mighty empire in the Far South.

IV

WHEN the three partners, Pizarro, Almagro and Father Luque were re-united, and sat down to discuss plans for the future, much thinking and calculating had to be done ; for, by this time, not only were their funds completely exhausted, but they had incurred heavy debts.

When the Governor was approached, he flatly refused to give his sanction for a new expedition to be made. No doubt he had heard rumours about the armies at the disposal of the *Inca*, and therefore feared that, should a disaster befall Spanish troops which might attempt an invasion of Peru, the King of Castile would hold him responsible. Possibly also, the fact that Pizarro had only brought back a few trinkets and ornaments made of gold and silver, led the authorities to suspect that the stories concerning the wealth of Peru were grossly exaggerated. Therefore, in summing up the reasons for refusing to sanction a further expedition to be organized, the Governor flatly told Father Luque that he had no intention to depopulate the region under his jurisdiction by sending troops and settlers to new lands, and that he would see to it that no one would be tempted to leave Panama by the display of " little camels " and the few trinkets of gold and silver Pizarro had brought back with him from the expedition which had caused so much suffering and cost so many lives.

The Governor's attitude was most disheartening, but although his drastic decision cast a gloom over the three partners, they were as determined as ever not to give up their scheme at this point. It was then that the resourceful Father Luque was suddenly struck by a brilliant idea. Why not appeal to the king, and from him obtain authorization for another expedition to be made? Surely if somebody made the journey to Spain, and gave the Court a detailed account of the discoveries, the needed royal command would be given, and then no further obstacles would hold up preparations for the conquest of Peru. Furthermore, if the king's enthusiasm could be aroused, the necessary capital would be found with ease. The priest, who knew the characters and respective abilities of his two partners, was of the opinion that it would be advisable to place so delicate and important a mission into the hands of a specially selected man ; but Almagro argued that Pizarro was the indicated man to make the voyage to Spain, it having been he who had done most of the work, besides being the only person who could give the king a first-hand account of the discoveries made. On the other hand, Pizarro—who evidently was fully aware of his lack of social standing and education—suggested that the only man who had the necessary attributes and qualifications to undertake such so delicate and important a mission was Father Luque. As duties made it impossible for the priest to leave Panama, he finally, though with reluctance, agreed that Pizarro should go to the court alone. Being a fine judge of character, and a man of foresight he evidently realized that, to avoid trouble, Almagro should go as well. " God grant, my sons, that you will not defraud one another of His blessing, as did Jacob and Esau. I should feel happier if you went to Spain together," were the prophetic words he uttered.

The needed funds for the journey having been procured with great difficulty, Pizarro, together with one of his most trusted soldiers and several Peruvian Indians, among them Felipillo, crossed the isthmus of Panama to take ship on the Atlantic side. Among many other things, the travellers took with them a number of golden vases, plates and ornaments, a quantity of silver, samples of finely woven and embroidered cloth, and two llamas.

Towards the middle of 1528, after an uneventful journey, the discoverer landed in Seville : but hardly had he stepped ashore than his old enemy Enciso had him arrested and thrown into jail for an alleged debt incurred a long time before in the Darien Colony.

However, Pizarro's imprisonment was of short duration, for when the Government heard about his predicament, indignation was great, and immediately orders were issued for his release. News about his discoveries had preceded him, and King Charles V was so keen to interview the popular hero that he sent him a sum of money to facilitate and speed his journey to Toledo.

In due time, when, together with his Indians bearing the gifts brought from Peru and other newly discovered parts of the New World, Pizarro appeared before the king, he and his entourage were at once impressed. Tall and broad shouldered, the discoverer was a striking figure of a man, and despite his lowly birth, he had the refined gestures of a Castilian gentleman. Though quiet and measured in his conversation, he could, when occasion called for it, use elegant and convincing language. Modestly he proceeded to tell the assembly about his travels, fights and sufferings he had endured in endeavours to widen Spain's possessions overseas. When he briefly told the story of the terrible months he and his few companions had spent on that lonely island in the Pacific, he deeply moved all his listeners.

Pizarro's appearance before the Court could not have taken place at a more opportune moment, for at the time Charles V was at the peak of his glory. In addition to his recent victory over France, Mexico had been conquered for the Crown of Castile. Cortez,* the famous captain who had achieved this astonishing feat of arms with only a very small force, was among those who now listened to Pizarro's tales of heroism and wonder.

As the king was about to depart to Italy to be crowned emperor by the Pope, he gave orders to the Council of the Indies† to attend to Pizarro and his Peruvian enterprise. Unfortunately for the discoverer, things moved very slowly with the Council, and eventually, anxious to speed up its decisions, he successfully appealed to the queen, who looked after affairs of the State during her husband's absence.

Pizarro was nominated Governor and Captain General for life, of two hundred leagues (600 miles) of land extending from the island of Puna towards the south along the coast of " New Castile ", as Peru was named by the Council of the Indies. In addition to these posts he also obtained the titles of Major High Constable and *Adelantado* (a kind of admiral-governor), and he was given the honour of the robes of St. Jago (St. James). Furthermore, in spite of his illegitimacy, he was allowed his father's coat-of-arms, to the original design of which were incorporated symbols of the discoveries he had made.

* Cortez, the conqueror of Mexico, was some ten years younger than Pizarro. Both were born in Estremadura, in Spain, and had a great deal in common. The former, however, came of an ancient and distinguished family, and in his youth had enjoyed a good education. From him Pizarro received most useful advice, for during his recent campaigns in Mexico, experience had taught him a great deal about warfare against Indians. Cortez had returned to Spain to place certain grievances before the King. The foremost of these, and the one that affected him most, was the fact that, after he had subdued the formidable Aztecs, and conquered their land, for the Crown, he had not been conceded the political mandate of it.

Perhaps it was due to advice given to Pizarro by Cortez that a new ambition was awakened in him, and that he took good care that no outsider would be placed into a position superior to him, should he succeed in conquering Peru.

† Legally all lands discovered were considered to be part of the Spanish monarchy, and not as colonies. Therefore the king himself regulated all the affairs connected with the New World, assisted by officials appointed by him to constitute the " Council of the Indies." The laws and regulations made were almost endless in their numbers, and though their conception was as near perfection as human laws can be, their execution and enforcement were a very different matter.

53

Pizarro's two partners in Panama, and his navigator whose services and skill had greatly contributed towards the success of the explorations, were very poorly rewarded by the Council. Almagro was made Commander of the fortress of Tumbez (which the Spanish explorers had only seen) and was granted only a fraction of Pizarro's salary, and he was raised to the rank of *Hidalgo*.

The navigator was nominated " Grand Pilot of the South Sea," but only a beggarly salary went with this high-sounding title. The survivors of the gallant little party who had stayed with Pizarro on the tiny island in the Pacific, were made *Hidalgos*, and those among them who already held this rank were raised to that of " Cavaliers of the Golden Spur." Pending the Pope's arrival, Father Luque was made Bishop of Tumbez, and " Protector of the Peruvian Indians."

If one considers that not an inch of Peru had been conquered when this contract was signed (26th of July, 1529), some of its clauses are astonishing, to put it mildly, and the impudence of its signatories is fantastic.

In fairness to Pizarro it must be stated that no evidence exists that he deliberately cornered for himself all these titles which were probably given him because he had captivated the admiration of the queen and of the members of the Council.

Despite the apparent lavish rewards in this memorable document, it is not so promising on close examination. The very fact that the Crown offered to contribute nothing towards the expenses of the proposed conquest, leads one to suspect that, in official circles, little confidence was placed in Pizarro's proposed enterprise. After all, it was easy to sign away parts of an empire about the wealth of which the Council had only the discoverer's word, and it only cost a few sheets of parchment, ink, and the labour of sharpening quills to promise salaries out of revenues, if ever such should be forthcoming. Certainly, in writing, things augured well for Pizarro, that is, should his daring gamble come off ; but, first of all, it was up to him to find the money, ships and men.

If in this he succeeded, the next step would be to venture into the Peruvian Lion's den, fight hard, suffer much, and hope for the best.

The large sums of money allowed to Pizarro, as well as the rather meagre salaries to be paid to Almagro, Father Luque, the navigator, and others, were to be derived from revenues, once Peru had been conquered, and not one ducat was to leave the Spanish treasury to contribute towards the payment of these salaries. According to this contract, Pizarro undertook to leave Spain within six months from the date of its signing, and to start out from Panama to conquer his newly discovered land within a further six months. He also agreed to take with him from Spain a force numbering at least one hundred and fifty men, and, in addition to these, to recruit a minimum of a further hundred soldiers in Panama.

Having settled his official affairs, Pizarro left Toledo to visit his birthplace, Trujillo. Although memories of his youth cannot have been happy, the homing instinct, so prevalent in most men, must have been strong in Pizarro. During the many years he had spent abroad, no one had ever bothered to enquire if he were still alive ; but in spite of this he wished once more to see his people, breathe the air of his native town, and to see what changes had taken place there during his long absence. Many years before, when he had wandered away as a poor outcast, no one cared where he had gone, but now that his name was on everybody's lips, Trujillo was proud to claim him as one of her worthy sons. Brothers who had hitherto ignored his existence, now suddenly stepped forward into the limelight, and, as always happens under such circumstances, many people claimed kinship or intimate acquaintance with the popular hero of the day.

It is quite evident that, in his day, Pizarro's father must have been a gay dog, for of the four sons he is known to have had, only one, Hernando, was legitimate. The others, Juan and Gonzalo, were both full brothers to Francisco, the discoverer of Peru, but to complete the family mix-up, this last also had a half-brother on his mother's side. (Francisco Martin de Alcantara).

As no records have been handed down with regard to the family reunion in Trujillo, it is left to imagination to picture what happened when Pizarro returned home.

But there was no time for idleness and prolonged merry-making. One hundred and fifty men must be found, and with them the discoverer must sail for the New World within the few months specified in his contract with the Council of the Indies.

Hair raising stories about hardships endured by members of previous expeditions to Peru had spread throughout Spain, and in consequence recruits came forward very slowly and with a certain reluctance, for although everybody admired Pizarro, few were those who now volunteered to accompany him on an enterprise which promised to be highly dangerous. Among the first to join him were his four brothers (two full and two half brothers) as well as a cousin.* It is probable that these were tired of a dull and moneyless existence in their hometown, and now saw before them a golden future with possibly social standing and power thrown into the bargain.

The raising of the necessary capital to equip the two ships was no easy a matter, but fortunately Cortez took an interest in Pizarro's plans. It is thought that he, to a large extent, made it possible for Pizarro to leave Spain, and that without his assistance the funds for transporting the expedition across the Atlantic would never have been forthcoming. This vital matter settled, Pizarro hastened to Seville to make final preparations for his return to Panama. And good reasons he had for being in a hurry, for besides the worry of not having found the stipulated number of recruits, the time limit set for his departure by the Council of the Indies, had almost been reached. Furthermore, a number of creditors were clamouring for money he owed to them, and,

* This cousin, Pedro Pizarro, was only fifteen years of age at the time, and went as the discoverer's page. He was of good family, and later in life distinguished himself as a chronicler. Eventually he settled down in Peru where he died at the age of about sixty.

worse still, officials from the Council were expected to arrive any day to see that all the clauses of the contract had been duly carried out. If they discovered the various deficiences, they would withdraw permission to sail, and all hopes would be dashed to the ground, perhaps for ever.

In view of these seemingly unsurmountable obstacles and difficulties, Pizarro, to whom adversity only seemed to serve as a stimulant, made a bold and desperate decision.

Without waiting even for a number of officials the Government had specially appointed to accompany him to Peru to act as witnesses during the proposed conquest, he clandestinely sailed from Seville, on the 19th of January, 1530. Before sneaking away like a fugitive, it had been arranged between him and his brother, Hernando, that the latter, together with the main batch of recruits, should follow in the other ship, as soon as the inspectors from the Council for the Indies had made their visit. Should they suspect the shortage of men, Hernando was to tell them that the main force had gone ahead, and thus bamboozle the officials. The ruse succeeded, for when the inspectors arrived to make their investigation, Hernando told them the tale so well that he and the remainder of the expedition were allowed to depart.

In the meantime Pizarro pursued his course, and in due time dropped anchor outside Nombre de Dios, soon to be joined by Hernando and the main batch of recruits. As soon as news of his arrival reached Panama, Almagro and Father Luque crossed the isthmus to welcome him, and to hear what had happened during his visit to Spain.

Quite naturally, both were dissatisfied with the share-out of appointments and honours, especially Almagro who, having only been given the post of " Commander of the Fortress of Tumbez ", felt so humiliated that he accused Pizarro of having deliberately taken the lion's share for himself. Although the latter assured his two partners that he had done his best for them, and that he was in no way responsible for the decisions made by the Council in Toledo, his explanation failed to satisfy the offended parties.

Another circumstance which greatly annoyed and disturbed Almagro was the appearance on the scene of Pizarro's brothers, whom he suspected of being opportunists who had come to the new world to acquire lucrative positions. Hernando, the oldest of these, was tall, and, though not good-looking, his presence was impressive, and it was evident that he was by far the most cultured and refined of the Pizarros.

Soon the rift between Almagro and Pizarro became so great that it was only with great difficulty Father Luque and a lawyer (who had invested considerably in the partners' previous expeditions) managed to bring about a reconciliation. According to an agreement signed by all concerned, Pizarro promised not to solicit from the king any post for himself, nor for any of his brothers, until Almagro had been conceded a Governorship for himself. It was also agreed that all gold, jewels and other valuables obtained during the conquest of Peru should be equally divided among the three original partners.

Somewhat reconciled, preparations were then begun for the expedition. Three small ships were conditioned, food-stuffs, armaments and twenty-seven horses were procured, mostly on credit. Ever since Pizarro's return from Spain, survivors of his previous expeditions, and colonists in general, told such hair-raising stories about the difficulties, hardships and dangers that awaited the foolhardy who might attempt to conquer Peru, that a number of the recently arrived recruits deserted, and that the enlisting of new ones was slowed up considerably. Despite all the promises made to possible candidates who happened to be in Panama, so few threw in their lot with Pizarro that by the time he was ready to sail, only one hundred and eighty-three men were on board his vessels. Fortunately, however, there being no zealous inspectors to interfere with plans, in January 1531 the expedition departed unmolested, after a religious ceremony during which the blessings of Heaven were invoked on the enterprise.

" Mad, fantastic, suicidal," said those who from the shore watched the three tiny ships sailing towards the south.

V

ROUGH seas and strong contrary winds slowed up Pizarro's ships, and made life on board so intolerable that, upon nearing the equator, it was decided to land the men and horses, in order to give them a much needed rest. Upon exploring the nearby lowland which was covered by dense jungle forests, a large settlement was discovered. During his previous visit to Peru, Pizarro had taken every precaution not to show the natives his real intentions, and in consequence he had even forbidden his men to accept gold, should such be offered to them as gifts by the Indians. But now things were different, and as this expedition was one of conquest, the Spaniards pounced on the settlement before its inhabitants had time to prepare for so unexpected an attack. To the white men's joy, a large quantity of gold, silver and precious stones was found, and when the customary fifth had been set aside for the king, the rest was divided among the officers and men.

Most of the precious stones found in the settlement were emeralds, but as the soldiers knew little, or nothing about lapidary matters, a Dominican friar who accompanied the expedition, told the ignorant men that emeralds were harder than steel, and that the best way to test them was to pound them between two large stones. If they broke, he affirmed, they were only bright-green stones, and of no value, but if they resisted the blows they were valuable emeralds. Naturally, the jewels submitted to this test were shattered to pieces, and in this way many large and fine specimens were lost. Later, when the soldiers found out that, in having taken the friar's advice, they had thrown away much wealth, they were very resentful, and it was even rumoured round the camp fires that he had cunningly kept many of the precious stones which had been given him to test.

This veritable wind-fall gave Pizarro an idea. Supposing he sent his three ships back to Panama ? Surely the sight of so much gold and silver would be an infallible bait to bring in more recruits. In the meantime, he and the main force would march in the direction of the Bay of Guayaquil where, later on, his ships with their cargo of reinforcements in men, armaments and supplies, could easily make contact with him.

No sooner planned than done, and, accordingly, whilst the ships were away on their errand, he started on his three hundred mile march through country he had only seen from the sea.

Through ever evil-smelling mud and slime, over infernally hot sandy stretches, and across rivers and innumerable streams the column advanced, all the time followed by clouds of mosquitoes and other tantalising insects. Soon the inevitable happened ; disease broke out. Exhausted men who lay down to rest awoke with fever, and others fell victims to a mysterious epidemic.* Horrible warts and painful ulcerous growths made their bodies swell, and when these were lanced to get relief, some of the sufferers bled to death. Even the most hardened veterans who had accompanied Pizarro on previous expeditions began to lose heart, and in loud voices cursed the day when they had left Panama.

For seven long and dreadful months the little army slowly advanced, and when the situation seemed to have become hopeless, a ship was sighted sailing along the coast. Smoke signals having been exchanged, the vessel dropped anchor near the mouth of the river. On board were several officials who had been appointed by the Council of the Indies to accompany the expedition, but who had been left in Seville, owing to Pizarro's hasty departure. Besides food and other supplies, the ship also brought a few volunteers who were desirous to try their luck in the Peruvian campaign. When these saw and spoke to Pizarro's starving

* Most likely this was *verruga*, a febrile disease characterized in warty eruptions or tumours of the skin. This disease is sometimes called Oroya fever, but whether these two are the same is doubtful. Oroya fever attacks between January and March, and is most common in a sector of the Andes, to the east of Lima. Verruga spreads along the coast, cases having been known far north of the equator. During the period of the conquest a severe epidemic of this horrible disease must have raged, for Pizarro's army was decimated by it.

and fever-stricken men, and heard about the death of many others, their hearts sank, for now there was no turning back for them.

Refreshed by a much needed rest and by the food the ship had brought, the overland march was resumed in somewhat better spirits, and when the expedition reached the Bay of Guayaquil, hopes were further raised when another ship arrived with some thirty new recruits. Whilst awaiting the arrival of his third ship, and making preparations for the invasion of Peru, Pizarro thought of pitching camp on the Island of Puna. His interpreters—who were natives of Tumbez on the mainland, and hated their traditional enemies of the island—warned Pizarro against the chieftains of Puna, whom they described as being very treacherous. Instead of frightening the listener, this warning gave him an idea : he would take advantage of this feud between the native tribes, and, if possible, he would play one against the other to suit his own ends. First of all, he would transport his whole force to the island, and if there he met resistance, force would be used ; but if not, everything possible would be done to befriend the islanders whose aid might be invaluable to gain a solid foothold on the mainland.

Things were made unexpectedly easy for the Spaniards when several island chieftains called in their camp and offered to convey them to their territory in *balsas*, a service which was immediately accepted.

The white men's movements so puzzled the Indians on the mainland that, trusting in Pizarro's protection, several *balsas* filled with minor chieftains and warriors from Tumbez, arrived under the pretext of paying him their respects. Naturally, the islanders strongly resented the intrusion of their old enemies ; but, with the Spaniards present, they kept their feelings in check.

Having been warned that the chieftains of the island were plotting against the white men, Pizarro had a number of them brought before him. Since those who acted as interpreters in the ensuing interrogation were natives of

Tumbez, and therefore hereditary enemies of the accused, it is quite possible that their interpretations did not correspond to what was said. Pizarro, finding the island chieftains guilty of conspiracy, handed all of them, except the principal chief, over to his visitors from the mainland, who murdered them in a matter of moments.

The fury and indignation of the islanders was such that about five hundred warriors assembled, and immediately attacked the Spaniards, who repulsed the first onslaught with heavy losses to the enemy. Again and again the brave though badly armed natives threw themselves at the white men whose cross-bows, firearms, lances and swords cut them down by the score. Those of the Spaniards who were mounted on horses, dashed into the fray, and when the Indians saw these terrifying apparitions, they were thrown into confusion and fled. Pizarro then ordered their principal chief, whom he held as a prisoner, to appeal to his warriors to cease fighting. This having been done, the natives confined their animosity to shouting threats at the white men, only a few of whom had been killed in the mêlée, though many were wounded, including Hernando Pizarro, who had fought with great bravery.

Hostilities had hardly ceased when, to the joy of the Spaniards, two ships, under the command of a very gallant Don, named Hernando de Soto, arrived with reinforcements of men and horses.

Being a shrewd diplomat, Pizarro immediately released some six hundred captives the islanders had made during recent wars against the Indians from Tumbez. In triumph, these and their kinsmen who had visited the Spanish camp, returned to their homes across the bay.

Two days later, certain that a most cordial reception would be accorded him, Pizarro embarked his whole force, partly in his own ships, and partly on *balsas*, and headed for Tumbez. The first three soldiers to reach the shore, travelled on one of the latter, together with a few horses and baggage. Some of the many Indians who were assembled on the beach, enthusiastically helped with the landing, whereafter they led the way towards a copse where it was shady and cool. No sooner arrived there than the seemingly friendly and joyous Indians sprang upon the unsuspecting soldiers whose eyes were gouged out, and arms and legs hacked off in a few moments.

Soon other members of the expedition, ignorant of what had happened, landed cheerfully, only to be attacked by hordes of natives into whose hands, among other booty, fell the major part of Pizarro's personal luggage. The soldiers, having recovered from the first shock of the unexpected assault, resisted the attackers with great bravery, and at the same time cried for help and warned their arriving comrades of the peril. Hernando Pizarro who was on a *balsa* with his horse, leapt into the saddle and jumped into the water. Within a few moments the animal began to sink into a quicksand, but fortunately it managed to extricate itself from the peril. The Indians who had never before seen a horse and rider, fled in terror when Hernando came dashing towards them, dressed in glittering armour, and brandishing his sword. Thus, for the moment, he saved the situation.

Shortly after these events, Pizarro and the main force landed, and immediately a council of war was held. No one could explain, or even guess, what had happened to change the natives who had been so friendly during the previous expedition's visit. Why this hostility? Why this sudden breach of faith?

When the mutilated bodies of the three soldiers were found in the nearby copse, a wave of wrath spread through the Spanish force, and to a man its members swore to avenge the natives' treacherous deed. Though Pizarro fully expected to have to do some serious fighting, he had not been prepared to run into trouble at this early stage of the campaign. His plans for the immediate future were badly upset, and now needed readjusting.

Cautiously entering the town of Tumbez, the Spaniards found that most of its inhabitants had fled, and that practically all the houses were in ruins. Even the fort was severely damaged, and the temples had been stripped of all their gold. The sight of all this desolation had a most depressing effect on the soldiers, especially so in the case of those who only recently had joined Pizarro's ranks. Some of the men still suffered from the effects of the recent march along the coast, and disease still claimed an occasional victim. And now, after all these dangers and tribulations, they had arrived in what had been described to them as a paradise filled with gold, only to find a scene of desolation. Whisperings of dissatisfaction soon became loud murmurs of mutiny, for most of the soldiers felt that they had been enticed to join the expedition under false pretences.

A party, sent out with orders to bring back prisoners for the purpose of interrogation, had the good fortune to capture the *Curaca* (Chief) himself. Although the captive replied to questions freely, his answers were so vague, and in some cases contradictory, that very little useful information concerning the destruction of the town, and the cause of his people's hostility, was obtained from him. When asked what had become of the two Spanish soldiers whom Pizarro had left behind during his previous visit, the *Curaca*, and all the Indians who were questioned, had different stories to tell. According to some natives both had lost their lives during fights against the men of Puna, others said they had been taken away to be shown to the *Inca*, and according to another version, an epidemic had been the cause of their death.

One Indian who presented himself to ask for Pizarro's protection, revealed that he had travelled widely throughout the land about which he gave some most valuable and encouraging information. He informed his listener about the greatness of the *Inca*, and told many tales about the size and beauty of certain towns in the interior of the country, declaring that gold was to be seen everywhere, especially in temples of which there were many.

Pizarro saw to it that these stories should reach the ears of his dejected troops; but, upon hearing them, the soldiers merely laughed, and mockingly replied to go and tell these yarns to some one else.

During a long interview with the *Curaca*, the Spaniards obtained some information that was of vital importance to them. According to the native Chief, a few years before Pizarro first arrived in Tumbez, a good and mighty *Inca* named Huyana Capac, had died. During his glorious reign the borders of his empire had been greatly extended, especially towards the north, or what is now the republic of Ecuador, where a kind of second capital has been established in the flourishing city of Quito. Roads had been built, the agricultural system had been improved; in fact, the empire enjoyed the most prosperous and happy days it had yet known. According to Huyana Capac's wishes, after his death his two favourite sons, Huascar and Atahualpa,* were to share the reign of the Empire. The kingdom of Cuzco was to pass to the former, and that of Quito to the latter. For a few years after the great *Inca's* death, all went well, but then the two heirs began to envy one another, and soon this led to open strife. With varying fortunes a bloody war was waged, but eventually Atahualpa, thanks to the skill of two experienced generals, defeated his brother's armies in a terrific and bloody battle. Atahualpa's victorious army then entered the city of Cuzco where numerous

* The name Atahualpa has been spelt in several different ways. Some early Spanish chroniclers set it on paper as Atabalipa, Atabaliba, Atabaliva, Ataoguallpa, etc. For the sake of simplicity the author uses Atahualpa. According to some ancient records this name derived its origin from the Brazilian Indians' imitation of the domestic cock's cry of defiance. Though perhaps far fetched, this theory may be correct, for in 1500 Cabral landed on the coast of Brazil where he set ashore two convicts, and probably also some fowls. Years immediately following this, other expeditions visited the Brazilian coast, and several more convicts were left behind. When, in 1543, Anton Correa and Hector Acuña reached the Upper Rio Paraguay, as emissaries sent by Nuñez Cabeza de Vaca, they found fowls among the Indians, though, as we have already seen, these birds were not known among the Quichua Indians (Incas) along the Pacific coast. Montesinos says Atahualpa's real name was Huallpa Titu Yupanqui, and he also states that he was called Ataguallpa after the nurse who gave him milk, and who was from a village near Cuzco, a name meaning " righteousness " or " strength." (Name of village : Atau.) A certain wild bird is known as huallpa, and the same name stands for a liana with a yellow flower. In the Quichua language this flower is called huallpa-huallpa. Ata means " beautiful," and some historians say that originally it must have been " Atua," meaning " fortune of war." (See Erland Nordenskiold : *Deductions suggested by the Geographical Distribution of some Post-Columbian Words used by the Indians of South America.* Oxford University Press, 1922.

E   65

people were massacred, among them many of royal blood who had favoured Huascar's cause, and palaces and houses were burnt or razed to the ground. Apparently the warriors of Puna still only recognized the defeated Huascar, although, not long before the Spaniards' arrival, Atahualpa had tried to defeat the islanders. This attempt having failed, it had been left to the people of Tumbez to deal with their old hereditary enemies of Puna. Huascar fell into the hands of his brother who had him removed as a prisoner to a fortress situated among the mountains. After his victory, Atahualpa had then declared himself *Inca* over the whole empire, and the few among his enemies who had escaped his terrible vengeance were glad to submit to his rule.

Pizarro listened to the *Curaca's* story in rapt attention, for in the rift between the two *Incas* he saw a chance he had not even hoped for. There was good reason for him to believe that resentment must still be smouldering among those Atahualpa had vanquished, and he knew that if he succeeded in taking advantage of this circumstance, the conquest of Peru would be made easier for him.

The *Curaca* and his fellow prisoners pleaded for mercy and peace, and when Pizarro promised these to them, most of the Indians who had fled towards the mountains, flocked back to their ruined town, where reconstructions were immediately begun.

The Spaniards would not have been mystified as to why the town of Tumbez had been destroyed, and why all the gold had disappeared, had they known that a very efficient and rapid means of communicating messages existed in Peru. In relays, fleet-footed runners, called *chasquis*, carried messages and even light goods from *posta* to *posta*. Months before, when Pizarro had first landed at Tumbez, news about the arrival of strange white men had been speeded to the *Inca* who had immediately sent instructions to all his chiefs along the coast, warning them to be on their guard. Though, during his previous visit, Pizarro had given his men strict orders not to betray their interest in gold, perhaps remarks carelessly made by members of the expedition were overheard by the interpreters who told their kinsmen about the Spaniards' real intentions.

After the recent attack on the Indian settlement in the north, during the march down towards the Bay of Guayaquil, news of this and of the looting of gold, silver and emeralds, very quickly reached the *Inca*, who immediately sent orders to the coast that everything possible be done to prevent the white men from gaining a foothold in the land.

Of all these happenings, however, the Spaniards were ignorant, and the cunning Indians in Tumbez said nothing.

．　．　．　．　．　．　．

Before venturing into the interior of the country, Pizarro thought it wise to befriend the people where he was, for enemies at his back would prove very dangerous. A strong base from where operations would be conducted having to be found, it was decided to explore the country lying south of Tumbez. Also, a great deal more had to be discovered about Peru and its people, before it would be possible to form a proper plan of campaign. The total Spanish force numbered only a little over two hundred men, many of whom were still ill or weakened by recent hardships. Leaving these in Tumbez, Pizarro set out to find a suitable locality for his base. The soldiers were given strict orders to treat all natives with respect and kindness, for, at this stage of the campaign, trouble had to be avoided at all costs.

Whilst Pizarro with the main force explored the regions between the coast and the Andes, de Soto, in charge of a small party, was sent to do likewise in the nearby mountain sectors. All went well with Pizarro, who met no opposition from the Indians who lived in prosperous settlements along the banks of different rivers, for evidently they had heard about the white men's terrible weapons, and therefore took good care not to interfere with them. When de Soto rejoined Pizarro's force, he reported that some of the inhabitants in the mountains had been hostile, but that whenever he and his party had been attacked, the indifferently armed native warriors had been routed with ease. He gave an account of how he had pushed on into the *cordilleras* until a well-constructed highway was reached. The most welcome news de Soto brought was that gold seemed to abound everywhere in the interior, and, better still, he brought back with him a considerable quantity of that metal.

After a month of exploring, a suitable place was found in the valley of the river Piura, close on a hundred miles south of Tumbez, and there it was decided to make the main base. The country near the river is fertile and pleasant, though the climate is hot. Trees afford shade during the broiling hours of day, but at night refreshing breezes from the sea cool the atmosphere. Quite near, towards the east, rise the first densely wooded ranges of the Andes, among which are many beautiful valleys and stretches of grassland. Only a few miles south of the river Piura the country changes completely, for there begins the vast Sechura desert, with its billows of hot sand which continually shift with the winds. From there on, towards the south, the coast is nothing but sand, sand, and more sand, excepting in places where rivers come down from the Andes. Where such traverse the broiling desert, welcome oases are to be found.

In choosing the region along the river Piura for establishing his headquarters, Pizarro realized that the Sechura desert would be as good as a rampart on one side of the settlement, for an attack from that quarter would be most difficult owing to the complete absence of water in that hot sandy waste. The place he chose for founding the first Spanish colony in Peru is situated about thirty miles inland from the bay of Paita, and was named San Miguel de Piura ; to-day generally called Piura for short.

Pizarro, who feared that possibly the *Inca* might send an army down from the mountains to oust him from his land, took every precaution against a possible surprise attack. Among the first of these he ordered his men to build a strong fort, and whilst this was being done, he sent for the sick soldiers who had been left in Tumbez. The fort completed, a church, a court-house and quarters for the troops were constructed. The land in the vicinity of the settlement was divided up among those of the soldiers who were chosen to garrison the fort, and every recipient of land was given a number of Indians to do the work for him.

Ever since the expedition had started from Panama, Almagro had remained there, it having been agreed that he should try to enlist further recruits, and generally safeguard the enterprise's interests there. Pizarro, who had heard rumours that his partner was attempting to organize an expedition on his own, wrote a letter imploring him to forget their old differences and to come to join him, and at the same time to bring as many men as possible.

When the gold, so far obtained in Peru, was about to be divided, Pizarro called together his men. Having pointed out that enormous riches awaited the expedition in the interior, he explained that for the campaign about to be undertaken, more men, armaments and supplies were badly needed. He then told his audience that to obtain these, gold would be required, and that already the expedition was heavily in debt in Panama. In continuation, he quite frankly admitted that before this debt was paid off, it was unlikely that supplies and reinforcements could be obtained. Having made the situation quite clear to his listeners, he appealed to them not to claim their respective shares of the gold, but to release all of it to him on loan. In doing so, he explained, they would make it possible to conquer Peru, and thus enrich themselves a thousandfold, and he assured them that their labours and sufferings of the past would not have been in vain. Without hesitation the men agreed to this proposal, for no one doubted that the speaker's words were true, and that his promises would be fulfilled.

An officer having been appointed to take charge of a small ship which lay at anchor in the Bay of Paita, the gold was transferred on board, and whilst the vessel was away on its important mission in Panama, Pizarro kept his men busy with constructional work. For some time all went well in the newly-founded colony, but, as time passed, and still no ship appeared with the, by this time, sorely needed supplies, dissatisfaction broke out among the soldiers, some of whom threatened to leave Peru at the first opportunity. Realizing that inactivity was chiefly responsible for the rapidly sinking morale of his troops, and fearing that if this state of affairs continued, mutiny might break out, Pizarro boldly decided to stake everything on a daring throw of the dice.

News had reached him that the *Inca*, with a huge army, was encamped near a town situated in a high plain, far away towards the south, among the high mountains. Instead of making preparations for the defence of the colony until reinforcements should arrive from Panama, Pizarro mustered his force, selected about fifty men to remain where they were, and then, with only one hundred and seventy-seven, about sixty of whom had horses, he set out, banners unfurled, and trumpets blaring defiantly, to march into the lion's den.* (September 24th, 1532).

The officials who had been especially sent to Peru by the Spanish Government to supervise the conquest, did not fancy the prospect of so dangerous a move, and, accordingly, preferred to remain in the relative safety of the colony, from where, should the worst come to the worst, they had at least a chance to make good their escape to Panama by sea.

VI

WITHIN three or four days, Pizarro reached the first densely wooded ranges of the Andes. Then began many long heart-breaking ascents to higher regions, and descents into deep, awe-inspiring valleys where mud and intertwined roots of colossal lichen covered trees made progress difficult and slow. In many valleys the heat was stifling, and clouds of insects made life intolerable. Upon approaching high passes, the atmosphere became bitterly cold, for in such places the rising hot air condenses, and fogs shift up the mountain side like broad strips of smoke. The change from heat to cold is so sudden that the traveller must keep on

---

* Only about twenty men were armed with cross-bows, and a few had clumsy, unreliable arquebuses, the only fire-arms available, besides two cannon, known as falconets.

moving, for even a short spell of inactivity allows the body to become chilled, making it shiver, and the teeth to chatter horribly. Clad in armour, as most of the Spaniards were, they felt these extremes doubly, and it was a herculean task to drag the horses and cannon up those steep and slippery mountain sides, zig-zagging along narrow Indian foot trails that wind in and out of dripping forests, and over rocky parts which are as difficult to scale as slate roofs.

The expedition now fought its way through regions that are difficult to describe in words, for there nature works on so gigantic a scale that it passes common understanding. Range upon range of the Andes extend towards the south, and here and there these are intersected by others running from east to west. In such places the confusion is almost terrifying to behold. Standing on a peak and looking in any direction, one sees nothing but deep, winding valleys over which tower jagged peaks which give one the impression of having been torn asunder in a cataclysm. The high, cold, windswept regions are known as *páramos*. There nothing but coarse grasses grow, and here and there low stunted bushes, no higher than heather. These are the favourite haunts of the shy vicuña, an animal of the llama species, prized for its soft silky fur which is woven into a rare and valuable cloth. The llama and its woolly sister, the alpaca, also thrive in these inhospitable parts, and in even higher regions, near the snow-line, is to be found the chinchilla of almost priceless fur.

From the mountain tops which the Spaniards attained, the view was impressive to the point of being overpowering. Out of a sea of clouds below them, rose innumerable snow-capped peaks, looking like so many glittering white islands in the midst of a stormy sea. Though in these heights the tropical sun was blinding on account of the crystal-clear atmosphere, the cold penetrated to the marrow, and the men looked forward to descending once more to warmer parrot infested regions. At night, ugly vampire bats fastened on to the horses, sucking their blood, leaving them exhausted and limp in the morning. Occasionally, in the hours of darkness, the sleepers were disturbed by the snarls of jaguars and other wild animals, while in the day condors majestically circled high up in the azure sky, looking for a dead animal or man upon which to whet their appetite.

Here and there among the mighty ranges of the Andes, the Spaniards came to beautiful fertile table-lands and high sheltered valleys where lush grasses, fruit trees, and beautiful flowers grow, strongly contrasting with the forbidding rough mountains which shut in these little paradises. Wherever possible, the industrious Indians had constructed terraces or *andenes* which were irrigated by canals, hewn out of the rocky mountain sides. For miles, tier upon tier of these *andenes* extended along the mountain slopes, and everywhere the white men saw evidence of the Peruvians' industry and thrift. High up in the cold windswept *páramos* and in the *puna* grasslands they came upon Indian shepherds tending flocks of llamas.

In villages and hamlets the expedition was given friendly receptions, and food was plentiful. Indians came flocking from afar to see the strange bearded white men whom they believed to be semi-divinities. With awe and wonder they gazed at the glittering armour, flags, trumpets and weapons, but what amazed the natives most were the horses ; fearsome beasts hitherto unknown in the land.

One evening, upon cautiously approaching some of the horses to have a closer look at them, a group of Indians intently observed the animals champing at the bits. Seeing that the strange contraptions were made of metal, the Indian chief hastily disappeared, soon to return with a few plates made of gold and silver, which he laid on the ground before the horses. When questioned why he had done this, he replied that he wished to befriend the dangerous beasts which ate metal, and that he thought gold and silver would be more to their taste than the iron he had seen them chew. Taking advantage of the chieftain's innocence, the Spaniards asked an interpreter to tell him that the horses ate a great deal of gold of which they were very fond. Whilst the natives ran to fetch a further supply of gold plates, the cunning Spaniards took away and hid those which had previously been placed before the animals.*

As the Spaniards advanced, further alarming news concerning the *Inca's* formidable armies reached them; reports, Felipillo, the interpreter, with malicious delight handed on to the soldiers, many of whom began to accuse Pizarro of leading them to certain death. When half his force threatened to march back to the coast, he assembled all his officers and men and tactfully told them that the colony on the banks of the river Piura needed volunteers to defend it in the event of an attack, so if any of those present wished to return there, they were at liberty to do so. At so critical a moment, when he needed every man and horse of his small army, this was an astonishing attitude to adopt; but it is evident that he wished to rid himself of cowards and malcontents without offending them. Five of the cavalry, and four of the infantry took advantage of his offer, and, accordingly, set out on their return journey to the colony. Then, with the army purged of the most faint-hearted and worst trouble makers, the march was resumed.

Every day the expedition discovered new evidences that the land was much more civilized than any until then discovered in the Americas. In several places were seen strong stone-built fortresses, the walls of which, in particular, attracted the Spaniards' attention. The huge stone blocks, though of different sizes and shapes, were fitted together so ingeniously, and with such precision, that nowhere could even the finest blade of a sword be inserted. How these

* The following story well illustrates the impression made upon American Indians by horses. A few years before Pizarro set foot on Peruvian soil, Cortez, the conqueror of Mexico, made an expedition to the interior of Aztecs' land. In a mountainous region his horse was lamed, and when Cortez met some friendly Indians, he left the animal in their care. The natives—who had never before seen a horse—took it for some supernatural being, and after the Spaniards' departure housed it in a temple where they tried to feed the unfortunate animal on savoury dishes of game, and even flowers, with the result that it soon died. Close on a century later, when two Spanish friars went to those remote and almost forgotten regions of Mexico where since Cortez and his expedition had passed through, no white man had been, the two missionaries found a stone effigy of a horse in a temple, and to their amazement discovered that the natives adored it as the god of lightning and thunder. (No doubt, the Indians thought the horse was responsible for the thunder made by the Spaniards' fire-arms.)

huge blocks had been transported up to some of the peaks which commanded strategic points, mystified the explorers as much as the amazing skill with which they had been joined together. Here and there along the route, they saw palaces which the Indians said were used by the *Inca* when, at intervals of a few years, he travelled through his empire to inspect its state and progress. The Spaniards were told that on such occasions the Indian monarch was carried in a magnificent litter glittering with gold and precious stones, and went accompanied by an escort of nobles and many soldiers. The palaces they saw were large and very solidly built of stone. Like the Indians' houses, they had roofs made of wood or bamboo, covered with rushes or dry, fibrous palm or cactus leaves. The interiors were breath-taking in their magnificence. Everywhere glittered gold in the shape of artistic vases, plates, and figures representing flowers, plants and animals of the country. Masses of finely woven and beautifully embroidered rugs and carpets further adorned these royal dwellings, the wealth of which by far surpassed anything ever seen or heard of in Europe. But these were as nothing, the Spaniards were told, when compared with the treasures to be seen in or near Cuzco, the capital of the *Inca's* empire. Even more promising was the information that all the gold and treasure they had seen in various royal dwelling places had been amassed during the reigning *Inca's* time, for it was the custom in Peru that after a monarch's death all his palaces were closed permanently, with all their treasures in them. This was done because, according to the natives' belief, their deceased monarchs occasionally returned to earth, and therefore everything they needed for their comfort and joy must be in immediate readiness for them.

All information concerning the *Inca* was of vital and paramount importance to Pizarro, who realized that his only hope of success and salvation lay in the execution of a lightning coup that would shake the empire, and demoralize its population to such an extent as to leave the *Inca* and his people stunned and helpless.

As the Spaniards cautiously advanced further and further into the tremendous mountains, they feared that a trap might be set for them. Along their route they not only found State granaries and forts, but also well-built *tambos* or barracks. These were used by the *Inca's* armies when on marches across the country, and were also at the disposal of Peruvian travellers when on official business. Run on lines of inns, attendants saw to it that visitors were comfortable, and the establishments kept clean and in good repair. In such *tambos* which were situated all along the highway, at distances of twelve and fifteen miles from each other, the Spaniards made their quarters, and provisions were obtained, either from the natives, or from State granaries, many of which they entered by force, to help themselves freely to what they required.

In most of the valleys and villages Pizarro's little force passed through, very few men were seen, and when the interpreters gave the news that most of the able-bodied Peruvian men had been called up for military service, even the bravest Spaniards' hearts sank. However, having ventured so far into the country, to turn back at this point would have been fatal. Nearly two months had passed since the expedition had left the coast when news reached Pizarro that a vast Peruvian army was encamped among the mountains, not far ahead. For the Spaniards, who at the time found themselves in a deep valley among awe-inspiring mountains, this was ominous news ; but dauntless Pizarro did not flinch.

Though, so far, native chieftains and inhabitants had received the expedition with kindness, he suspected that this was only intended to give him and his men confidence, and to lure them into an ambush from which escape would be impossible, and, accordingly, he and his officers were constantly on the alert for a surprise attack.

At the head of a small detachment, de Soto was sent ahead to investigate the lay of the land, and, if possible, to ascertain what were the Peruvian army's intentions.

Several days passed, and Pizarro began to fear that something must have happened to the reconnoitring party, when, to everybody's relief, de Soto returned with the report that the regions he had visited were fertile and well populated, and that everywhere he had seen evidence of wealth.

Shortly after de Soto's return, a Peruvian nobleman, accompanied by a number of servants, presented himself in the Spanish camp. He explained that he had been sent by the *Inca*, Atahualpa, from whom he brought a number of presents, such as llamas, vicuñas, game (alive and dead), different brightly plumaged birds, Indian pepper, parrots, macaws, monkeys, emeralds and turquoise. The visitor said that the *Inca* had charged him to inform Pizarro that he was waiting to receive him near Cajamarca, a town situated on a high plain beyond the wall of mountains ahead.

Even less cautious persons than Pizarro would have suspected that the real purpose of the Peruvian nobleman's visit was to find out as much as possible about the Spanish army and its strength. However, he took good care not to show his feelings of suspicion, and pretended to be delighted with the presents, and the *Inca's* friendly messages. He requested the visitor to inform the *Inca* that he was aware of the recent war he had fought against his brother, and that the Spanish army was at his disposal, should he need assistance in the campaign against the rebels who still offered resistance in different parts of the empire. Above all, Pizarro charged the envoy to inform his lord and master that he had come as an ambassador of the only true and living God, and of the king of Castile, the mightiest and most powerful monarch on earth. In order to impress the visitor, he was treated as if he were a king, and invited to remain in the camp and rest before setting out on his return journey. However, anxious to report to the *Inca* as soon as possible, the envoy did not accept the invitation, but made ready to depart. Pizarro then presented him with a linen shirt, a red cap, knives, scissors, and a few other articles. The knives and scissors especially delighted the visitor, for although the Peruvians knew how to make a remarkably hard alloy by mixing gold and copper,* they did not use iron.

The *Inca's* envoy having departed, Pizarro sent the presents he had received from the Peruvian monarch, together with a quantity of gold and fine cloth, to his colony. At the same time he gave news about his progress, and once more urged his men garrisoned there to do everything possible to remain on friendly terms with the Indians, for the colony was the expedition's only life-line, and should this be cut out by antagonizing the natives there, Pizarro's hopes of survival would be very slender indeed.

Every precaution against a surprise attack having been taken, the expedition once more pushed forward. So far no opposition had been encountered, but upon reaching a wide and turbulent river, it was found that a mass of Indians assembled on the opposite bank, were preparing to impede the Spaniards' progress. Pizarro still hoped that reinforcements would arrive from Panama, and catch up with him; but when this hope proved to be in vain, he decided to cross the river, despite the natives' lively demonstrations of hostility.

During an exceptionally dark night, Hernando Pizarro and a few soldiers swam across the river, in order to hold the left bank until, by day, their comrades could follow them without interference from the natives. When these discovered Hernando and his men, they fled in dismay, which permitted Pizarro and his main force to follow the advance guard without opposition, the crossing of the river being affected by means of roughly improvised rafts, alongside which the horses swam, led by ropes.

In order to discover why the Indians had suddenly become hostile, Hernando Pizarro, accompanied by a few horsemen set out to take some prisoners. Soon he returned, his object achieved, but when the captives he brought back with him

* This process of mixing gold and copper has been lost, and although to this day scientists are trying to discover how the Peruvians mixed that tough non-corroding alloy, in the Quichua language called *champi*, the riddle remains unsolved.

Iron, called *quillay*, though known, was not used, as was also the case with glass; *cquespy* in the Quichua tongue. Lead in its native state was known as *titi*, copper as *anti* and tin as *yuractiti*, meaning white lead.

were questioned about the *Inca* and his intentions, they refused to speak, or, if they did, their answers were so evasive that Pizarro decided to adopt severe and brutal measures to obtain information which might mean life or death to him and his men. Accordingly, one Indian—who happened to be a local Chief—was taken aside and tortured until he declared that the *Inca* was very wroth with the Spaniards, and that he was determined to kill them all. The unfortunate Chief also divulged that three armies were lying in wait for the expedition, at different points ; one at the foot of the next mountain range, the other near the summit of the pass, and the third near Cajamarca.

Another chieftain who was interrogated gave the alarming and somewhat contradictory information that a Peruvian army of more than fifty thousand men was encamped among the mountains somewhere in the south.

The two prisoners' stories were so conflicting, as far as localities were concerned, that, in order to learn the truth, Pizarro sent one of his most trusted interpreters to go and spy on Atahualpa, and, if possible, find out what were his likely movements and plans. The Indian, a native of the coastal regions, explained that he preferred not to go as a spy, and that it would be much better if he were sent as a messenger, for if he went as such he would possibly be allowed to speak to the *Inca*, in which case he would be able to obtain much more reliable information. Agreeing with this suggestion, Pizarro asked the interpreter to convey his greetings to the *Inca*, and to tell him that the white men's visit was one of friendship, and that he was looking forward to the day when he could personally explain the nature of the mission which had prompted him to cross the wide seas, and to visit his empire. Taking advantage of this opportunity, Pizarro again offered to help the *Inca* in his war against such of his brothers' armies as had not yet been defeated in the field.

No one in the Spanish camp doubted that soon things would come to a climax, and every man was aware of the seriousness of the situation. However, Pizarro's unflinching courage and determination so inspired his officers and men that now no one thought of turning back. Accordingly, the interpreter having departed on his mission, the march was resumed, and after three days the foot of another towering Andean range was reached. By this time, thanks to a number of natives who had been interrogated during the advance, Pizarro knew for certain that the *Inca* and his army were encamped somewhere on the eastern side of the range which now barred his way.

At this point he could have chosen to follow the main Peruvian highway which ran due south, more or less parallel with the mountains. Though this would have made progress easy, a great détour would have had to be made to reach the *Inca*, and, furthermore, and most important, if a trap had been set for the Spaniards, in all probability this had been done at one or two suitable places along the highway.

As usual when faced with a difficult problem, and on occasions when every man's full support was needed to win through, Pizarro called together his whole force, and without mincing words or facts, put the situation before all of its members, officers and men alike. Having discussed the pros and cons of following the highway, he explained that at all costs every Spaniard must help to preserve the natives' illusion that the mysterious white visitors from overseas were supermen. Therefore, he proposed that there was only one thing to do : march straight across the seemingly impassable mountain range, and thus impress the *Inca* and his army.

Having listened to their leader, all the Spanish soldiers enthusiastically agreed that he had spoken well, and swore that, wherever he might choose to guide them, they would follow.

Pizarro then selected forty horsemen and sixty of the foot to begin the difficult climb with him, whilst the rest, who were in charge of the baggage, were to follow behind, as quickly as they might. Leading the horses, sometimes dragging and pushing them, this vanguard slowly scrambled up the precipitous mountain side, cursing and sweating. After some hours, to everybody's consternation and dismay, it was discovered that on a high rocky prominence dominating the narrow and precipitous trail, stood an awe-inspiring, stone-built fortress. When it was ascertained that it was not manned, the Spaniards felt greatly relieved, for if only a few Indians had been there to impede their advance by rolling down some rocks, every one of the invaders would have been killed. Struggling on towards still higher regions, Pizarro and his men came upon another fort, and as this was also unoccupied, they took shelter in it for the night. Before daybreak the Indian interpreter, who a few days before had been sent as a kind of spy-messenger to the *Inca*, appeared in the fort with the welcome news that he had seen no signs of an ambush along the route he had followed to the Peruvian camp, and that, apparently, for the time being, the *Inca* had no hostile intentions. When, in continuation, the messenger reported that the Peruvian monarch was about to despatch two special envoys to the Spanish camp, Pizarro immediately sent a message to his rear guard, urging its commander to catch up with him with all possible haste, for he feared that if the *Inca's* ambassadors found him with only a hundred men, they would not be impressed. Meanwhile he proceeded with all speed towards the summit of the pass, for there, should treachery be intended, he could at least defend himself. In order to find out more about the movements of the Peruvian army, he once more sent his interpreter to the *Inca* with a message.

Shortly after Pizarro and his men had reached their immediate objective, the rear guard caught up with him. Though the long and arduous climb to the high, cold and wind-swept heights left horses and men exhausted, all were proud to have won a victory over nature.

Soon after the rear guard had rejoined Pizarro's detachment, the envoys from the *Inca's* camp arrived. They presented the Spaniards with ten llamas, and enquired in the name of their ruler when the white men expected to arrive at Cajamarca, it being the *Inca's* intention to send them further supplies. Pizarro courteously replied that he would march with all possible haste, and that he was looking forward to greeting their ruler as a friend. When the Peruvian ambassadors praised the *Inca*, and with great pride recalled the victories he had recently won over his brother's armies, Pizarro arrogantly told them that the monarch who had sent him across the seas was greater and mightier than any *Inca* ever had been, and in order to impress his dumbfounded visitors he vaunted that in war white men were invincible.

Twenty-four hours after the *Inca's* envoys had departed to deliver these messages, another royal ambassador, accompanied by a number of servants who brought ten more llamas as gifts, arrived in the Spanish camp. The visitor—who must have been a nobleman of rank—had a golden vessel filled with an alcoholic beverage made of fermented maize, whereupon he toasted the assembly. This done, he said that he had been sent to accompany the white men to Cajamarca where the *Inca* was waiting to receive them. In continuation he then proceeded to ask a number of questions which sounded somewhat suspicious, and when he wound up a long harangue about the glories of his monarch by vaunting the Peruvian armies' power and prowess to the skies, the Spanish officers who listened to him, felt sure that this was done to impress and frighten them.

When the interpreter-spy Pizarro had for the second time sent to Cajamarca to deliver a message to the *Inca* returned and saw the Peruvian nobleman, he threw himself at him in a fury, and began to kick and beat him. Having separated the two struggling men, Pizarro asked the aggressor to give his reason for thus assaulting a representative of the *Inca*, to which the interpreter hotly replied : "Why do you expect patience from me when you honour this spy and liar. The *Inca* gave me no audience and no food, and I was ill-treated, and barely managed to escape with my life."

The infuriated interpreter went on shouting that Cajamarca had been evacuated, and that Atahualpa and his army were encamped out in the open country. He warned Pizarro not to trust the Peruvians, and related that when he had tried to impress a chieftain by telling him about the irresistible arms possessed by the Spaniards, his listener had merely laughed, and replied that the white men's army was much too small to be taken seriously.

Having somewhat recovered from the shock of the interpreter's assault, the Peruvian nobleman said that in view of the fact that the *Inca* was keeping a fast, he could grant no audiences, and he assured Pizarro that his ruler's intentions towards the Spaniards were friendly.

Not knowing what to believe, Pizarro put a stop to the heated argument between the two antagonists, but upon resuming his march he took every precaution to avoid being caught unawares.

Descending from the high mountains, the Spaniards came to beautiful fertile regions where the climate was delightfully mild. After several short days' marches, Cajamarca was sighted in a green valley of about fifteen miles in length and nine in width. The town, with its symmetrically arranged rows of low straw-roofed houses, and the many neat cultivations in the vicinity, surpassed anything seen on the other side of the Andean range. Far away, on the opposite side of the valley, on the green slopes of a hill, Pizarro and his handful of men beheld a sight that filled the bravest among them with consternation, and not a few with fear. Grouped in perfectly straight rows, masses of tents could be seen, illuminated by the brilliant afternoon sun.

Although the Spaniards had been prepared for a surprise, the sight of so vast and well organized an encampment filled them with serious apprehension, especially so because hitherto the opposition they had encountered during different expeditions in the New World, had amounted to nothing more than undisciplined mobs of badly armed savages. But evidently the Peruvian army was a very different proposition, and therefore, as Pizarro and his men stared at the sinister looking sea of tents on the opposite side of the valley, everyone realized that it was too late now to retreat, and that the only hope of salvation lay in showing a bold front.

Having divided his little force into three groups, two of which he entrusted to his most reliable officers, Pizarro put himself at the head of the foremost, and then gave orders to march forward, with banners unfurled and trumpets blaring defiantly.

Entering the town, it was found to have been deserted by its inhabitants, excepting a few old men and women who wailed and otherwise demonstrated grief and fear. Judging by the number of houses, and the general aspect of the place, the Spaniards estimated that, normally, it must have contained about ten thousand inhabitants. The houses were well built, mostly of *adobe*, that is, baked clay, and they were covered with neatly thatched roofs, but a number of the larger constructions were made of stone, among them two strong fortresses. A vast triangular *plaza* was shut in by low, though spacious buildings, the doors of which faced the open space. The rooms of these had been constructed in such a manner that the Spaniards guessed they must be barracks.

The mountains were beginning to assume tints of red when the Spanish troops had installed themselves in their new quarters. Every precaution to guard against a surprise attack having been taken, Pizarro sent de Soto with fifteen horsemen to visit the *Inca*. In order to impress him, the soldiers wore the brightest armour available, and their steeds were adorned with the finest trappings. Felipillo (the Indian youth from Tumbez who had made the voyage to Spain with Pizarro) accompanied the party as interpreter. Shortly after de Soto had departed, Pizarro, fearing that his envoy might be attacked by the Peruvians, sent his brother Hernando and a further twenty horsemen to act as rear-guard.

As de Soto and his escort with palpitating hearts reined up at the *Inca's* camp, the Indian warriors stood motionless, staring with amazement at the horses. When Felipillo inquired where the *Inca* was to be found, a white building was pointed out to him. It was situated a little beyond the mass of tents, against the side of the hill on the gentle slopes of which the Peruvian army was encamped. Upon approaching the low though spacious edifice, the Spaniards guessed that it must be a kind of pleasure house, for it had a large courtyard, and near it was a thermal bath, hewn out of the rocks.

Shortly after de Soto had brought his fiery horse to a standstill outside the *Inca's* temporary dwelling place, Atahualpa, surrounded by many of his noblemen, appeared with great pomp and dignity. As he happened to be keeping a fast, he only wore the simplest of clothes, his chief garment being a kind of shirt called *uncu ;* but in dazzling contrast his courtiers were attired in flowing robes, dyed and embroidered in brilliant colours and hues. They were bedecked with magnificent ornaments made of gold, and studded with precious stones, and all wore heavy pendants which hung from their ears, the lobes of which were so enlarged and distended that they reached down to the shoulders, and in some cases even half-way down to the chest.

The Spaniards were so amazed by this display of colour and wealth that they gazed at the scene, bewildered and in utter amazement.

The *Inca* was easily recognized, for round the top of his head was wound a crimson strip of cloth with fringes that hung over the forehead, down to the eyes. About thirty years of age, Atahualpa was strongly built, and although his head was somewhat large for his height, and his eyes were bloodshot, Spanish chroniclers describe him as having been good-looking and a striking figure of a man. His sphinx-like, totally expressionless countenance was partly assumed, and he moved with the dignity befitting a ruler of undisputed authority, and of one who by his subjects was thought to be a divinity.

Having seated himself on a richly decorated low stool, he remained motionless and silent, his eyes fixed to the ground, and after a while asked what his visitors desired. De Soto then dismounted, and having made a respectful obeisance, politely answered through Felipillo that his captain, Pizarro, desired to meet the *Inca* personally, in order to pay his respects, and also to tell him what had brought him across the seas. He went on to say that his commander would consider it a great honour if the *Inca* would deign to dine with him in Cajamarca that night, or on the morrow. In continuation, de Soto explained that although the white men were strangers in the *Inca's* land, they desired to treat him with all the reverence and honour due to a great and mighty prince.

To this Atahualpa replied that he appreciated the kind thoughts of the white men's captain, but that, being the hour late, and he was keeping a fast, he would visit Pizarro next day. De Soto then inquired if the *Inca* wished him to take any further message to his commander. Atahualpa then said that he wished to have Pizarro informed that, although he would arrive in Cajamarca with his army in full marching order, the Spanish leader need not be alarmed.

At this stage Hernando Pizarro rode up, and when the *Inca* was informed that the new arrival was the brother of the white men's commander, he raised his eyes for the first time and told Hernando that a certain chieftain had informed him that he had killed three of the white men, and one of their horses. This, the *Inca* added, had been done because the Spaniards had ill-treated some of his subjects in that neighbourhood. At the same time he explained that, in spite of this, he wished to be the white man's friend, and repeated that, on the following day, he would visit their commander.

To this Hernando Pizarro arrogantly replied that the chieftain who had sent this information was a braggart and a liar, and he asked Felipillo to tell Atahualpa that the Indians in the valley in question were like so many old women, all of whom one horseman of his could rout single handed, as the Inca would discover if ever he saw a Spaniard fight. Hernando then assured the *Inca* that, notwithstanding the white soldiers' invincibility, his brother wished to be his friend, and that he offered his aid against any prince who might wage war against him.

" Four days' journey from here," Atahualpa replied, " are some very formidable foes of mine, against whom I can do nothing. There you can go and assist my soldiers."

Hernando then boasted: "Ten of our horsemen shall go. This number will suffice. Your soldiers only need to show us where the foe lies hidden!" For an instant a faint sarcastic smile flickered across the *Inca's* sphinx-like face.

Presently, a number of young Indian beauties appeared with large golden goblets filled with an alcoholic beverage. The Spaniards who had previously discovered that this was made from maize that had been well masticated and mixed with saliva, hesitated for a moment, but, to avoid offending their hosts, drank sparingly of it. Throughout this interview, in order to be ready in the event of an act of treachery, all the visitors, with the exception of de Soto and Hernando Pizarro, had remained mounted, ready to spring into action instantly.

Ever since the *Inca* had raised his eyes off the ground to look at Hernando Pizarro, he had kept them fixed on de Soto's fiery charger who, keen to be on the move, neighed, snorted and pawed the ground. Having observed Atahualpa's curiosity, de Soto—who was a great rider—leapt into the saddle, and proceeded to put his well-trained mount through his paces. In those days every Spanish Don practised the art of *haute école* riding, and as de Soto was the best mounted man in the Spanish camp, and famed for his horsemanship, he gave a performance which not only astonished the *Inca*, but one even his own countrymen watched with admiration. Every now and again, in order to show the animal's speed, the rider spurred it into a fast gallop, and raced down an avenue between the tents. Some of the frightened onlookers withdrew hurriedly when the horse tore towards them, but although on several occasions de Soto purposely only checked his animal's wild career so late in dashing straight towards the seated *Inca*, that the breath moved the fringes of his crimson *borla* (headband), and flecks of foam from its mouth fell on Atahualpa, he remained stock still and unmoved. The soldiers and noblemen who showed signs of fear, the *Inca* ordered to be reprimanded, and those who fled from the horse, he had punished severely. According to one Spanish chronicler, indeed, two Peruvian soldiers were immediately executed for having run away in terror.

Soon after this fine display of horsemanship, de Soto and Hernando Pizarro took their leave of the *Inca*, and with loud trumpet blasts rode through the Peruvian camp. The Spaniards had done their best to impress Atahualpa, but his expressionless, sphinx-like countenance had never betrayed what he thought. Though the Spanish trumpets sounded gay and defiant as the little cavalcade passed through the Indian camp, de Soto and his men rode towards Cajamarca in silence, for every man realized that against an army such as the one they had seen, they stood no chance, should it come to an open combat. As the sun dipped behind the peaks of the *cordillera*, heavy black clouds collected overhead, and cold winds began to sweep down from the frozen heights, the icy blasts carrying with them sleet and rain, which added to the gloom and despondency of the men who thought their doom was near.

This feeling spread throughout the Spanish camp when it became known what de Soto and his escort had seen that evening. The only person who remained calm and undaunted was Pizarro, who summoned his officers to a council of war. Although he had made certain plans before crossing the mountains, he had kept those plans to himself. Now, as he revealed them to his officers, they sat speechless with astonishment, for their leader's resource and daring were almost beyond their comprehension. When Pizarro had spoken, all his listeners agreed with him that, desperate as his plan was, it offered the only possible chance of success and survival.

Sentries and guards having been placed at different points, in and around the town, Pizarro spent a sleepless night, making great efforts to cheer his men, and to restore their faltering courage. In the distance, hundreds of little fires could be seen flickering along the hill side where the *Inca's* army was encamped. The night was pitch-dark, and the only sounds heard by the dejected Spanish soldiers, were the mournful whistling of the wind, and at regular intervals the prolonged throaty cries of sentries as they called their *rondas*, making it known in the guardroom that there was nothing to report, and that every sentinel was at his post.

VII

THOUGH the Spanish soldiers felt the strain of recent forced marches over high and incredibly rough mountains, nervous tension among them was so high that few of them nodded off to sleep during the long and anxious hours of watching and waiting. Already before the first faint purple-green streaks of dawn silhouetted the jagged peaks in the east, there was great activity in Pizarro's camp, and when the sun rose in all its glory (Saturday, November 16th, 1532), over the snow-capped mountains, trumpets called the soldiers to muster in the *plaza*. Solemn mass having been performed by the priests who accompanied the force, the men were given a good meal, whereafter Pizarro carefully explained his plan in detail to the assembly. His address ended, he divided his calvary into three sections, numbering about twenty horse each. The rooms of the buildings which practically walled in the square, were so spacious that the cavalry could easily be accommodated in them. Rattles and little bells—brought from Spain to be given to Indian chiefs who always took a delight in such presents—were fastened to the horses' trappings, armour and swords were polished, and gay plumes fixed to helmets. The three sections of mounted troops having taken their positions inside different buildings, the infantry was likewise stationed in a number of houses, all the doors of which faced the *plaza*. The few arquebusiers and cross-bow men were given orders to hide themselves on roofs, and the two cannons were dragged up the steps which led into the stone fortress which dominated the *plaza*. Having placed the cannons in position, they were carefully loaded. Then, at a few points from where a good view of the valley could be obtained, look-outs were posted, to observe and report the movements of the *Inca's* army.

The sun was nearing its meridian, and still there appeared to be no movement in the Peruvian camp, and as the hours dragged on, suspense became almost unbearable to the Spanish soldiers who waited in their hiding places. Then, at long last, the look-outs who were stationed on the top of the fort, shouted down that the Peruvian army was moving, and excitement grew tenser and tenser as, at intervals, further news about its progress was given.

The advanced guard, numbering about twelve thousand men, was armed with copper maces, and slings ; primitive weapons not to be scoffed at when used by strong arms and dexterous hands. Behind this body followed a few thousand warriors whose weapons consisted of long poles to which were fixed lassos. The huge rear-guard was entirely made up of lancers, and finally came the servants and numerous women of the royal household. In the centre of this enormous procession was the *Inca*, seated on a golden throne, placed on a litter carried by noblemen.

Pizarro hastily went round to give final instructions to his officers and men, upon whom he once more impressed the vital importance of remaining hidden and silent until a signal was given. He then selected twenty of his most trusted soldiers to stay beside him, ready to take his orders, or to follow him wherever he might be needed. Having taken his position in the interior of a house through the practically closed door of which he could see the *plaza*, Pizarro, like all his men, waited.

The shadows of evening were beginning to lengthen when it was reported that the Peruvians had halted about three miles out of the town, and that it looked as if they intended to camp there for the night. This information puzzled Pizarro who realized that if his troops had to stand to another night, they would be wearied in the morning, for two sleepless nights, after the exhausting forced march across the mountains and all the recent suspense and worry, would

be more than they could stand. It being a clear case of
" Now or Never ", he immediately sent a messenger to
inform the *Inca* that everything was prepared for his
reception, and that the white men would be most
disappointed if he put off his promised visit for another
day.

When the envoy returned with the news that Atahualpa
accepted the invitation and would be on his way as soon as
possible, all those who heard it felt relieved, though their
excitement and nervous tension grew as time slowly passed.
The messenger further reported that the *Inca* intended to
leave the bulk of his army encamped outside the town, and
that he would come accompanied by only five or six thousand
men. This information sounded too good to be true, and
therefore filled Pizarro with grave suspicions, for previously,
from different Indian chiefs, he had heard that Atahualpa
was sagacious and cunning, and that, in war, his cruelty
and ruthlessness knew no bounds.

Once more, hearts palpitating with excitement, and in
some cases fear, the Spaniards waited and listened, and the
few who were in positions to peep out of their hiding-places
did so very cautiously. For some time the only noises that
occasionally broke the deadly silence were the snorts and
stampings of impatient horses whose masters stood beside
them, swords drawn, or lances tightly gripped, ready to
mount and sally forth.

At last, in the distance, weird chanting could be heard,
slowly coming nearer and nearer. The *Inca* was approaching.
Another seemingly interminable spell of waiting followed,
and then, at last, a stream of hundreds of Indians entered
the *plaza*, still chanting, and at the same time sweeping the
ground with small branches of trees, figuratively to clean
the path for their monarch. Behind them, clad in robes of
various bright colours, came a body-guard, followed by an
array of richly dressed noblemen. For some time this
impressive procession slowly streamed into the spacious
plaza which began to fill with a mass of humanity. Without
a word of command being given, the Indians then opened

a wide path, and stood in silence as the *Inca* appeared, seated on his golden throne.

As customary on State occasions, he wore a dazzling mantle known as *llacolla*, round his head the imperial crimson *borla* (a band with fringes), and he was bedecked with golden ornaments and precious stones. In his left hand he held a sceptre of gold and silver (allusions to the sun and moon), and with his right arm he carried a golden shield, embossed with the image of the sun. The designs worked into his mantle were of extreme delicacy, being in several colours and shades, interwoven with threads of gold, and engraved knee coverings and sandals of the same metal completed his costume. A few dwarfs held *achihuas*, that is, many-coloured parasols made of bright feathers from regions far beyond the mountains, over his head.

Like the *Inca*, the courtiers and noblemen who surrounded or carried his litter, wore many ornaments which sparkled and glittered as the last rays of the evening sun played on them.

Having reached the middle of the *plaza*, the bearers of the palankeen halted, whereupon Atahualpa stood up, and majestically looked round, as if demanding that the white man appear at once. At this juncture a Dominican friar, named Valverde, accompanied by Felipillo, the interpreter, stepped out of a house, and, carrying a large wooden cross in one hand, and a Bible in the other, approached the *Inca*. Having made a respectful obeisance, the friar held up his cross before the astonished and mystified *Inca*. Then, with the doubtful assistance of Felipillo (who himself probably did not comprehend a word of what he was supposed to translate) Valverde said that he was a servant of the only true God, and that, as such, it was his duty to teach His word, as set down in the Holy Gospel. With this, for the *Inca's* inspection, he held up the Bible. Atahualpa looked on, and listened in silence, his sphinx-like face betraying nothing of what he thought. The Friar then tried to explain a few of the mysteries of the Christian Faith, and when he thought that his stolid listener had comprehended at least something of what he had said, he proceeded to tell him that the Pope and the King of Castile had entrusted Pizarro with the Governorship of Peru. He urged the *Inca* to abjure his heathen gods and to embrace the Christian Faith, and to swear allegiance to King Charles the Fifth, and to submit to Pizarro who, Valverde assured Atahualpa, had come as a friend, for the true God abhorred war. With this he again held out the Bible which the *Inca* now took in his hand. Having examined the, to him, strange and unattractive object, he flung it to the ground, with a gesture of disdain and annoyance, and exclaimed in a fury : " Tell those rascals to come here ! Well do I know what they have done on their march, how they have ill-treated some of my chieftains, and how they have plundered my store-houses. They shall not move from here until they have given me satisfaction for their misdeeds, and until they have paid for what they have stolen ! "

The friar attempted to make excuses, but it was of no avail. Even though the *Inca* had failed to comprehend the speech regarding the Christian Faith, he certainly had understood that a, to him, unknown Pope and a King, powerful and mighty as they might be in their own lands across the seas, had had the audacity to give away an empire that did not belong to them, and, furthermore, one they had not even conquered. It was absurd, intolerable.

Realizing that nothing would pacify Atahualpa, Valverde hastily retrieved his Bible, in so doing dropping the cross, and with bowed head hurried towards the house in which Pizarro was hiding. " You have seen the action of this haughty heathen dog ? " he exclaimed. " At him—I absolve you ! "

Pizarro—who like his men was a sincere though, according to to-day's standards, fanatical believer—crossed himself and bowed. Then stepping outside the door, he raised his sword—the fateful signal. Almost at the same instant the cannons in the fortress thundered, muskets and arquebuses responded, trumpets blared, and out of the many doors which faced the *plaza*, sprang soldiers yelling the old Spanish battle-cry : " Santiago y cierra España ! "* From three sides the cavalry charged, the rattles and bells that had been fixed to the horses' harness jingling loudly, thus adding to the Peruvians' terror, and causing them to stagger back towards the centre of the *plaza* in a panic. In the wild commotion, thousands of Indians, blind with fear, swirled round like so many harassed sheep.

Spanish chroniclers who took part in this onslaught, maintain that although Atahualpa had sent word that he would come unarmed, his warriors carried weapons concealed under their clothes.

One of Pizarro's brothers, as well as other writers of that period, even affirm that, so certain was the *Inca* of capturing the whole Spanish force, that some of his men had brought with them implements wherewith to gouge out the white men's eyes. On the other hand, some eye witnesses contradict these statements, declaring that the Indians were unarmed, and therefore entirely at the mercy of the Spanish soldiers.

The tightly serried mass of panic-stricken Indians swayed to and fro, and eventually a section of them was thrown against a high wall that stood between the houses on one side of the *plaza*. There hundreds were trampled underfoot, and the onrush was so violent that in a matter of seconds, a heap was formed against the wall, causing it to collapse. Through this gap hundreds fled wildly into the open, hotly pursued by a section of the Spanish cavalry. Sensing disaster, the bulk of the Peruvian army and the royal entourage which

---

* This battle cry is somewhat difficult to translate into English, but perhaps the following version is acceptable : " St. James, and shoulder to shoulder Spain." In this case the Spanish verb *cierra* corresponds to the English adjective " serried," applied to ranks of soldiers.

Santiago (or San Jago) is the Patron Saint of Spain. According to a legend, St. James the Greater, as he is known in England, died in martyrdom in Jerusalem, in the year A.D. 42. His body was brought to Spain where he is said to have preached during his lifetime. His remains were buried in a marble coffin, and subsequently forgotten for some eight hundred years, when a shepherd miraculously discovered the grave. King Alfonso the Chaste ordered a chapel to be built on the ground where the apostle had been buried, and later the cathedral of Santiago de Compostella was erected there. This cathedral became a favourite place of pilgrimage for thousands of European Christians.

were encamped some three miles outside the town, were thrown into confusion, men and women fleeing towards the mountains. Meanwhile, in the town, confusion was indescribable. Borne by his nobles, and surrounded by a mass of Indians, the *Inca* was still on his litter which swayed perilously as the Spaniards charged, cutting down those of his subjects who made heroic efforts to shield him.

Fearing that Atahualpa might be killed in this wild *mêlée*, Pizarro, accompanied by his chosen twenty, slashed his way through the sea of Indians, towards the litter which was being tossed about like a raft during a storm. Shouting loudly, he commanded his men not to kill the *Inca*, and upon reaching the litter he seized Atahualpa's robes, and dragged him down to the ground. Whilst Pizarro's arm was outstretched, one of his own soldiers accidentally wounded him in the hand, and another Spaniard—who must have been a bit of a souvenir hunter—tore the imperial *borla* off the *Inca's* head.

Seeing their monarch fall, immediately to be hustled into a house as a prisoner, the horrified Indians scattered in every direction. By this time it was getting dark, and when the massacre came to an end, as suddenly as it had started, a heavy, cold rain began to fall, drowning the moans of the wounded and dying Indians who lay thickly strewn about the *plaza*. The sun had set for the last time on the *Inca's* Empire, and the icy blasts from the mountains sang its threnody.

The news of Atahualpa's captivity soon reached thousands of his subjects who continued their flight in every direction. Many hundreds of their comrades had been slain ; but, incredible as it may seem, the only Spaniard who had been slightly injured in this bloody *coup de main*, was Pizarro with his accidental hand-wound.

Though ankle-shackles were placed on Atahualpa, and he was kept under the watchful eye of a strong guard which made escape impossible, he was well and respectfully treated. He accepted the misfortune so philosophically that, after the massacre, when he was seated next to his conqueror at a banqueting table, he was calm, composed, and even talkative. When Pizarro apologized for having to hold him as a prisoner, he replied that there was nothing unusual about this, for in war it was natural that one army should be victorious, and the other vanquished. Through Felipillo's interpretership the *Inca* declared that from the first day the Spaniards had set foot on Peruvian soil, he had constantly been informed as to their movements. He even admitted that, having heard that they were so few in numbers, he had purposely allowed them to cross the mountains unmolested, for besides being curious to see men from another world, he had felt confident that it would be an easy matter to overpower them, and to take their novel arms and horses.

That night, before the Spanish soldiers lay down for a much needed rest, mass was said. After this, in a brief address, Pizarro told them that although Providence had assisted them to gain a victory, dangers still existed, and that it was necessary to be on the alert, ready to spring into action at once, should the Indians rally and attempt a surprise attack. However, the night passed without incident, and next morning, with the assistance of Indians who had been rounded up, the dead were buried, and the town generally put to rights. On the previous day, at the end of the interview with the *Inca*, Friar Valverde had dropped his large wooden cross in the excitement. Believing that this mysterious object held supernatural powers, and was the secret of the white men's invincibility, throughout the night, and for several days after the massacre, Indians were seen to adore it, the cross having been planted in an upright position where the friar had dropped it.

With the *Inca* in his hands, and the imperial army utterly demoralized, Pizarro now began to formulate his plans for the future. First of all, he sent a party of soldiers to bring back the booty left in Atahualpa's camp. They found that everything had been abandoned, the reason for this being that no one had dared to remove anything without orders from the *Inca*, whose belongings were held as sacred by his subjects. Therefore a rich booty of massive gold plate, precious stones, ornaments, and an enormous quantity of finely woven cloth, fell into the hands of the Spaniards. Of the many prisoners taken, a number, including some noblemen and women of the royal household, were kept to attend on Atahualpa. The others were released with the warning that, should they ever make war against the white men, a terrible fate awaited them.

Being well treated, the *Inca* soon settled down to his new mode of living, and appeared to be so indifferent to his lot that occasionally he even laughed and joked with the Spanish officers who taught him how to play with dice. The game he liked best was chess, the intracacies of which he soon mastered to such an extent that he became an excellent player, for he had a quick understanding of things. Among various articles some of the Spaniards gave to him was an ornate Venetian glass. Examining the gift with visible signs of delight, he asked if such fine drinking vessels were only used by the King in Castile. The donor who probably wished to impress Atahualpa, replied that not only kings, but noblemen and even common people drank out of such vessels in his homeland. Hearing this, the *Inca* let the glass fall from his hand, breaking it into many pieces, and at the same time haughtily exclaimed : " Then such a common thing does not merit the esteem of anyone ! "

During some of his long conversations with Pizarro, he told him that a few years previously a bright comet was seen in the heavens, earthquakes shook the land, and a thunder-bolt struck one of the royal palaces, causing a fire which burnt it to the ground. In the sky, high up above the conflagration, an eagle fought against several hawks, and the aerial combat ended in the king of birds crashing to the ground among the mass of people who watched it. Apparently all these extraordinary happenings had filled the Peruvians with awe and dismay, and in them wise men and priests saw predictions that terrible calamities were about to befall the *Inca* and his empire.

Momentous events had followed one another with such

lightning speed, and everything had gone so well for the Spaniards, that they could hardly believe that all this was not part of a fantastic dream. With the mighty Peruvian army defeated and scattered to the four winds, and the *Inca* in their hands, Pizarro's seemingly hopeless position had been reversed to one of strength, especially so because the natives believed their monarch to be a divine being without whose orders they dare do nothing. Another factor which greatly favoured the Spaniards was the fact that during a recently fought battle between Atahualpa and his brother, Huascar, the latter's main army had been defeated, and that the rival *Inca*, after having been captured, was detained as a prisoner in a fort somewhere among the nearby mountains. Despite Huascar's defeat, his supporters still hovered about certain sectors of the country, and until the Spaniards had arrived on the scene, had occupied the attention of Atahualpa's forces, and had taxed to the utmost the skill of his most able generals. Of this state of affairs Pizarro now hoped to make good use to his own advantage, for besides being an excellent soldier, he was a cunning diplomat.

Not only from Atahualpa, but also from some of the noblemen who were given permission to visit him, was obtained much valuable information, based on which Pizarro gradually formulated his plans for the future. For the time being, until reinforcements from Panama should arrive, he thought it unwise to venture further into the country concerning which his royal captive told him many amazing tales, especially about the capital, Cuzco. During many long interviews with Atahualpa and some of his visitors, these corroborated stories about temples filled with gold and precious stones, stories previously heard from different native chieftains. However, despite being convinced that fabulous wealth existed in Cuzco and in many other parts of this vast empire, Pizarro—who, though reckless and dashing at times, knew when to be cautious—decided that to move now would be dangerous, for his army was small, and a large proportion of it was required to guard Atahualpa who, at all costs, must not be allowed to escape.

Hoping to speed up the arrival of reinforcements who, in the meantime, might have reached the colony (San Miguel) at the coast, a messenger was despatched to give the news about the recent victory of Spanish arms, and to give as glowing an account as possible concerning the prospects of the future. The messenger having departed, Pizarro, realizing that inactivity presented many dangers, ordered his soldiers to fortify the town and to build a church. Whilst his troops were thus engaged, he and his most trusted officers continued to collect as much information about Peru as possible, questioning the *Inca*, chieftains who came to visit him, and, in fact, any native, man or woman, who was likely to throw light on different subjects and matters which were of importance to the conquerors. Foremost among these was the information gathered regarding the feud between Atahualpa and Huascar, and the war which had split the Inca empire into two factions. Months before, in Tumbez, the local *Curaca* (chief) had told Pizarro about this rift between the two brothers ; news which, at the time, had made him hope that, some day, he might be able to take advantage of this state of affairs.

After the recent defeat of Huascar's army, Atahualpa's victorious legions had entered the city of Cuzco where they massacred many people, and looted and burned many houses ; a bitter experience that was still fresh in the minds of the city's inhabitants who hated their conqueror who came from Quito in the far north.

From different sources Pizarro now heard that Huascar's supporters secretly rejoiced at the thought that Atahualpa was held a prisoner by the white men upon whom, he was further informed, they looked as saviours, sent by the sun-god to deliver them from their enemies.

Atahualpa—who was astute and very cunning—soon guessed why his captors took so keen an interest in the feud between him and his brother, and he began to fear that if his rival—whom he still held as a prisoner in the fort among the mountains—managed to escape, or if the Spaniards freed him, might easily be proclaimed sole monarch of the whole empire. As it turned out, Atahualpa's suspicions and fears were well-founded, and therefore, as time went on, he became more and more desperate to regain his liberty, and when he heard that Pizarro intended to arbitrate between him and Huascar, the alarm he felt was great. No one knew better than he that his brother's case against him was a strong one, and being a man possessed of sound reasoning powers he realized that Huascar's mild character was suited to make him an ideal puppet emperor for the Spaniards. Accordingly, in view of these disturbing facts and alarming developments behind his back, Atahualpa realized that he must do something quickly if he was to retain the throne for himself.

Ever since the first reports about the white men's arrival at the coast had reached him, he had suspected that gold was what most attracted them, and after the recent massacre when all the treasure was looted out of his abandoned camp outside Cajamarca, he was left in no doubt that his earliest suspicions had been well-founded. Based on the firm conviction that gold was his captor's greatest ambition, Atahualpa schemed and planned how to obtain his release.

One day, when Pizarro and some of his officers visited him, he suddenly made so staggering a proposition that, at first, they thought the prisoner had gone mad.

" If I cover this floor with gold and silver, will you set me free ? " he suddenly asked. Hearing this, the Spaniards looked at each other, and smiled incredulously, for surely this would be impossible, the room being twenty-two feet long, and sixteen wide. When Atahualpa noticed that the sincerity of his offer was received with doubt, he rose and walked towards one of the walls. Then, raising a hand, as high as he could reach, he made a mark, and at the same time exclaimed, " Not only will I cover the floor, but if you promise to give me my liberty, I will fill the room up to here ! "

The Spanish officers stood dumbfounded, staring in

amazement, and presently Pizarro spoke, his words being translated by Felipillo. A red line having been drawn along the wall, at the height the *Inca* had indicated with his outstretched hand, it was agreed that within the period of two months this space (some three thousand cubic feet) should be filled with gold, and, likewise, a smaller adjoining room with silver. A Spanish notary set on paper the terms of this astounding agreement, according to which Atahualpa was promised his freedom, provided the ransom was paid in full within the stipulated time, and under the further condition that he pledged himself to refrain from plotting, or any treasonable action against the Spaniards.

Immediately after having come to this agreement with Pizarro, the *Inca* sent messengers to the principal towns of his different States, with orders that all the gold and silver was to be taken out of palaces and temples, and be sent without delay to Cajamarca. To this order he added another equally important one, to the effect that his subjects were to refrain from any hostile act against the white men who were to be treated with the same honour, respect and obedience as he, the *Inca*, himself.

．　．　．　．　．

Unless in the company of Pizarro, or some of the Spanish captains, Atahualpa usually remained alone in a room, attended by his wives and concubines. His nobles only appeared before him when summoned. Before entering the royal chamber, they took off their *huarachos* (sandals) and on their bent backs placed a heavy bundle of sticks, in token of humility, submission and reverence. Atahualpa always treated his vassals with such indifference and haughtiness that even the most exalted of his nobles trembled with awe in his presence. He frequently changed his clothes and mantles which were made of finely woven vicuña wool, and some even of the silky skins of certain bats, carefully cured and stitched together. No garment, however costly, was worn more than once. The *Inca's* wardrobe being held as sacred, immediately after an article of clothing was taken off, female attendants packed it into a wooden box to be burnt without delay. Some of the cloaks worn by Atahualpa were of singular beauty, different patterns and colours being inwoven with great skill and artistry, and he was never seen without his peculiar *llautú*, a kind of turban of many bright colours. To this, in an upright position, set in a sparkling ornament, were affixed two plumes of a rare bird, only to be found in certain remote and desolate parts among the Andes.

Through the very doubtful medium of Felipillo, whose translations must have been all the more deficient because he himself had only a remote idea of the subject, Friar Valverde, assisted by Pizarro and some of his officers, diligently set themselves to convert Atahualpa to Christianity, but without success. Despite the fact that the intended convert expressed his belief that his deity must have forsaken him, and that he even went as far as to admit the possibility of his sun-god being inferior to the white men's God, he was convinced that he himself was of divine origin, being a pure and direct descendant of the first *Inca*, Manco Capac, and of his sister-wife, both of whom, according to his and his subjects' belief, had been sent to the earth by the Sun to civilize the inhabitants. Try as Valverde would, Atahualpa refused to forsake the deity of his forefathers.

As time passed, more and more noblemen and messengers visited the captive monarch, until, finally, Pizarro became suspicious that a hostile act was being plotted against him. At this stage, trouble with the Indians would have been a serious matter for the Spaniards who were desperately awaiting reinforcements from Panama.

Despite being kept in their respective captivities, both rivals to the Peruvian sceptre were secretly informed about events, and both managed to smuggle out, or receive messages. When Atahualpa heard that Huascar intended to promise the Spaniards an even larger ransom than he had undertaken to deliver for his release, he was greatly perturbed. Although his army had entered and sacked Cuzco, he himself had never been in that city, and consequently only relied on hearsay as far as the ancient capital's treasures were concerned ; treasures on which depended his release. When he sounded his captors to find out if his brother's intended offer had reached them, his spirits rose, for evidently they knew nothing of it ; but when he was informed that Pizarro thought of bringing Huascar to Cajamarca to examine which of the two was better qualified to occupy the Peruvian throne, he became so agitated that he lost his usual self-control and composure.

In the meantime, the Indian couriers who had been sent to various parts of the country to collect the gold and silver for the ransom, were on their way. One party which had been despatched to Cuzco was accompanied by three Spanish soldiers who, reclining in hammocks were carried by Indians. The distance from Cajamarca to Cuzco is well over six hundred miles, as the crow flies, and the highway followed led through some of the most extraordinary mountain regions in the world. Why Pizarro chose ignorant and irresponsible men for so important a mission is not known ; but possibly they were the only individuals in his force who by this time could speak and understand the *Quichua* language tolerably well. The three soldiers were sent to supervise and hasten the delivery of the gold, and also to bring back a report on Cuzco and the towns along the route.

Atahualpa's orders that the white men should be treated with the same honour and obedience as himself were carried out with such fidelity by his subjects that wherever the three Spaniards passed or halted, they were treated as semi-divinities. One can hardly be surprised that very soon this went to the ignorant adventurer's heads, and that they abused the Peruvians' servility, behaving in a most abominable manner. In Cuzco they were received with public festivities, and generally treated as if they were *Incas*, people believing that the white men had been sent by the Sun to lead them to happiness. The soldiers were amazed at what they saw, for Cuzco and its wealth surpassed anything they had anticipated. Taking full advantage of

Atahualpa's orders to his people, they impudently entered into palaces and temples which they ordered to be stripped of their gold, jewels and silver. Not satisfied with this, they humiliated noblemen and priests, and boldly made themselves at home in the sacred building where lived the Virgins of the Sun. The Spaniards, fully aware that no one dare lay hands on them, and that their orders would be obeyed instantly, made priests remove a mass of venerated ornaments, religious symbols, gold plate and other treasure from Peru's most sacred building, the Temple of the Sun. They were not satisfied with half measures !

Seeing all this sacrilege, and realizing that all the treasure that was being collected was to set free their hated enemy, Atahualpa, priests and noblemen hid away an immense quantity of gold and jewels, for why should they help one who was not the rightful heir to the throne, and one who only recently caused their town to be sacked ?

The sadly disillusioned people of Cuzco—who had acclaimed and welcomed the three Spanish soldiers as saviours—were glad to see them depart after a week, though they took with them two hundred loads of gold and twenty-five of silver ; a load being as much as four Indians could carry.

In the meantime, in Cajamarca, Pizarro heard rumours that an Indian army was assembling in a valley in the vicinity, and that an attack on the Spanish camp was imminent. He immediately sent his brother Hernando with twenty horsemen and twelve foot soldiers to reconnoitre the country. Should the report of the trouble brewing with the Indians prove to be without foundation, Hernando and his men had orders to travel south, to the holy city of Pachacamac, situated on the coast, near the city of Lima of to-day. There, according to Atahualpa, was to be found Peru's richest temple, dedicated to the deity Pachacamac,*

* Pachacamac signified " Giver of Life." Although the *Incas* and their people acknowledged Viracocha—embodied in the Sun—as their Supreme being, they never interfered with newly conquered peoples' religious belief. Accordingly, after having conquered the coastal regions near what is now the town of Lima, they merely built a Temple of the Sun alongside that of

worshipped by the inhabitants of those regions as the Creator of the world.

Atahualpa had told Pizarro so much with regard to the great temple in Pachacamac, and its spacious halls blazing with gold and precious stones, that he thought it advisable to supervise the transportation of this enormous treasure, and to make sure that it should be brought in its entirety to Cajamarca. Therefore, when Hernando found that everywhere he and his small detachment of soldiers went, the Indians were friendly, and that there was no sign of an uprising, he continued his march towards Pachacamac on the coast.

For a considerable distance, in the highland, a well constructed road was followed. This Peruvian highway was so good that, according to Hernando's own account, it was better than any in existence in Europe at the time. Rivers, streams and giddy canyons were crossed by means of bridges, some of which were made of stone. Others were of the suspension type, but even these were so strongly built

Pachacamac. Thus, with the passing of time, the two religions and their respective deities had fused into one, and the city of Pachacamac had become a kind of Mecca.

According to an old Peruvian legend, the god Viracocha appeared whilst one of the early *Incas* was travelling through the land. As in the story of Moses on Mount Sinai, the *Inca* is said to have been alone when the Divinity descended to earth to prophecy the fall of the *Incaic* empire. After the apparition had vanished, the *Inca* assembled his wise men and seers, and ordered a sanctuary to be built some fifty miles south of Cuzco, where the meeting between the two was believed to have taken place. In an inner chamber of this sanctuary he had placed a stone image of Viracocha, as he had appeared to him. Under the Inca's guidance, and according to his instructions, sculptors worked for some time until a tall figure, dressed in long flowing robes—unlike any worn by the Peruvians—was completed. But, stranger still, the figure had a beard, and held a large, strange animal, with claws like those of a lion, tied by the neck with a chain. Later, when some of the Spaniards saw this remarkable stone figure, they decided that it must be St. Bartholomew, who, they believed, must have been in Peru, preaching the gospel among the Indians. Unfortunately, both the figure of this bearded Viracocha as well as the sanctuary were destroyed by Pizarro's fanatical men.

As most of the Spaniards wore beards, and with their cannons and arquebuses could make noises like thunder, the Peruvians, convinced that they had descended from heaven, and had risen out of the sea, called them *Viracochas*, the name meaning "Foam of the Sea." (*Vira:* foam ; *cocha:* sea, or lake). Many Indians also called the Spaniards *Incas*, believing them to be sons of their god, the Sun.

that the horsemen could safely ride across them. Many beautiful and fertile valleys were traversed, and everywhere the Spaniards looked, there was evidence of the natives' industry and thrift. On the slopes of mountains grazed vast herds of llamas, tended by Indian shepherds who played weird music on reed flutes, or Pandean pipes, known as *pincullus* and *quenas*.

News that treasure was being collected to obtain the hated Atahualpa's release, and in all probability also information concerning the atrocious behaviour of the three soldiers Pizarro had sent to Cuzco to supervise the collecting of the ransom, had preceded Hernando's arrival at Pachacamac, *chasquis* (foot-runners) having been secretly dispatched from the capital to warn people in Peru's holy city against the white men and their ambitions. Therefore, when Hernando and his party arrived there, most of the gold and treasure had been hidden, and even the temple of the Virgins of the Sun was empty, its many attendants having been removed.

The city was of considerable size, and the majority of its houses were strongly built. The chief temple stood on a conical hill, and when Hernando presented himself at its main entrance, a number of excited priests barred his way. In vain they tried to explain that only the *Inca* and a few chosen holy men were allowed to enter into the sanctuary, and it looked as if Hernando would have to force his way in when an earthquake shook the region, making the priests and people flee in terror. Instead of being frightened by this unexpected occurrence, the Spaniards felt convinced that the Divine Hand was intervening on their behalf. Therefore, undismayed, they rushed up the hill, and tore open the door of the *sanctum sanctorum*. Instead of seeing, as they had hoped, a hall with walls lined with gold, and a mass of sparkling jewels, all Hernando and his men found was a crude wooden idol representing Pachacamac. The fanatical Spaniards then proceeded to wreck the place, and to smash the idol into many pieces. This done, a wooden cross was erected, whilst from the distance the Peruvians looked on in horror.

Having recovered from their first shock, a delegation of priests and noblemen came forward to tender their homage to Hernando whom they now regarded as a supernatural being who even had control over the elements. Taking advantage of the situation, he told them that they had been adoring false gods, and in a brief address, urged them to mend their ways, and to pray to the only true God, symbolized by the wooden cross his soldiers had erected.

A considerable quantity of gold having been discovered buried near the temple, Hernando decided to depart without delay, for he had heard the alarming news that one of Atahualpa's two ablest generals, with an army of over thirty thousand men, was encamped in Jauja, a strongly fortified town situated in the mountains, about one hundred and twenty miles east of Pachacamac. Taking with him twenty-seven " loads " of gold, and a considerable quantity of silver, he boldly set out, determined to capture the redoubtable Peruvian general whom he suspected of standing to with his army, waiting for a secret order to march on Cajamarca to destroy Pizarro's force. Considering that Hernando only had thirty-nine men with him, it seems suicidal that he should have marched against so vast an army, commanded by a general who was famous throughout Peru. However, by this time the Spaniards had full confidence in themselves, and, above all, they relied on the *Inca's* order that no one should molest them.

The forced march from the coast into the mountains was not accomplished without difficulties, and when the last of the spare horse shoes had been worn out on the rocky ground, Indian smiths were ordered to make new ones of a mysterious hard silver alloy.

Jauja was a large town, and upon arriving there the Spaniards found that the Peruvian army was camped some miles outside. Messengers were immediately sent to invite its commander to visit Hernando, but it was only after several vain efforts that the suspicious Indian finally presented himself in the Spanish camp, bringing with him a quantity of gold he had collected as a contribution towards

Atahualpa's ransom. After some persuasion he agreed to accompany the expedition on its return journey to Cajamarca, and there to visit the Inca. Being a person of royal blood, the Peruvian general was carried in a litter, surrounded by many chieftains, and everywhere he passed or halted, the natives issued forth to pay him homage.

VIII

SEVERAL months passed, and Atahualpa was still a prisoner in Cajamarca. From different parts of his empire columns of carriers brought contributions towards his ransom, and as the treasure mounted up, the members of his faction looked forward to the day of his release.

For some time Pizarro had suspected that his royal prisoner was secretly communicating with his generals, and he feared that Indian armies were massing among the mountains, making preparations to attack Cajamarca. When he accused the *Inca* of being the instigator of such a plot, his captive denied it, and assured him that his orders to be friendly towards the Spaniards were being obeyed by all his subjects. However, despite these assurances, Pizarro still had his doubts, and when tidings were received that, on Atahualpa's orders, Huascar had been put to death, this came as a bitter blow and disappointment to those of the Spaniards who had hoped to make the victim a puppet emperor.

According to reports, when the murderers dragged Huascar out of his prison, he vainly tried to soften their hearts, and as he was being thrown into a turbulent mountain river—from which his body was never recovered—he had exclaimed, " My reign has been short, but the traitor who disposes of my life, though he was my subject will reign no longer than I."

Huascar's assassination coincided with several other important events.

News reached Pizarro that, at last, his partner Almagro had arrived from Panama with four vessels and two hundred men, including fifty horse, and two or three experienced captains. Apparently the newcomers had suffered great hardships during their sea journey, and the disheartened men were clamouring to return to Panama when, in the bay of Guayaquil, they received the first news about Pizarro and his expedition whom they had given up for lost. Having reached the colony (San Miguel) on the banks of the river Piura, Almagro and his men heard about Pizarro's successful campaign, and when they were told about Atahualpa's captivity and the enormous ransom offered for his release, discontent gave way to wild enthusiasm.

Almagro had with him an official Government secretary who proved to be a cunning intriguer. He must have known that two years before, when Pizarro had started out from Panama on his last expedition, he and Almagro had not parted on friendly terms, due to the fact of jealousy over the appointments of the Council of the Indies in Spain.

Shortly after the newcomers landed in Peru, this secretary —who evidently intended to run with the hare and with the hounds—secretly sent Pizarro a note, warning him that Almagro had not come to join him, but to make an expedition on his own account, and that it was his intention to establish an independent government in the lands he hoped to conquer. When this note reached its destination, Pizarro, instead of being alarmed or annoyed, immediately sent a message of welcome to his partner, and asked him to hurry to Cajamarca and share in his good fortune. When Almagro discovered his secretary's malicious intrigues, he brought him to trial, and, finding him guilty of treachery, ordered him to be hanged.

Ever since Pizarro had set out from the colony on his memorable march into the unknown to meet the *Inca* and his vast army, the officials who had been sent to Peru by the Spanish Government to supervise the sharing out of treasure and land, had snugly and cautiously remained behind the stockades of San Miguel near the coast. When the newly arrived reinforcements made ready to depart to Cajamarca, these careful officials, very true to type, as well as a few soldiers who had preferred to remain in the colony, thought the moment had arrived in fair safety to venture into the interior of the country. Accordingly, when Almagro and his force set out in the direction of the forbidding-looking mountains, these cautious gentlemen seized the opportunity to travel under his protecting wing, for now all were most anxious to be present at the share-out of the rich spoils.

After an uneventful march, as Almagro approached his destination, Pizarro, accompanied by a number of his men, rode out of the town to meet the new arrivals, and when the two commanders met, they greeted one another with demonstrations of sincere joy and friendship. (April 1533).

Pizarro was delighted to hear that, since last he had seen his old associate, the King of Spain had conferred on him the title of " Marshal ". Side by side the two friends then rode into the town, followed by the soldiers, many of whom were now reunited with old friends and former companions-in-arms. Upon arrival in Cajamarca, Almagro lost no time in calling on the *Inca*, who was the object of great curiosity to all the newcomers.

Although the appearance of more Spanish soldiers added to Atahualpa's fears and apprehensions, he did not betray his thoughts, but when, shortly after Almagro had arrived, a bright light was seen drifting across the heavens, superstitious fears cast him into a deep gloom, for he remembered that a few days before his father died, a similar sign had been observed.

Old differences between Pizarro and Almagro seemed to be forgotten, and as more and more gold flowed into Cajamarca, the Spanish soldiers' spirits rose higher and higher, and all looked toward a life of ease and opulence.

About a month after the reinforcements had arrived, news was received that Hernando Pizarro was approaching the town on his return journey from Pachacamac. Pizarro, accompanied by Almagro and a number of officers, joyfully rode out to meet the men who had been to the Holy City after gold. When Hernando saw Almagro (whom he had hated ever since their first meeting in Panama) he turned away from him, and to such an extent showed his feelings of annoyance, that Pizarro had to intervene, and force him to offer his apologies. Although Almagro accepted the offender's outstretched hand, this incident was to be like the spark which smoulders until, eventually, it causes a conflagration.

The Indian general Hernando brought with him had behaved in a most dignified and even haughty manner during the long march, but upon arriving in Cajamarca, he became a different man. Before entering the room in which the *Inca* was to receive him, he took off his sandals, and placed the customary bundle of sticks upon his bent back, thus demonstrating his submission and respect. Upon approaching Atahualpa he trembled violently, and after having raised his hands as if greeting the rising sun, he knelt down to kiss his feet. Then, weeping bitterly, he lamented the disaster which had befallen his master, and exclaimed that this would never have happened if he had been with him. The Spaniards who were present at this interview, observed the Peruvian general's expressions of loyalty and submission in silence, and they were amazed to see that not for one moment did Atahualpa lose his customary composure, but, without uttering a word, received these respects as if he were a god.

A few days after these events, the three soldiers who had been sent to Cuzco, arrived with their enormous treasure and many breath-taking stories about the marvels they had seen during their long journey. When their companions heard these, and saw the two hundred loads of gold—among them seven hundred plaques which had been torn off the walls of the Temple of the Sun—they went wild with excitement.

Despite the enormous quantity of treasure so far brought to Cajamarca, the two rooms in which it was deposited were not yet filled up to the line that had been drawn along the walls, and the time set for the payment of the ransom had elapsed. When reproached for the delay, the *Inca* explained that on account of the great distances his couriers had to travel, it would take some time to bring in the full requirements. This explanation, however, failed to satisfy Pizarro who suspected that the delay was part of a scheme to give Atahualpa's armies time to rally. On the other hand, his prisoner may have guessed that, despite his orders, much of the gold in temples and palaces had been hidden away by followers of his late brother, who bore him no goodwill.

As, at intervals, Indian carriers brought in more gold, the greedy Spanish soldiers' demand that the treasure so far collected should be shared out, became louder and louder, and as their impatience grew, and some of the officers joined in their demand, Pizarro eventually expressed his willingness to satisfy their desire.

The official opening of the treasure room was preceded by a solemn religious ceremony during which divine guidance was invoked. All those who were present realized that the share-out would involve great difficulties, if every man's claims and hopes were to be satisfied.

The treasure consisted of many different articles ; vases, plates, and a mass of ornaments, made of gold and silver of different degrees of purity. Therefore in order to make the division fair and accurate, it was decided to melt down everything, and to reduce the articles to bars of uniform metallic standard, gold and silver. Before the process of melting down was commenced by expert Indian goldsmiths —who worked day and night for a month—a number of articles, such as vases, plates, goblets, imitations of plants and figures of animals that were of special artistic merit, were put aside to be sent to the Court in Spain. Unfortunately, the bulk of delicately and ingeniously made masterpieces of Peruvian art went to the melting furnaces, and thus the world lost for ever many fine and interesting pieces.*

* Greatly as this is to be lamented, it must, however, be pointed out, that in Pizarro's time art *connosseurs* were few and far between in Europe, and that men who ventured into unknown parts in the newly discovered world, were not collectors of masterpieces.

The distribution of the ransom caused a great deal of controversy, especially so because the soldiers who only recently had arrived on the scene with Almagro, claimed their full share. When Pizarro's men argued that they had done all the dangerous work, and captured the *Inca*, the newcomers maintained that, before enlisting in Panama, they had been promised an equal share in the gains of the campaign. After much haggling, it was finally agreed that the *Almagristas*—as Almagro's men were called—should receive 100,000 *pesos* of gold, to be divided among them as they pleased, and that in future they would be entitled to their full individual share of treasures obtained.

All the gold and silver bars having been stacked up, and the religious ceremony concluded, the distribution of the richest booty known in history was commenced.

Pizarro conducted the difficult and delicate task with such skill and fairness that, even though no records exist about various other men who had financed his expeditions in Panama, it must be assumed that none of them were overlooked.*

The next important step to be taken was to inform the Court in Spain about events and happenings in Peru. After some debating, it was agreed that Hernando Pizarro should make the voyage, and personally deliver the royal

* It must be borne in mind that in those days gold was scarce in Europe, and that in consequence the purchasing value of one *peso de oro* was very much higher than it would be to-day. For this reason it is almost impossible to ascertain in modern monetary terms and values what Atahualpa's ransom was worth in Pizarro's time. It must be sufficient, then, to state that the total amount of gold was 1,326,539 *pesos de oro* (gold) and 51,610 *marcos de plata* (marks of silver).

The customary royal fifth having been deducted, most of the cavalry-men received an average of 9,000 *pesos* of gold, and 300 marks of silver. The share of those who belonged to the infantry was about half of these amounts per head. Certain soldiers who had especially distinguished themselves, received extra rewards, whereas others, in particular those who had remained in the colony at the coast, had to be content with very little. According to rank and merit, officers and captains received their shares and rewards, Pizarro topping the list with 52,222 *pesos* of gold, and 2,350 *marcos* of silver, besides the Inca's golden throne, valued at 25,000 *pesos*. Among the captains, his brother, Hernando, and de Soto, came off best. Whether Pizarro shared his part of the treasure with Almagro is not known, but as the two remained on very friendly terms, it is to be presumed that the latter had reason to be satisfied. The third partner, Father Luque, had died in Panama.

fifth of Atahualpa's ransom and of the other treasures obtained during the campaign. The moment being opportune, Hernando was to seek further powers of administration for Pizarro, and honours and titles for some of those who had particularly distinguished themselves in the field of action. It is probable that Hernando was chosen for this delicate mission because he had the necessary polish for appearing before the Court, and, perhaps, also on account of the differences between him and Almagro, for ill-feeling still smouldered in both men's minds, despite their forced reconciliation. From the fact that Hernando received a surprisingly large share of the treasure, it may be surmised that it was hoped that he would remain in Spain, satisfied with the wealth he had obtained. He was to ask the King to appoint Almagro Governor of the yet unconquered lands, situated south of Pizarro's jurisdiction. Almagro so distrusted Hernando that he secretly urged two friends—who were also to make the voyage to Spain—to keep watch on him, and, if necessary, to plead at the Court on his behalf.

When Hernando departed, he was accompanied by several officers who had decided to retire from active service, and to return to their homes in order to enjoy the fruits of their campaigns.

Rumours concerning Indian armies massing in different parts of the *Inca* empire kept the Spanish soldiers constantly alert, and caused much uneasiness among them. It is possible that these alarming reports were spread by the late Huascar's party, and that this was done with the intention to injure Atahualpa, who had as many enemies among the Peruvians as he had friends and supporters. On various occasions Pizarro's prisoner asked to be set free, but every time he did so, the answer was evasive, and eventually, as further reports concerning contemplated Indian uprisings were received, he was put in irons and placed under a very strong guard. Soon the nerves of some officers and men became so frayed that they suggested that Atahualpa be put to death without delay. They maintained that this step would fill the Peruvians with dismay, and that, being left without a leader, it would then be possible to march on Cuzco, and complete the conquest of the country.

With the passing of time, rumours became so alarming that Pizarro called on the *Inca*, and angrily accused him of treachery. In an effort to calm his accuser's suspicions and fears, the prisoner replied, "Are you jesting? I do not know why you take me for a man so dull witted that, holding me as you do, in your power, weighed down by chains, you believe that I think of treason. If I commanded my people to march against you, you surely would cut off my head. Indeed, you are ill-informed as to my subjects and the power I have over them, if you believe that they would do anything contrary to my orders. In my land neither the birds fly, nor the leaves stir against my will."

Despite these assurances, uneasiness grew daily in the Spanish camp, and soon other officers and the officials who had come to supervise the conquest, joined in the soldiers' now loud demands that Atahualpa be executed without delay. In spite of all the vociferation, Pizarro refused to take so drastic a step, for he maintained that no conclusive evidence existed to prove the prisoner's complicity in any act of treachery, or breach of obligations. De Soto and a few captains strongly supported their leader in this view, and when a new rumour circulated that a strong Peruvian army had assembled about a hundred miles from Cajamarca, and that an attack would be made at any moment, de Soto, accompanied by a detachment of cavalry, hurriedly set out to ascertain what truth there was in this latest alarming report.

No sooner had this reconnoitring party left than a great tumult broke out in the Spanish garrison, soldiers and officials angrily demanding that Atahualpa be brought to trial at once. At first Pizarro refused to listen, but when the agitation grew, and he realized that serious trouble was about to break out among his troops, he gave way.

A court of justice having been organized, the *Inca* was brought before Pizarro and Almagro, who acted as judges. The prosecution accused the prisoner of his brother's murder, and of being the instigator of an insurrection against his captors. Among other charges were those of polygamy, idolatry, and incestuous marriage. To-day these can only be described as farcical and unfair, but in the eyes of the fanatical Spaniards they were of great importance.

When the court retired to consider the verdict, a majority of ten to one declared the *Inca* guilty. The defence expressed the opinion that evidence against the accused was insufficient, and requested a delay until de Soto should return with a report as to the movements of the Peruvian armies. The defence furthermore maintained that only the King of Castile himself had the right to pass sentence on a monarch, and therefore urged the prosecuting party to send the *Inca* to Spain. Some members of the tribunal expressed the fear that, if Atahuapla were executed, it might have very serious repercussions throughout Peru, and they pointed out that the Spanish forces were insufficient in numbers to face such a situation. Eventually, after a heated debate all these objections and suggestions were over-ridden, and it was decided that the verdict of " Guilty " should stand, and that the sentence be carried out that very night. The judgment of the court was then taken to Friar Valverde for his signature, which he affixed without hesitation.*

Upon hearing the sentence, Atahualpa frantically exclaimed, " What have I done, or my women and children, to deserve such a fate ? " Then, recovering his self-possession, he stoically awaited the hour of death.

On the 29th day of August, 1533, two hours after sunset, trumpet blasts echoed over the fateful *plaza* of Cajamarca

---

* It was most unfortunate for Atahualpa that Felipillo acted as interpreter during this trial, for later it was rumoured that the cunning Indian youth maliciously distorted declarations made by the *Inca* and by a number of his subjects who were examined as witnesses. It is not definitely known whether or not the legends regarding Felipillo are true ; but, according to them, he distorted his translations in order to bring about the conviction of the *Inca*. This he has been said to have done because he had fallen in love with one of Atahualpa's concubines who, having rejected his amorous advances, had reported the matter to her master. According to one tale about Felipillo, Atahualpa indignantly, but in vain, appealed to Pizarro to punish the offender, and from that time on the guilty youth harboured a deep hatred for the captive monarch, whose life now depended upon the accuracy of his translations.

where the Spanish soldiery was assembled. A number of torches gave a red flickering light, casting weird shadows against the walls, as, surrounded by a guard of soldiers, Atahualpa slowly shuffled out of a doorway, ankle-shackles and chains making his progress difficult. Immediately in front of him walked Friar Valverde, carrying a cross. Having reached a pile of faggots, in the middle of which stood a stout post, the short procession came to a halt. Addressing the *Inca* through an interpreter, Valverde made a last effort to convert him to Christianity. He pointed out to the unhappy monarch that if he accepted baptism, instead of being burned at the stake, he would suffer the milder form of death by the *garrote*, or, in other words, by strangulation. During the nine and a half months the *Inca* had been held in captivity, the friar and others had made many efforts to convert him to Christianity, but he had refused to renounce the faith of his fathers. Now, for a few moments, the stoic victim stood in silence, considering his hopeless situation. Then, upon having expressed his willingness to embrace the cross, a short ceremony of baptism was held, Atahuapla receiving, according to some chroniclers, the name of Juan, and, according to others, that of Francisco. The baptism completed, he was handed over to the executioners who placed a rope round his neck, and strangled him by tightening it from behind, twisting it round by means of a stick.

When the Indian population of Cajamarca heard that their monarch was dead, the air was filled with cries of lament. Members of the *Inca's* entourage, especially his concubines, rushed about the streets in a frenzy, and implored the Spaniards to execute them; for, according to their belief, if this were done, they would follow their master to the Mansions of the Sun. When their wishes were refused, some of the distraught women hanged themselves, in some cases with their own hair; and many more would have done likewise, had not Pizarro immediately taken steps to guard against a mass suicide.

After a solemn funeral mass, Atahualpa's body was

interred alongside the graves of Spanish soldiers who had died of sickness, but a few nights later Indians secretly removed their monarch's remains. According to some rumours, they were taken to Cuzco, but according to others they were re-buried somewhere in the mountains, together with an enormous quantity of treasure. Although the Spaniards questioned numerous Indians, and extended their searches for the body far and wide, their quests proved to be in vain. Its mysterious disappearance gave rise to many legends, some of which, with the passing of time, have become firm beliefs among many people.

When the news of Atahualpa's death spread through the land, demonstrations of grief and loyalty were such that many men and women laid violent hands on themselves, and everywhere—save in parts inhabited by adherents of the late Huascar—cries against the Spaniards were raised to the Sun.

A few days after the execution, de Soto and his party returned to Cajamarca from their reconnoitring expedition. Everywhere they had passed, the Indians had been friendly, and no sign of a Peruvian army had been seen. Upon learning what had taken place during his absence, de Soto was filled with indignation, which he expressed in no uncertain words. Pizarro—who now realized that in executing the *Inca* he had made a grave mistake—blamed certain captains and Valverde for what had been done, and excused himself in saying that no one in his position could have opposed the garrison's demand, without running the risk of mutiny. To this de Soto angrily replied that, even if Atahualpa had been guilty, no one but the King of Castile had the right to condemn him, and that the *Inca* should have been sent to Spain for trial. This well-founded statement sounded so much like a dangerous accusation that all those who had anything to do with the recent trial and execution, began to blame each other for what had been done, with the result that a heated quarrel broke out among the officers and ecclesiastics, who now feared an official investigation, with its attendant consequences.

IX

ATAHUALPA's death and Huascar's assassination left the Peruvians like a flock of sheep in a storm, without a shepherd to keep them together. Commanders dispersed their armies to different parts of the land, and soon the hitherto meek and servile Indians lost all respect for authority. Then disorders broke out, the formerly oppressed masses rising against the nobility and priesthood, and even religion lost its hold on the people. In the general tumult and upheaval, storehouses, temples and palaces were looted and set afire, and, taking advantage of the situation, certain truculent tribes who had been held in subjection by the *Incas*, now pounced on different regions like so many packs of wolves.

In some respects this sudden and complete collapse and dissolution of the *Incaic* system favoured the Spaniards' designs, especially in so far as the founding of a new monarchy was concerned. Realizing that, without an *Inca* to rule over Peru as a figurehead, turmoils would continue indefinitely, Pizarro called together a number of Indian noblemen, and, having informed them that it was not his intention to dissolve their monarchy, asked them who was best qualified to occupy the *Inca's* throne. The legitimate candidate was Huascar's brother, but as the noblemen whom Pizarro interviewed were of Quito, and therefore belonged to Atahualpa's camp, they proposed that the sceptre be handed to Atahualpa's brother Toparpa. This prince being very young and inexperienced, he suited Pizarro's plans admirably, and therefore, a few days later, with as much pomp as circumstances permitted, he was crowned in Cajamarca. Those who had hoped that this mock coronation would pacify the Indians were greatly disappointed when it was reported that armies were massing in different parts of the country. The people of Cuzco strongly resented the presence of a puppet *Inca* whom they regarded as a potential enemy, and, still more unpleasant for the *conquistadores*, within a month of Atahualpa's execution the influx of treasure ceased completely, whereupon the Spanish soldiers clamoured to march into Cuzco, hoping to fill their coffers with the city's riches. The men who had only recently arrived with Almagro were particularly eager to get there without further delay, for they had received only a tithe of the ransom, but had been promised an equal share of future spoils. Great, therefore, was the joy when Pizarro announced that the time had arrived to leave Cajamarca, and march on to the El Dorado of his men's dreams.

Young Toparpa and the Peruvian general Hernando Pizarro had taken to Cajamarca during his return journey from the holy city of Pachacamac, were carried on litters, surrounded by a retinue of noblemen and many vassals.

Though some of the roughest mountain country in the world had to be traversed on this long march, everything went well at first, but the Spaniards' optimism was somewhat dampened when news was received that further along their route a strong Peruvian army was assembled, determined to impede their progress.

This sudden hostility greatly disappointed Pizarro who had hoped to complete the conquest of the country without further opposition. Among the noblemen in Toparpa's retinue was one of his half brothers, and Pizarro now thought it convenient to send him ahead on a mission of pacification. Accordingly, the prince set out, but soon members of his escort returned with the news that, regardless of his royal blood, he had been slain as a traitor by his own countrymen. Suspecting the Peruvian general who travelled with the expedition of being the instigator of all the new troubles, the Spaniards put him in irons, and placed him under a strong guard which made any attempt of secret communication with the enemy impossible.

When the town of Jauja was reached, Pizarro decided that, it being well situated for defence, it would be advisable to wait there for a few days whilst stout-hearted de Soto with a detachment of sixty horsemen reconnoitred the country further ahead.

Between this town and Cuzco (a distance of about two hundred and fifty miles) the Andean ranges twist in every direction, their snow-covered peaks towering high above rocky valleys and deep sombre gorges which echo with the roar and thunder of rushing mountain streams and rivers. In low places the humid heat is stifling ; but upon climbing up incredibly steep and dangerous foot-trails, the atmosphere becomes cooler and cooler, until, upon nearing the wind-swept summits, the cold becomes unbearable.

Into such regions de Soto and his sixty had to venture in order to carry out a reconnaissance that promised infinite dangers. They had not ridden far when, in the distance, they saw a well-fortified encampment, its warriors preparing to impede their further advance. In the hopes of avoiding bloodshed by parley, de Soto dispatched a messenger to Pizarro, suggesting that he send him the puppet *Inca*. Unfortunately, meanwhile, young Toparpa had fallen gravely ill, and died, leaving Pizarro without a tool. As it was suspected that the Peruvian general—who was still kept in chains by the Spaniards—was responsible for this mysterious death, as well as for the presence of hostile armies, he was brought to trial, and although he denied all implication, the prisoner was declared guilty of treason, and condemned to death. Typical of his race, he remained stolid to the end, and bore the anguish of being burned at the stake unflinchingly.

When de Soto learned of the *Inca's* death, he immediately made a daring attack on the Indian encampment. Leading his men, he dashed at his enemies with such fire and fury that, after a short though bloody battle, they fled into the mountains. Joined by reinforcements, the Peruvians once more rallied, and took up positions in parts where a successful attack on them seemed impossible. The sight of horses still terrified them, but almost overnight they devised means whereby they seriously impeded the movements of cavalry. Along the steep tracks leading to high passes they dug holes in which they planted posts with sharp points, and in different places which commanded approaches to the heights, they piled up rocks, in readiness to be rolled down on the invaders.

Finding that his enemies increased in numbers as he proceeded into the labyrinth of mountains, de Soto dispatched a courier to Pizarro, urging him to send reinforcements with utmost speed. Then, without waiting for these to arrive, he daringly continued his advance, scaling range after range, and crossing rivers and streams, the bridges across which had been destroyed to impede him. Here and there bloody combats took place, and on several occasions it looked as if de Soto's little force would be wiped out. On one steep mountain slope, particularly determined opposition was offered by the natives who killed several of his soldiers, as well as a number of horses. Despite the rocks that were being hurled down upon the Spaniards, they fought their way up-hill with astonishing bravery, and eventually managed to reach a high plain where another fierce combat ensued. Only a few of de Soto's men escaped without injury, and all were so exhausted that only the falling of night saved them from being annihilated by the Peruvians. Withdrawing to the bank of a stream, the Spaniards prepared to pass the night as best they could, and within a few hundred yards of them the Indians did likewise, evidently with the intention of renewing their attack in the morning. For several hours the Spaniards dressed their wounds, shivering with the intense cold, whilst their leader made efforts to cheer them. But their despondency gave way to wild joy when trumpet calls from the valley below announced the arrival of reinforcements. They replied to the calls from their position on the heights, and when Almagro and a strong body of men reached the summit of the pass, they were received with jubilation by de Soto's soldiers who had given themselves up for lost.

When daylight appeared, and the Indians saw that the number of white men had been doubled during the night, they hesitated for a while, but presently attacked with great determination. As the battle was fought on a plain, horses could be used to full advantage, and thanks to them the Indians were soon put to flight, leaving behind many dead and severely wounded. De Soto and Almagro were now about twenty miles from Cuzco, but in order to avoid running unnecessary risks, they decided to encamp and await the arrival of the main force.

During the daring advance to this point, Pizarro had not remained idle in Jauja, where a new colony had been founded. Before setting out to catch up with the two advanced bodies of troops, he appointed the official Government treasurer to take charge of the newly set up administration, and forty soldiers were left behind to guard the town and the bulk of the treasure which was too heavy and cumbersome to carry with the expedition indefinitely.

Shortly after Pizarro had joined forces with de Soto and Almagro in the neighbourhood of Cuzco, the Spaniards had a pleasant surprise when a young Peruvian prince, attended by a large retinue, presented himself in their camp to offer his services. This prince was Manco, a brother of the unfortunate Huascar, for whose murder Atahualpa had been responsible. At this critical stage of the conquest, with the Spaniards about to enter the capital, the arrival of this prince seemed to come as a godsend to Pizarro who, ever since the recent death of the puppet *Inca*, had been desperately hoping to find a new, and, if possible, legitimate candidate to the vacant throne.

Foxy young Manco called on the Spanish commander because he realized that to continue the fight against the white invaders was a hopeless one, and he hoped that in joining sides with them he would be safe, and stand an excellent chance of being placed on the throne. Therefore, when Pizarro received him with much ceremony and honour, he had good reason to be pleased with himself, for everything promised to work out as he had hoped, though his vassals in Cuzco viewed this slick turning of coats with very different eyes.

It is evident that in placing puppet *Incas* on the throne to suit his own interests, Pizarro greatly underestimated the intelligence of the Indians who easily saw through his game, and who fully realized that the Spaniards had not come as friends, but as conquerors. Therefore, when the news about Manco's betrayal spread among the defenders of the approaches towards Cuzco, many of them abandoned their points of vantage, and in disgust flocked back to the capital where they hurriedly collected much gold, set fire to a number of buildings, and sacked several palaces and temples before leaving with their loot.

In order to prevent a general destruction of the city, Pizarro immediately despatched a strong detachment of cavalry, again under the command of the reliable de Soto. Two days later, towards the end of November 1533, after some minor skirmishes with isolated parties of natives who lay in wait among hills adjacent to the city, the main Spanish force marched into Cuzco, and during an impressive ceremony, Pizarro officially took possession in the name of the King of Castile.

(A description of Cuzco will be found in Appendix IV).

A few days later, with much pomp and glitter, Manco was placed upon the Peruvian throne in the main square of Cuzco. In order to impress the sullen natives and to make the illusion perfect, all the ancient *Incaic* coronation rites and ceremonies were observed, these being made even more magnificent by the presence of the Spanish troops, dressed in their full armour. The mock coronation, which was a cunningly calculated mixture of pagan and Christian rites, was followed by a banquet, presided over, as was customary, by the mummies of former *Incas* which were brought out of the Temple of the Sun. After this traditional item, there came public festivities during which strong native maize beer was consumed in great quantities. Although Manco had officially been handed over the Peruvian sceptre, not only he, but also all his noblemen and vassals had to swear allegiance to King Charles of Spain ; a mysterious personage about whom they knew nothing, though no doubt they were fully aware that this great overlord in a distant land was represented in their country by the commander of the white invaders whose terrible weapons it was unwise to oppose.

Pizarro's soldiers were given strict orders that the natives were not to be molested, and that there was to be no looting. Gold, silver and other valuables were only to be taken possession of under supervision, and all treasure thus collected was to be pooled. However, as soon as the men were allowed to roam through the city, they disregarded these orders, looting and plundering at will. Palaces, temples and noblemen's houses were entered by this swarm of human locusts who hungered for gold, and more gold. To the Peruvians' horror, Spanish soldiers forced their way into the sacred Temple of the Sun which they stripped of whatever valuables were left. Not even the venerated mummies of *Incas* and *Coyas* were respected, these being dragged out into the open, to be searched for treasure which was suspected to be concealed in them. Everywhere, not only within the city, but also in its vicinity,* the Spaniards rummaged for gold which was suspected to have been hidden. Indians were questioned, and a number of them were even tortured to make them reveal what was thought to be their secret. Despite most of the victims' stubborn refusal to speak, considerable quantities of gold were found, and it is an astonishing fact that, despite the previous visit of the three soldiers whom Pizarro had sent to Cuzco to supervise the collecting of Atahualpa's ransom, and the exodus of masses of the young people who took with them

---

* Among the various rich treasures believed to have been hidden is one which deserves special mention. During the reign of the *Inca* Huayna Capac, when his eldest son, Huascar, attained the age of seven, he ordered a colossal chain of gold to be made. Many Indians told the Spaniards that this chain was eight hundred yards long, and as thick as a man's wrist, and that it was used to encircle the great square of Cuzco during the feast of equinox, or *raymi*, as it was called by the natives. The fact that a granite wall which surrounded the square was pierced with two hundred loopholes (said to have been made to hold the chain), left the Spaniards in no doubt that the tales about this gigantic golden chain were true. Many Indians were questioned to find out what had become of all this gold, but in most cases they pleaded complete ignorance. When, at last, one told his questioners that the chain had been carried some distance out of the town, and that it had been thrown into a small lagoon, a detachment of soldiers and two hundred Indians went there and dug canals, in order to drain the lagoon. However, after long and fruitless efforts the task had eventually to be abandoned.

the greater part of the city's wealth, the loot now found by the Spaniards was still so great that it amounted to more than the ransom delivered by Atahualpa.

When the gold and silver had been melted down into ingots, four hundred and eighty soldiers received their share which, on an average amounted to 4,000 *pesos de oro* per man, as well as a quantity of silver and precious stones. As usual, one fifth was set aside for the king, and, in addition to this, a number of articles, including several life-size figures of llamas and women—all made of gold and silver—were kept intact to be sent to the court as samples of Peruvian art. Besides precious metals and stones, enormous quantities of finely woven cloth and garments were found in storehouses. Some of the robes—probably intended for ceremonial occasions—were made entirely of bright featherwork, and others of gold and silver thread. " To see how marvellously these were made, was an almost terrifying wonder," an eye witness wrote.

The booty in gold was so great that the soldiers gave their silver and precious stones to any companion who would take them, for the transportation of such bulk and weight was difficult. Gold being of no commercial value in Peru, the Spanish soldiers could only use it among themselves ; and now, there being such a glut of this metal, its value went down accordingly. Within a few hours of having received their share, many of the soldiers had gambled away their last *peso*. A golden image of the sun, that had been taken out of the temple, is said to have changed hands at one throw of the dice.

The demand for certain articles and commodities that were necessary to the Spaniards, became so great, and the available supply among the expedition's stores was so small, that prices soared sky high. Thus, for instance, a handful of writing paper sold at ten *pesos* gold ; a pair of half-boots for thirty ; a black cloak for a hundred ; and a horse for anything between three and five thousand *pesos*. This extraordinary state of affairs made many of the men regret that they had not returned to Spain when they had been given the chance, immediately after the division of Atahualpa's ransom in Cajamarca.

If the acquisition of gold had been Pizarro's main desire, he could have retired after the taking of Cuzco, to spend the rest of his life in ease and luxury. However, far from doing so, he fixed his eyes on the future. Peru must be colonized, and to accomplish this, the whole of the country's social and political structure must be re-built from its very foundations. Therefore, without losing time, a Spanish police force was organized, a municipal government appointed, and, idols having been removed from temples, one of these edifices was immediately consecrated to be used as a Christian church.

The few priests who accompanied the expedition, with great zeal set to work, spreading the Gospel among the natives, and laying the foundations for their education.

Among Pizarro's first concerns was the division of property and land among those of his officers and men who intended to settle in the newly conquered land. A number of Dons who had left their homeland penniless, or to avoid being thrown into a debtor's prison, now suddenly became owners of palaces and mansions which hitherto had been occupied by *Incas* and Peruvian noblemen. But since, from a European point of view, even in those days, these straw-roofed palaces were far from comfortable to live in, much had to be done to them to please the conquerors' various tastes. Accordingly, the prospective new occupants immediately set to work, reconstructing the edifices allotted to them, in most cases new storeys being built on the basement of old walls. Indian labour—forced and otherwise—was easily obtained, and thus Cuzco began rapidly to change in appearance.

Despite the fact that during the two years which had passed since Pizarro had begun the conquest, hundreds of miles of the Andes had been explored, and Cuzco had been taken, only a fraction of the vast Peruvian empire had been trodden on by Spanish boots, and its second capital, Quito, situated over a thousand miles north of Cuzco, was only known to the *conquistadores* by hearsay. According to many reports and stories told by natives, the splendours and the wealth of Quito surpassed those of Cuzco ; but in order to reach that distant city, strong armies would have to be defeated in the field of battle, for, in the north, the late Atahualpa's supporters had rallied to defend their land against the white invaders.

With Cuzco in his hands, and young Manco installed as puppet *Inca*, Pizarro hoped that his immediate tasks would be made easy, and that with cunning and diplomacy the full and complete conquest of the Peruvian Empire would only be a matter of time.

X

PIZARRO'S optimism regarding prospects for the future was suddenly dampened when it was reported that one of Atahualpa's former generals was assembling a formidable army among the mountains in the north. Almost at the same time he received the staggering news that Don Pedro de Alvarado—a very gallant and famous captain who had formerly distinguished himself during the conquest of Mexico under Cortez—had landed at the coast near the equator with a very strong and extremely well-equipped expeditionary force ; not to join Pizarro, but to make conquests on his own account.

The garrison in Cuzco was thrown into a state of alarm by this report, and immediately *chasquis* (Indian runners) were dispatched to Pizarro's colony at the coast, with written messages asking for further information regarding the new arrivals and their intentions. Whilst waiting for the reply, Cuzco fairly hummed with rumours and agitation. Every Spaniard there knew that the rival expeditionary force had the full right to make conquests in the regions where the landing had been effected, for, according to the document signed between Pizarro and the Council of the Indies (five years previously, when he had been in Spain) the northern boundary of territory placed under his jurisdiction, began at a line drawn from east to west from the island of Puna in the Bay of Guayaquil, and extended about six hundred miles to the south. From there on, still further to the south, Almagro had been assigned any land he might conquer, i.e., the southern sector of Peru, as well as Bolivia and Chile.

Alvarado, the leader of the rival expeditionary force, was known to every man in Pizarro's camp, and, indeed, a number of them had fought under him in Mexico where, on account of his fair hair and skin, the Aztecs had called him *Tonatiu*, meaning " Son of the Sun." Beneath a lively temperament and engaging personality, he was known to be madly ambitious and hard-hearted, though the men who had fought under him gave him full credit for always having been first in danger, and for shunning no discomforts when such had to be faced and braved to attain seemingly impossible goals during campaigns. Upon his return to Spain, after the successful conclusion of the conquest of Mexico, honours were bestowed on this radiant captain who took advantage of the situation in planning new exploits which he hoped would bring him further fame and glory. The Court having been captivated by his charms, he had no difficulty in equipping an expedition, the object of which was to explore the Pacific Ocean. In the name of the king, the Council of the Indies had given him permission to do this, and, furthermore, the right to conquer any islands or mainland. In addition to this, Alvarado was appointed Governor of Guatemala from where he had originally intended to commence his exploration of the Pacific.

By the time he arrived in Central America to take up his appointment, and to begin his activities, breath-taking tales about the wealth of Quito had spread as far as Guatemala, and therefore, instead of carrying out his original intentions and plans, he decided to try his luck in South America. He had such faith in the outcome of the enterprise that he put a large sum of his own money into it, and when everything was ready, he sailed with twelve ships, five hundred soldiers, two hundred and twenty-seven horses, many Guatemalan Indians and a number of negroes. Some of the Dons who had joined his expedition were so optimistic regarding prospects that, hoping to settle in the rich land to be conquered, they took with them their wives and all their belongings.

When Pizarro and his men in Cuzco heard that Alvarado, together with the most formidable expeditionary force yet seen in South America, had left the Bay of Caraques (situated a little south of the equator), and was marching towards the Andes with the intention of conquering Quito, all were filled with fury and indignation, especially so Almagro who had not yet had the opportunity to explore any of the regions in the far south (Bolivia and Chile) that were to be his. Indeed, despite his labours and exploits, so far he had derived but little benefit from them, and therefore it is not surprising that he, as well as the entire force in Cuzco, resented the presence of a rival expedition which looked like snatching from them what promised to be the richest prize yet heard of in the world.

Here, indeed, was a worrying situation for the Spaniards in Cuzco. The distance from this city to Quito is well over a thousand miles over the most difficult terrain imaginable. On one hand, there were the intruders from Guatemala, almost at the entrance to the rumoured sesamé, and on the other there was Atahualpa's redoubtable general who, with his hordes of warriors, threatened to march on Cuzco at any moment. If only this Peruvian army could be annihilated or scattered, Pizarro and Almagro could hurry on to Quito, and there dispute the spoils with the newly arrived Spanish army.

In view of the seriousness of the situation, and realizing that something must be done without delay, it was decided that Almagro should take the war into the enemy's camp, i.e., boldly attack the Peruvian army, and, if victorious, proceed in the direction of Quito with utmost haste.

Accordingly, Almagro set out with a detachment of horsemen and a large body of Indians headed by the puppet *Inca*, Manco. When one considers that, at the time, the battle-scarred, one-eyed Almagro was nearing his seventieth year, it is amazing to think that he did not shun the prospects of a terrific battle, and, if from this he emerged victorious, the thousand-mile march to Quito, over mountains and through regions with every diversity of climate.

Once more Spanish audacity paid rich dividends. Appearing suddenly and unexpectedly, Almagro set on his foe with such fury that, after a brisk encounter, the opposition was routed and scattered in every direction, survivors seeking refuge in different Andean valleys. Disheartened, the Indian captains urged their general to make peace, and when he called them cowards, they killed him with lance thrusts and hatchets. Thus died the last of Atahualpa's greatest generals.

Immediately after his victory, Almagro advanced in forced marches towards San Miguel, the colony at the coast, for there he intended to pick up reinforcements. Some months before, shortly after Atahualpa's execution, Pizarro had sent one of his most trusted captains, Belalcazar, to take charge of the colony, and Almagro now needed every man before venturing anywhere near the army from Guatemala which, by now, he feared to be near Quito, if not actually in possession of the city and its riches. And so, Almagro, accompanied by only one hundred and forty soldiers, but supported by the puppet *Inca* Manco, and a large body of Indians, hurried towards San Miguel. Little did he dream that, in the meantime, a most amazing situation had developed in the north, and that soon this situation would become even more involved.

. . . . . .

In order to follow events, and to comprehend what led to the extraordinary situation just referred to, let us go back to the time when the army from Guatemala landed in the Bay of Caraques, situated a little south of the equator.

It was not long before the hopeful and enthusiastic

would-be conquerors bitterly regretted that they had come to this part of the world. To begin with, all went well, but soon incredible difficulties and misfortunes beset the expedition's path. Penetrating inland towards the Andes, a number of primitive Indian tribes were met, and considerable quantities of gold and emeralds fell into the white men's hands. These tribes had only recently been subdued by the *Incas*, and therefore remained uninfluenced by Peruvian civilization. The only guide available deserted, making off into the jungle, leaving the expedition with its army of negro and Guatemalan Indian porters to advance without knowing what lay ahead, nor exactly what direction to take. In the low parts the humid heat was oppressive, swarms of insects made life intolerable, and soon malaria and other fevers began to claim victims. Swamps, rivers and tropical forests were slowly and painfully traversed, and when the expedition entered in to the indescribably vast and intricate network of mountains, sufferings became even worse. Dense dripping forests made progress almost impossible, gigantic trees with their mass of creepers and lianas forming a veritable wall along the foothills of the mountains, and in the high regions, sleet, snow, ice and terrific gales took their toll in human lives. The ill-clad Indians, accustomed to a mild climate, were the first to suffer seriously. Due to frost-bite, many lost fingers and toes, and soon victims began to die like flies. Baggage, supplies, arms, and even gold and emeralds were abandoned or thrown away as encumbrances. What was the use of treasure when empty stomachs were craving for food ? During nights, in high regions where fuel was lacking, the unfortunate wretches, white men, negroes and Indians, huddled together in order to prevent being frozen to death, but usually a number were found dead in the morning. Whenever a horse perished, or had to be killed, men pounced on the carcase like so many ravenous wolves. Several Dons whose wives could proceed no further, remained behind to die with them, whilst their companions staggered on, further and further into the unknown.

As the crow flies, from the Bay of Caraques to Quito, the distance is only about one hundred and fifty miles, but the regions to be traversed are extremely difficult and mountainous; and it must be remembered that the expedition had no guides, and therefore marched hither and thither in different wrong directions, following valleys and traversing places which they mistook for high passes. To make things even worse, a distant volcano was in eruption at the time, filling the atmosphere with fine ashes and acrid fumes, which gave the regions the appearance of being enveloped in a thick black fog.* Eyes and respiratory passages were affected by these choking fumes, adding greatly to the sufferings of the wretched explorers who wearily trudged on, urged by their unfaltering leader who stubbornly refused to acknowledge defeat by turning back.

Time and again, before an ascent to some snowed region was commenced, Alvarado assured his followers that this would be the last, and that beyond the mountain they would come to more hospitable regions. Disappointment followed disappointment, and finally, after five long months, the starved and bedraggled survivors of this veritable death-march reached the high valley of Riobamba. There the climate was delightfully mild, and the vegetation brought back memories of better days. When, in this neighbourhood, the *Inca* highway was struck, everyone gave a sigh of relief, for it was realized that safety had been reached at last, and that the final goal was not far distant. Feelings of joy soon gave way to bitter disillusionment and utter futility when it was discovered that shod horses had travelled over the highway not long before, for the hoof-marks seen there were fresh. Everyone present realized that another Spanish army had forestalled them, and that all the sufferings and sacrifices of the fateful march had been in vain. Eighty-five Spaniards and several of the Dons' wives had died, and no fewer than

* In the year 1925 when the author travelled through the mountains in Southern Ecuador, similar conditions prevailed in one region. It was said that a volcano, situated far away in the interior towards the east, was in eruption at the time.

two thousand Indians, besides a number of negroes and many horses.

The miserable starvelings stared at the hoof-marks in utter dismay.

.   .   .   .   .   .

Almagro received a shock when, upon reaching San Miguel, he was informed that the colony's commander, Belalcazar, together with most of the garrison, had set out to conquer Quito. This having taken place without orders from Pizarro, Almagro became suspicious, and, without losing time, he continued his march into the northern Andes. On the way he had several sharp encounters with Indians, but as these operated in small groups, they were easily scattered. The terrible misfortunes met by the army from Guatemala on its march towards Quito, so slowed up its progress that Almagro reached the high land of Ecuador, and made contact with Belalcazar, before Alvarado and the emaciated survivors of his expeditionary force arrived at the *Inca* highway and discovered those awful tell-tale imprints of horses' hoofs.

Belalcazar explained to Almagro that although he had set out from the colony of San Miguel to conquer Quito without orders from Pizarro, his intentions were completely loyal. He recounted how, having intelligence of the arrival of a mysterious Spanish expeditionary force, and its departure in the direction of Quito, he had hastened to forestall whoever the intruders might be. In spite of opposition from the Indians, he had succeeded in entering Quito, where he had planted the Spanish flag on the principal palace, formerly occupied by Atahualpa. Almagro was bitterly disappointed when he learned that upon entering the town, Belalcazar and his men had found palaces and temples stripped of valuables, the Indians having hidden all the gold, silver and precious stones immediately after they had received news of Atahualpa's execution. Though many natives were questioned, and some even tortured, none would reveal where was hidden what is believed to be the world's greatest treasure, known as "Atahualpa's Treasure," sought to this day by hopeful adventurers.

In the town of Riobamba, situated on a high plain among mountain scenery of overpowering beauty, Almagro and Belalcazar now calmly awaited the arrival of the army from Guatemala, and when Indian scouts reported that it was approaching, Almagro sent messengers to open parleys. Eventually, after several exchanges of letters, some of which nearly precipitated hostilities between the two camps, the rival captains arranged to meet, in order to discuss the position, man to man. After much bargaining and haggling, Alvarado agreed to quit South America, in return for one hundred thousand *pesos de oro*. In exchange for this sum he was to leave his twelve ships behind, as well as all his horses, equipment and supplies. Whilst these discussions were being held, the soldiers and officers of the two camps intermingled freely, and when the newcomers were given the choice of returning to Guatemala, or of joining Almagro's forces, most of them joyfully accepted the latter offer. Among them were several splendid Dons, but the rank and file, though of a better type than the desperate adventurers who had originally come from Panama with Pizarro, were worse disciplined, a circumstance which was soon to lead to much trouble.

· · · · · ·

Pizarro was in the old sacred Peruvian city of Pachacamac when he received the welcome news that Almagro had made contact with Alvarado's army, and that an agreement had been reached between the two. Some weeks later, when the latter and his troops arrived in Pachacamac, they were received with great enthusiasm. Festivities continued for several days, and shortly after Alvarado had received the stipulated one hundred thousand *pesos de oro*, he boarded a ship and sailed back to Guatemala.

Pizarro had every reason to be pleased with himself, for now, with Quito in his hands, and Spanish troops firmly established in Cuzco, as well as in two or three other strategic points, the whole *Inca* empire had been conquered. On its ruins he was determined to build a colony which, he hoped, would some day be a sparkling gem in the Castilian crown, and a new pride of the Church. With a mere puppet emperor on the Peruvian throne, the actual reign of the *Incas* had come to an end, and what was left of the Incaic civilization, and of the Peruvian system of administration, was now rapidly to disappear. A new era was about to begin in Peru.

XI

ALL resistance on the part of the Peruvians having come to an end, excepting that of a few primitive tribes in remote parts, the Spaniards sheathed their swords, and Pizarro— who was still in Pachacamac—surveyed the neighbouring coastal regions, seeking to discover a suitable site whereon to found a city that was to become the capital of the new colonial empire. About twenty miles to the north, a plain near the River Rimac* appeared to offer everything he looked for. The site having been selected, on the 18th of January, 1535, the city of Lima was founded with pomp and ceremony. To commemorate the day when the site was chosen, the new Peruvian capital was named *Ciudad de los Reyes* (City of the Kings), for the decision to build there had been reached during the festival of Epiphany, in Spanish called *Fiesta de los Reyes* (Feast of the Kings). The name given to the city very soon changed to that of the river (Rimac of Limac), and in time this was corrupted to Lima.

The lay-out of the city, and an irrigation system having been carefully planned, sites were allotted to the colonists, whereafter work was commenced with energy and zeal. Facing what was intended to become the main *plaza*, the foundations for a large cathedral were laid, and on the other sides of the square it was planned to erect different

* Rimac, or Limac, a Quichua word meaning " Speaking River."

public buildings, and a palace to be occupied by Pizarro.

At about the same time a colony was founded along the coast further to the north, and in honour of Pizarro's birthplace in Spain the town-to-be was named Trujillo.

Not only among his own countrymen, but even among the native population, Pizarro became liked and respected, for he proved to be a fair and just administrator. Now, very wisely, he treated the Indians with consideration and leniency, thus getting the maximum of work out of them without the necessity of using force. Everything pointed to a rosy future ; the new colonies hummed with activity, and in the newly-founded towns, buildings and public works began to take shape ; but at the horizon dark storm clouds were gathering.

With a view of exploring Chile, Almagro had gone to Cuzco. He was accompanied by the members of the army from Guatemala who had visions of soon becoming rich. Like their new leader, they considered the old Peruvian capital to come under his jurisdiction, and therefore were delighted when, upon entering it, he assumed its administration. De Soto, assisted by two of Pizarro's brothers, Juan and Gonzalo, who had jointly governed the city, received Almagro with outward signs of honour and respect, and it seemed as if everything would proceed smoothly when news trickled through from Panama that Hernando Pizarro had arrived there on his return journey from Spain. It was also reported that the king had bestowed certain honours on Almagro, and that he had been granted the Governorship of all the lands he might conquer south of a line drawn from east to west where Pizarro's jurisdiction ended. The Dons and men from Guatemala who had attached themselves to Almagro's fortunes, were so elated by this rumour that they gave vent to their feelings by looting and robbing the poor Indians of Cuzco who had enjoyed peace and quiet under the government of de Soto. Very soon the Spaniards in the city split up into two camps, and even the Indians joined one faction or the other, only de Soto's prudence on one side, and Almagro's moderation on the other, preventing bloodshed. Troubles between the two camps continued until, after forced marches, Pizarro himself arrived in Cuzco. Almagro met his old partner as he came out of church whither, first of all, he had gone to offer thanks for his safe arrival. The two men having greeted one another as old friends, Pizarro reproached Almagro for having put him to the great inconvenience of so long and tiring a journey. To this the latter replied that there had been no need for such haste, and that, after all, the chief cause of the trouble was the jealousy of Pizarro's two brothers, Juan and Gonzalo.

A general reconciliation having been brought about, Almagro made preparations to explore Chile. His free and easy disposition, and his almost reckless generosity had won for him many friends who now eagerly rallied to his banner.

Before setting out on his proposed march, he sent for the Peruvian High Priest and a brother of the puppet *Inca* Manco. These two Indians were given instructions to prepare the way for the expedition, and to pacify Indians who might feel inclined to obstruct its advance into their territory.

No sooner had Almagro departed on his expedition than Pizarro, after having appointed his brother Juan to take charge of affairs in Cuzco, returned to Lima in order to supervise the building of the newly founded city, a task into which he had put his heart and soul.

At long last Hernando Pizarro returned with many interesting stories to tell.

His journey from Peru to Panama, and from there to Seville, had been uneventful. No sooner had he landed in Spain, and it became known that he had brought about half a million *pesos* of gold, besides much silver and other treasure, than the news spread far and wide like wildfire. Not only this, but the soldiers who had retired from service in Peru, and had travelled home with him, now proudly showed their riches to friends who fairly gaped at the sight of so much wealth. Adventurers gazed out to sea and dreamed about Peru. Not since Columbus had returned from his first voyage of discovery had Spain been so excited.

Hernando Pizarro was at once received by the king, whose different ventures in Europe had left his coffers in sore need of replenishing. The messenger from Peru was treated with great honour, and even lodged as an attendant of the Court. Whilst the sparkling treasures he had brought were being displayed, he recounted to his royal master the Peruvian expedition's amazing achievements and successes. The king was so delighted with the wealth and the good news, that Hernando was immediately made a Knight of St. Jago, and whatever petitions he made were immediately granted. Pizarro's southern boundary in Peru was extended seventy leagues (approximately 210 miles) further towards the south, and in addition to this he was raised to the rank of Marquis, the title given to him being that of *Marques de los Atavillos*, a province of Peru. Almagro was nominated Marshal, and was given the power to govern the land he might conquer for the distance of two hundred leagues (approximately 600 miles) to the south of Pizarro's jurisdiction.* Almagro's territory was given the name of *Nuevo Toledo* (New Toledo) and that of Pizarro *Nueva Castilla* (New Castile). The vases, plates, and figures made of gold, Hernando had brought with him for the king's inspection, proved to be of so little interest to the king that a few of the most remarkable specimens having been picked out, the others were smelted down, and thus lost for ever.

Taking advantage of the Court's enthusiasm for Peru, Hernando seized the opportunity to ask for a fleet and men to assist in making further conquests in South America. This request was immediately granted, the king ordering officials to assist Hernando in making preparations for his departure. This time there was no difficulty in finding recruits, for hundreds of men hoped to be given a chance of enriching themselves.

* The king nominated Almagro Governor and Captain General of 200 leagues (600 miles) of land he might conquer along the coast in an *easterly* direction towards the Straits of Magellan. *Easterly*, of course, should have read *southerly*. Owing to a contradiction in this royal grant of land, as far as names of places and distances were concerned, it could be argued that Cuzco came within Almagro's jurisdiction, or it could be claimed to be within Pizarro's territory.

Under the king's orders, ships, equipment, armaments and stores were quickly acquired. One hundred and eighty soldiers having been picked out of the many who offered their services, Hernando ordered his fleet to set sail for the New World. A violent storm so battered his ships that he was obliged to return to port for repairs, but eventually the Atlantic was successfully crossed, but upon putting into the small port of Nombre de Dios, where it was hoped to refresh the men who had suffered greatly during the voyage, food was so scarce that several died of starvation. Disease, fever and terrific heat claimed a number of other victims, but finally the Isthmus of Panama was reached, and, as was usual, crossed by land. On the Pacific side, Hernando was again held up for some time; a delay which caused great anxiety in Peru where his return was eagerly awaited.

.   .   .   .   .   .

Shortly after his return to Peru, Hernando left Lima to take over the government of Cuzco from his brother, Juan, in whom Pizarro evidently put little trust as an administrator. For it is clear that the brothers Juan and Gonzalo, though gallant in the field of battle, and liked by their companions-in-arms, lacked the qualities necessary for government.

In the meantime, Almagro pushed onwards south towards Chile, accompanied by more than five hundred Spanish soldiers, and hundreds of Indian porters. Untold hardships were suffered by all the members of this memorable expedition. Soldiers who were unable to march further, were carried by the Indians in hammocks, as also were the valuable colts born on the way across the vast windswept table-land of Bolivia, 12,500 feet above sea level.

When Hernando Pizarro arrived in Cuzco, he found that serious trouble was brewing there. Many of the Spaniards had behaved abominably towards the Indians, and even the puppet *Inca* had been treated so contemptuously that, together with some of his humiliated nobles, he secretly planned to overthrow his white oppressors.

American Indians are possessed of great cunning, and no

one in the world surpasses them at keeping a secret. In sending the High Priest of the Sun to prepare the way for Almagro's expedition to Chile, Manco had proved to be no exception to this general rule, for he had instructed him on the march secretly to instigate a general uprising against the *conquistadores*. At the crucial moment the High Priest was to desert Almagro, and take a leading part in the insurrection. In Cuzco the plot was only discovered after Manco left the city ; but very soon a pursuing body of Spanish horsemen captured the fugitive who was taken back and incarcerated in the fortress, where Hernando met him upon arriving from Lima.

Curiously, although Hernando was inclined to be haughty and arrogant with his own countrymen, he was always kind to defeated Indians. Therefore, without ado, he gave orders for Manco's immediate release. The *Inca* pretended to be most grateful to his protector, and won his sympathy and compassion by telling him of the many wrongs committed by the Spaniards during his prolonged absence. To prove his gratitude, he indicated Hernando several places where treasure and jewels lay hidden, and presented him with them. Seeing that this manœuvre produced the desired effect, Manco craftily went further and announced that a life-size statue of his father, the *Inca* Huayna Capac, had been placed into a secret cave, some distance away from Cuzco, and that, as a further token of friendship and gratitude, he desired to present it to Hernando. Blinded by these favours, and by the prospect of yet another almost incredibly valuable gift, the Governor gave Manco permission to leave the city. With him he took a number of Indians, and Hernando even sent along two of his soldiers as a special bodyguard, and one of his best interpreters.

Eight days passed, and when Manco failed to return with the promised treasure, it began to dawn on Hernando that he had been tricked, whereupon he sent his brother, Juan, with a strong body of cavalry to capture the fugitive, whom he now suspected of planning an insurrection.

Juan and his men found the country to be deserted of

human inhabitants ; a sign which promised that trouble was brewing. Having been informed as to the direction in which Manco and his party had travelled, Juan hastened to catch up with him. Upon nearing a mountain range, he met Manco's Spanish bodyguard. These men informed Juan that they had peacefully travelled with Manco to the locality, and that, suddenly, he had ordered them to return to Cuzco. Seeing that the whole Indian population of the region was up in arms, and loudly clamoured for the blood of every Spaniard in the country, they declared that they considered themselves lucky to be alive.

Determined to capture Manco, Juan and his men rode on until they reached a deep stream, on the opposite bank of which a force of Indian warriors greeted them with shouts of defiance. Despite the natives' overwhelming superiority in numbers, the Spaniards spurred on their horses, and plunged into the water, and upon reaching the other side charged the enemy with great courage. The ensuing fight was fierce and bloody, and for a considerable time the issue hung in the balance. Experience had taught the natives much about fighting against cavalry, and, furthermore, they were well armed, some even using copper swords copied from some previously taken from the Spaniards. Towards evening the Indians made a slow and orderly retreat towards hills nearby, and on the following morning when the Spaniards were about to renew their attack on them, they were dismayed to see that during the hours of darkness Manco had been joined by considerable reinforcements. Throughout that day, Juan's cavalry made daring charges against heavy odds, and although the Peruvians suffered severe losses, the Spaniards were unable to dislodge them from their advantageous positions on the heights. The terrible slaughter continued for three days, and still Juan was far from achieving victory. A number of his men and horses had been killed, and most of the others were wounded or completely exhausted, when a messenger arrived with the alarming news that another vast Indian army had surrounded Cuzco, where Hernando Pizarro and his small body of troops were in an extremely precarious position. Juan immediately gave orders to retreat towards the beleaguered city where his arrival was anxiously awaited. Upon nearing Cuzco, he and his weary men saw a sight which filled them with consternation. Everywhere surrounding the city were thousands upon thousands of Indian warriors, armed with lances, copper maces, swords, slings, lassos, bows and arrows and battle axes. Many wore protective armour and glittering helmets adorned with bright plumes, or fearsome looking head dresses made of the heads of jaguars and other wild beasts. The awe-inspiring din of cymbals and trumpets intermingled with the fierce war-cries of the Peruvians as Juan approached the ring of warriors which had been thrown around the city. Drawing closely together, the Spaniards charged without hesitation, and to their surprise they were allowed to pass without resistance being offered them, probably because the Indians hoped to destroy them, together with the garrison within the city, by starving them to death.

Hernando felt greatly relieved at seeing his brother back, for every man would be needed to face the beleaguering hordes which numbered some two hundred thousand Indians, whereas the total Spanish force only amounted to about two hundred men. Fortunately, in the capital there were about a thousand Indians of a warlike tribe which had only recently been conquered by the *Incas*. These Indians now joined the Spaniards, for at last they saw an opportunity to avenge the wrongs they had suffered under their conquerors and oppressors, the hated Peruvians, who had brought them captive to Cuzco.

Manco's cunning escape, and the whole insurrection had been planned with such secrecy that the conquerors were taken completely by surprise. Many of the Spanish troops having left on different expeditions, the Peruvians had not been slow in seizing the opportunity to strike at their white oppressors. The unsuspecting Spaniards had left the fort of Cuzco practically unguarded ; a carelessness and over-confidence which was to cost them dearly.

This fortress, with its massive ramparts, stood on a steep

hill, dominating the city below. It was a formidable point of vantage, from which the Indians harassed the beleaguered Spaniards.

Strong barricades having been placed in all the streets leading into the city, Hernando Pizarro made preparations to withstand a siege which was likely to last until assistance arrived from the coast. Fortunately for the Spaniards, it did not occur to the Indians to deviate the stream which provided the city with water, and thus, at least, thirst was not among the anguishes the beleaguered men and their horses had to suffer. There was sufficient food in store to last for some time, but of the eventuality of relief delaying, no one dare think.

With the fortress in the Indians' hands, the Spaniards' situation below was extremely uncomfortable, an incessant shower of arrows and stones obliging the soldiers to take cover, or to move with great caution. Although Juan Pizarro had been wounded in the jaw, he volunteered to make a desperate attempt to re-capture the fort. One night, when the masses of flickering camp fires made by the Indians had grown dim, he stole out of the city, accompanied by a body of picked soldiers. The Indians never fought at night, and usually left their camps poorly guarded ; a circumstance of which the Spaniards now hoped to take advantage.

Advancing with great caution, Juan and his men succeeded in reaching the last of the three formidable parapets without being discovered by the enemy. Finding the steep path which led to the narrow entrance, the Spaniards dismounted and followed behind their valiant leader. Suddenly a hail of arrows, javelins and rocks came down upon the attacking party. Disregarding the danger, Juan rushed forward, sword in hand, and was about to pass through the narrow gap leading up to the last parapet, when a rock struck him on the head. Though mortally wounded, he continued to cheer on his men who made valiant efforts to force their way through the narrow entrance. However, the odds against them were so heavy that after a few of the brave attackers were killed, and most of the others wounded, the survivors retired, carrying Juan back to Cuzco where, a few days later, he died in great agony. His loss was deeply felt by all his companions-in-arms, for he had always been a favourite among both officers and troops.

There was no time for mourning, for every day the situation in Cuzco became more critical. Arrows and stones with burning substances attached to them set a number of the thatched roofs afire, and soon the whole city was enveloped in flames, obliging the Spaniards to camp in the main *plaza*, which was like an island in this burning inferno. From the fort and other points of vantage, the Indians shouted defiance, and boasted that the whole country was up in arms, that all communications with the coast had been cut off, and that Lima, Trujillo and other Spanish colonies were besieged. When heads of white men were thrown over the barricades, the soldiers realized that the Indians' boasts were only too true, for some of these heads had been brought with fiendish intention from different parts of the country to intimidate the beleaguered garrison. The fire in Cuzco raged with unabated fury for several days, and when the flames had consumed everything but the solid stone walls, only the Temple of the Sun and the adjacent House of the Virgins remained intact. At the time, the former building was in course of reconstruction as the cathedral, while the latter had been set aside to be used as a convent. Several times the roofs of these buildings caught fire, but although no attempt was made to fight the flames, they soon extinguished themselves without doing much harm.

Several attempts to dislodge the Indians from the fortress ended in failure, costing the Spaniards a few lives and many wounded. One Peruvian nobleman in particular distinguished himself in repelling the Spanish attacks. This herculean warrior was armed with a heavy copper mace, and whenever it looked as if the attackers would gain a foothold on the ramparts, he was there to repel them. Hernando Pizarro so admired this nobleman's fighting qualities and bravery that he gave orders to the Spanish soldiers not to kill him, but, if possible, to capture him alive. At last, after a terrific struggle, the Spaniards managed to reach the top ramparts of the fortress by using scaling ladders, a form of attack the Indians had not expected. The ensuing fight was fierce and bloody, and when the Peruvian hero realized that the white men had won the day, he wrapped himself up in his cloak and flung himself from the southern parapet into the rocky valley below.

The re-capture of the fort temporarily eased the situation for the Spaniards, but soon the lack of food was severely felt. Most of the stores had been consumed by the flames, and in order to obtain new supplies, it now became necessary to raid granaries situated outside the city, trusting that the besieging Indians had not used or removed their stores. Throughout the night, the Spaniards, assisted by their thousand Indian confederates, cleared away *débris* and barricades which obstructed two narrow streets leading out of the city, and shortly before daybreak the cavalry made a successful sortie, attacking the surprised besiegers with such violence that they fell back in disorder.

By this time the Indians had become so accustomed to fighting against cavalry that the Spaniards had to be extremely careful. Pits containing pointed stakes, and lassos dexterously thrown at riders and horses, were a great danger, for if a man was caught in the noose, or his mount was brought down to earth, the Indians immediately pounced upon him with lances, battle axes, or maces. The *boleadora*, or *ayllu* as the Peruvians called this strange and typically South American weapon, was another danger the Spaniards had good reason to fear. It consists of three heavy stone balls fastened to the ends of three strong leather thongs which are tied together in the shape of a star, the balls being fastened to the points. When thrown by an expert, these balls wrap themselves round a horse's legs, bringing him crashing to the ground.

Thanks to several successful sorties made by the Spaniards, a certain quantity of food was brought back, but this was not accomplished without losses the small garrison could ill afford. Weeks and months passed, and still Hernando and his contingent held on. As no relief arrived from the coast, it was feared that Lima and Trujillo had fallen to the enemy, and that, therefore, the only way out of this hopeless situation lay in battling their way to the coast. When some of the men and officers suggested this to their leader, he flatly refused to retreat, and expressed his determination to die rather than abandon Cuzco.

This state of affairs could not continue indefinitely, and therefore Hernando thought out a plan which he hoped would put new vigour and courage into his troops. Lack of food and sleep, and frequent minor engagements with the enemy, apart from wounds, showed their effects on all the beleaguered men's bodies and faces, and Hernando realized that only a bold stroke would re-animate them to hold on longer. Knowing that Manco had established his head-quarters in a fort situated in the neighbouring mountains, he made a desperate plan to strike there ; the heart of all the trouble.

Accompanied by seventy horsemen, he dashed out of the city, annihilating all enemies who attempted to bar his way. Upon reaching the ramparts of the fort, a cloud of arrows and stones descended upon the Spaniards, obliging them to beat a hasty retreat. On a flat stretch of land nearby, ranks were re-formed and council taken, but in the meantime, encouraged by their initial success, hordes of Indians poured out of the fort, and with fearful war-cries threw themselves upon the white men whose consternation was increased when it was discovered that the natives had opened the irrigation sluices of a nearby stream, the waters of which now rapidly flooded the little plain, impeding the movement of the horses. It was evident that the Indians had anticipated an attack, for even horse-traps had been dug in the vicinity, and now these claimed a number of victims. A few of the Indians even possessed fire-arms, which, though used with little or no effect, constituted an element of surprise to the Spaniards. These weapons had probably been taken from soldiers killed in previous encounters; and it has been said that several Spanish soldiers who had previously been taken prisoner by the Peruvians, taught their captors how to use firearms, and how to fight against cavalry.

Hernando and his men fought with the fury of desperation, and under cover of the night eventually managed to retreat towards Cuzco. Despite this very serious reverse, Hernando the indomitable, still thought that he could capture Manco, and accordingly made plans for a second attack.

One night, after the last flickering Indian camp fires around the city had died down, he stole out unobserved, and advanced rapidly towards the *Inca's* fort. This time he had with him eighty of his best mounted men, a number of picked infantry and a body of Indian auxiliaries. It was pitch dark when the Spaniards cautiously approached the fort which they intended to storm at the first break of dawn, when Indians usually fall into their heaviest sleep; a racial characteristic of which Hernando hoped to take advantage.

In the Peruvian highland, nights are bitterly cold, and therefore, shivering and with chattering teeth, the Spaniards silently stole up a steep and slippery incline, at the top of which the fort was situated. The site for this stronghold had been so well chosen that it could only be attacked from one side, the other being considered impregnable.

The first streaks of dawn faintly silhouetted the jagged mountain peaks and the ramparts which surrounded the fort, when Hernando and his men reached the first outer wall. Not a sound was heard above, and the Spaniards thought the day was as good as won when, suddenly, like a thunderclap, an unearthly din of horns, symbals, war-drums and wild yells echoed and re-echoed through the semi-darkness. At the same instant thousands of dark shapes appeared on the ramparts above, and a cloud oi arrows, javelins and rocks was hurled down upon the startled attackers who, after a futile attempt to scale the outer wall, were compelled to fall back, carrying with them those of their comrades who had been severely wounded.

To the Spaniards' astonishment, on one of the terraces Manco could be seen, mounted on a horse, lance in hand, directing operations. The animal had evidently been captured during a previous encounter, and the white men now admired the adroit manner in which the *Inca* handled it, as if he had ridden all his life.

Encouraged by their success in repelling the Spaniards, thousands of Indians rushed out of the fort, and threw themselves at the white men with such valour that, throughout that long day, they were obliged to fall back. Time and again the Indians renewed their assaults, some recklessly catching horses by the legs, and pulling them to the ground ; but the Spaniards fought back with such effect that only a few of their number were seriously wounded. After every encounter the ground was strewn with dead and mortally wounded Peruvians who had fallen to better arms and superior skill. It was getting dark when, bloody and exhausted, Hernando and his men staggered into Cuzco. The enemy had harassed them throughout the retreat, and a few days later the city was attacked with such determination that the Spaniards had to fight as they had never fought before to stem the fierce assault. Weeks passed, and still neither relief nor news came from the coast, and eventually even the bravest of the beleaguered men began to think that their inevitable doom approached.

During one of the sorties made in search of food, the severed heads of several Spanish soldiers were found. From Lima, Pizarro had sent these unfortunate men with letters and dispatches for the besieged garrison in Cuzco. From the dispatches, which fortunately had not been destroyed by the Indians, it was learned that Lima and Trujillo were besieged, and that the whole of Peru was in a state of revolt. Apparently Pizarro had made several attempts to communicate with his brother in Cuzco, but all these attempts had ended in disaster, the soldiers who were sent on the dangerous errands having been killed by the Indians, who held all the mountain passes. Only two or three of the men who had set out to re-establish contact with the beleaguered garrison in Cuzco had succeeded in returning to their starting point to tell the sad story of their companions' death, or how others were captured by the Indians to serve as slaves for the *Inca*. From the letters found near those gruesome heads, it was also learned that in different parts of Peru some seven hundred Spanish soldiers, as well as a number of colonists, had lost their lives.

In Lima the situation was so serious that a number of officers and men suggested the immediate evacuation of the city, and retreat by sea to Panama. But Pizarro was not the man to act like the proverbial rat in a sinking ship, and therefore he flatly refused to leave any of his garrisons to their fate. Instead of using the available ships to seek safety, he sent them, manned by skeleton crews, to appeal for assistance in Panama, Nicaragua, Guatemala, Mexico, and in the West Indies. In his urgent calls for immediate help, he stated that Peru would be lost, unless troops and supplies arrived without delay, and in writing to Alvarado in Guatemala he even promised that if he returned to help, he (Pizarro) would return to Panama or Spain, after the quelling of the Indian insurrection.

Whilst these events took place at the coast, Hernando and his men stubbornly continued to defend Cuzco. Nearly six months had passed since the siege had begun, and still the ring of Indian warriors held fast. Thanks to successful sorties made, starvation claimed no victims, though lack of food had weakened even the strongest bodies. Acts of individual bravery and gallantry on both sides became almost daily events. Challenges for single combats were occasionally made, and accepted, the two antagonists meeting in the open and fighting to the death whilst their comrades looked on.

That armies march and fight on their stomachs, the Peruvians knew well. With the passing of months, granaries were depleted of their stores, and therefore, with the coming of the planting season, the *Inca* had to release the greater part of his warriors to till the land in their respective home regions. Keeping sufficient men to hold the mountain passes, and to continue the blockade of Cuzco, Manco confidently settled down to starve out the white men who obstinately continued to defend the charred ruins of what had formerly been the proud and flourishing capital of his ancestors' mighty empire.

The weary Spaniards felt great relief at seeing thousands of their enemies depart, and immediately seized the opportunity to raid regions nearby where they knew food was to be found. During one of these sorties they rounded up some two thousand llamas, which were successfully herded into Cuzco, where their arrival was greeted with scenes of wild rejoicing.

XII

IGNORANT of the serious situation in which his countrymen found themselves in Peru, Almagro and his expeditionary force advanced towards the unknown south, crossing wind-swept tablelands and mighty snow covered mountain ranges. Here and there primitive Indians attacked the white intruders with great ferocity, though on all occasions the Spaniards' superior arms prevailed. In high places, *sorroche*, as mountain sickness is called in Peru, affected the soldiers, who were unaccustomed to such high altitudes. Lack of atmospheric pressure made them gasp for air, many felt limp and exhausted, and others staggered in fits of giddiness which often were accompanied by profuse bleeding of the nose. Hunger and bitter cold added to the Spaniards' sufferings, and even more so to their unfortunate Indian porters, who had not the necessary clothes to afford protection against the cutting winds, icy squalls and whirling snow frequently encountered on the march. As porters died, Indians captured during fights were chained together, and forced to carry the baggage.

The expedition had covered over a thousand miles when its starved and bedraggled members descended from the last westerly Andean range towards the shore of the Pacific

Ocean. One fifth of the soldiers, and an even larger proportion of the Indian porters had miserably perished on the march. Upon reaching Coquimbó, the survivors' relief was great, for there the fields were green, and the vegetation and climate a delight to man and beast.

Used to easy acquisition of treasure, the soldiers were sadly disappointed, for nowhere they had passed had they seen, or even heard of a temple or a palace where loot was likely to be found. Judging by reports gathered from Indians who lived along the coast, no gold was to be found further towards the south, though the narrow strip of land between the Andes and the ocean was said to be fertile, and inhabited by many different Indian tribes.

In order to ascertain if these stories were true, Almagro sent an officer in charge of a body of soldiers to explore the coastal regions further to the south. Shortly after this party had set out, the sick and weakened men who had remained in Coquimbó with Almagro, were overjoyed when reinforcements arrived. It is amazing how, on several occasions during the conquest and exploration of the New World, such forces managed to meet in vast and totally unknown regions.

The captain who was in charge of the new arrivals, brought Almagro a copy of the royal warrant Hernando Pizarro had taken to Peru on his return from Spain.

Almagro's sadly disappointed men in Coquimbó were delighted with the intelligence brought, confirming their leader's Governorship and title to land, for by this time every member of the expedition had firmly attached himself to Almagro's fortunes, and therefore looked upon the Pizarro brothers and their followers as rivals who had the luck and the advantage of having been first to arrive in Peru.

After an absence of about two months, the officer who had been sent to explore the coastal regions to the south, returned with the report that nothing worth while was to be found there. Officers and soldiers alike now urged Almagro to return to Cuzco, all being convinced that the city fell into his jurisdiction. "Why isolate ourselves near the end of the world," they argued, "when neither gold nor treasure is to be found in the land we have reached after so many hardships and perils?"

In order to avoid the hardships of the expedition's recent mountain route, Almagro decided to make the return journey to Cuzco by more or less following the coast for about nine hundred miles, and then, from what to-day is the port of Mollendo, to turn east, and reach his destination via Arequipa, about half way between the coast and Lake Titicaca. The coastal regions to be traversed were unknown at the time, and therefore the Spaniards set out with the idea that the return journey was bound to be easier, and that, if nothing else, the intense cold in the Andes would be avoided.

Nearing what is now northern Chile, they came to hot, sandy regions, and later marched into the dreaded Atacama desert, nearly three hundred miles in length, where nothing is to be seen but a cloudless light-blue sky, and rolling billows of shimmering sand. Not a drop of water is to be found there, and the heat is terrific. How Almagro and his men—many of whom wore armour—managed to traverse this broiling inferno, shunned by man and beast, is a mystery to anyone who has ventured a few miles into it.

But iron determination, a fanatical belief that they were on a holy crusade, and light-hearted spirits, raised the *conquistadores* above physical discomforts, and often even fear of death, and enabled them to accomplish seemingly impossible feats of endurance.

Upon reaching Arequipa, Almagro heard the first news about the siege of Cuzco. When informed that Manco was leading the insurrection, he immediately sent an envoy to his headquarters, in order to arrange a meeting. As Almagro had always been on friendly terms with the *Inca*, the messenger was well received. Manco bitterly complained about the behaviour of Hernando's followers, and laid the total blame on them. At the same time he expressed his willingness to meet Almagro, and, under certain conditions, even promised to cease hostilities.

The news that Almagro had returned from Chile and was about to make a separate peace with Manco, was shouted to the Spaniards in Cuzco by the besieging Peruvian warriors. When Hernando Pizarro realized that this was no mere bluff, he became seriously worried, and in despair decided to make an attempt to forestall his rival's move. Accordingly, he sent a young mulatto to the *Inca* with a message urging him on no account to make peace with Almagro who was not the master of Cuzco; but, instead, to come to terms with him, Hernando Pizarro, legitimate Governor of the city.

It was well for the mulatto that Almagro's envoy was still with Manco when he arrived, for the *Inca* was so annoyed with Hernando's messenger that he would have cut off his right hand, had it not been for the intervention on his behalf by the Spaniard from Almagro's camp. As it was, Manco contented himself by only cutting off one of the mulatto's fingers, and with this as an answer, sent the unfortunate youth back to Cuzco.

Having failed in his attempt to make peace with the *Inca*, Hernando tried to reach a compromise with Almagro who was encamped in a small Indian town situated about eighteen miles south of Cuzco. When Manco heard that messages were being exchanged between the rival leaders, thinking he was being double crossed, he refused to have any further dealings with Almagro whom he regarded as one who had acted in bad faith.

In view of the fact that Almagro had four hundred soldiers at his disposal, and several excellent and experienced captains, Hernando knew that he must act with caution. Therefore, he promised that, for the time being, he was prepared to give half of the city to his rival, and he also assured him that a great welcome awaited him in Cuzco.

Out in Almagro's camp, most of the officers warned their leader not to trust Hernando, and strongly advised him not to accept any compromise regarding the governorship of the city, but to seize it, if necessary by force. They pointed out that in Cuzco there were only two hundred soldiers who, after the long siege, were so weakened and demoralized that they would offer no resistance. Almagro readily agreed with the officers' views, but in order to avoid a civil war, and being branded as the aggressor, he refused to take so drastic a step. Instead, he sent an emissary to Hernando, with a letter in which he stated what he considered to be his rights. The message was so strongly worded that in Cuzco no one doubted that the situation was becoming hopeless. Hernando made great efforts to animate his faltering men and officials, a number of whom he knew to be in favour of his rival. He pleaded, made promises, and argued ; but most of his listeners remained unmoved. When he attempted to explain that the provisions of the royal warrant were clear enough, they replied that the question was most debatable, and when he made efforts to convince them that Cuzco undoubtedly came within his brother's jurisdiction, some of his luke-warm partisans answered that, being no geographers, they preferred not to take sides in this controversy which looked like leading to unnecessary bloodshed. Hernando then realized that his only salvation lay in playing for time, for surely, sooner or later, reinforcements would arrive from Lima, and save the city for him.

After further parleying between Hernando and Almagro, it was agreed that both factions were to remain in their present quarters until experts had definitely settled the question of the boundary. According to this truce, Hernando promised not to strengthen the fortifications of Cuzco, but, instead, to proceed with the restoration of buildings damaged or destroyed by the disastrous fire Manco's warriors had caused early in the siege.

For some time all went well, but with the coming of the rainy season, Almagro's idle troops became dissatisfied with their uncomfortable quarters in the small Indian town. It was also rumoured that, contrary to agreement, Hernando was strengthening his fortifications, and that a relief expedition, sent by Pizarro from Lima, had crossed the mountains, and was about to join the garrison in Cuzco. Almagro's captains now urged their leader to act without delay. This time they were successful, for Almagro immediately gave orders to march. Darkness and rain favoured the stealthy invaders, who managed to penetrate into the city without difficulty, only twenty loyal soldiers defending the house in which Hernando and his brother, Gonzalo, were asleep. Hearing the noise outside, both jumped out of bed, buckled on their armour, and fought with such valour that even their enemies were filled with admiration. An offer to surrender having been refused, the attackers set the thatched roof of the building on fire. Despite being enveloped in a dense cloud of choking smoke and whirling sparks, the two Pizarros and their handful of loyal supporters fought on like demons, and only when the roof threatened to collapse, they rushed out of the door, immediately to be overpowered and disarmed. Hardly had this been done than the burning roof collapsed with a loud crash.

Together with a number of their leading supporters, the two Pizarros were detained in a house under a strong guard. The majority of their officials, who preferred to run with the hare and with the hounds, lost no time in acclaiming Almagro as their new and rightful governor.

The army from Lima was reported to be some forty miles from the city, so Almagro sent an envoy, escorted by a number of soldiers, to inform the leader that he, Almagro, was master of Cuzco, and that he would tolerate no interference. He also warned the commander of the relief force that, if he advanced further, he would unlawfully enter into territory outside Pizarro's jurisdiction.

When, after eight days, the envoy and his escort failed to return, Almagro rightly guessed that they had been detained by the men from Lima. This thought so infuriated him that he marched out of the city to fight those whom he regarded as arrogant intruders. Before he left, his friends urged him to execute the two Pizarros, and when he refused, one of their number prophesied that, some day, he would regret having missed so good an opportunity to be rid of a pair whose ambition was merciless revenge.

Almagro and his followers knew that many old friends of theirs were in the relief army from Lima, and therefore they were confident that the majority would refuse to fight, and that, in all probability, many would pass over to them. Upon reaching the Abancay river, it was found that the bridge and two available fords were well defended, and that the opposing army was encamped on the opposite bank. Almagro waited until nightfall, and then, although the river was deep and swift, this seventy year old warrior plunged into the turbulent waters, followed by eighty of his best horsemen. At the same time a detachment of his troops assailed the bridge, whilst another body awaited the signal to force a passage across one of the fords. Several of Almagro's men were swept away by the swift waters, but thanks to the darkness the others managed to reach the opposite bank without opposition, immediately harassing the enemy who offered stubborn resistance. Shortly after daybreak the fierce encounter came to a sudden end, many of the men from Lima passing over to Almagro, as had been expected. Although the battle had been fought with great fury, casualties were not heavy on either side, and the victors treated the vanquished with lenity, a rare happening in civil wars.

With Pizarro's Lima force disarmed, Almagro marched back to Cuzco, where he proved to be both humane and generous, in ordering that all the prisoners' belongings, including arms, be restored to them, and that they be allowed to move about as free men. To those who had lost their possessions, he made presents out of his private funds, and generally showed such sympathy that most of his former enemies joined his ranks.

Some members of Almagro's council again clamoured for the two imprisoned Pizarros' lives, and all expressed the opinion that the time was opportune for a march on Lima, where Pizarro was anxiously awaiting the arrival of reinforcements from Panama and Nicaragua. Almagro's officers argued that Pizarro would never rest until he had reconquered Cuzco for himself; but although their leader agreed that his rival in Lima was an enemy not to be taken lightly, he thought it advisable first of all to strengthen the defences of Cuzco, and to proceed with the reconstruction of the city which still presented a sorry sight after the long siege.

Manco and his warriors—now greatly reduced in numbers —was still in the neighbourhood, awaiting the return of the thousands he had temporarily released to attend to their crops. Although the Indians troubled the Spaniards but little, Almagro thought the moment opportune to deal the enemy a blow. Accordingly, he sent his ablest captain and a strong body of cavalry to attack the *Inca*, who still had his headquarters in the mountains. The campaign was so successful that, after two or three encounters, the disheartened Indians deserted the *Inca*, who escaped with difficulty into a remote sector of the Andes.

Nearly a year had passed since the Indian insurrection had broken out, and still communication between Cuzco and Lima was interrupted. The only information about happenings at the coast had been gathered from officers and men of the defeated relief army, and as news it was antiquated. Almagro was busy making preparations to march down to the coast when an embassy arrived from Lima with news about the situation there, and with an offer to reach a compromise regarding the governorship of Cuzco. Unfortunately, however, when it looked as if the matter would be peacefully settled, the principal spokesman of this embassy died, whereafter Almagro sent the other mediators back to Lima. He asked them to inform Pizarro that he was about to march down to Chincha at the coast, in order to despatch to Spain the royal fifth, amounting to 600,000 *pesos* gold, and that he would take Hernando with him as a prisoner, whilst Gonzalo would remain under close arrest in Cuzco.

Having reached his destination at the coast, Almagro

immediately set to work fortifying Chincha, and to build a port which was to make him independent of Lima. It was his ambition to develop the settlement into a city which should soon overshadow the capital founded by Pizarro, and to become the main point of communication between Peru, Panama and Spain.

In the meantime, Gonzalo Pizarro and several fellow prisoners managed to bribe their guards, and to make good their escape from Cuzco. After a perilous flight across the mighty Andean ranges, the fugitives eventually succeeded in reaching Lima in safety. Infuriated by Gonzalo's escape, Almagro now regretted that he had not executed his prisoners ; and, had it not been for the intervention of one of his captains, he would have killed Hernando there and then.

A number of angry communications having been exchanged between Pizarro and Almagro, they finally agreed on a priest as arbitrator. Very soon, however, this well-meaning ecclesiastic realized that it would be impossible to come to an agreement, unless the quarrelling parties met. Accordingly, a meeting was arranged at a place situated half-way between Lima and Chincha, from where the priest conducted the arbitration. Relations between the two camps were so strained that, as a special precaution, it was agreed that no troops were to be moved from their respective quarters, and, moreover, that each leader was to be accompanied by only twelve officers.

Pizarro was first to arrive at the house of the priest, soon to be followed by Almagro, who courteously greeted his rival, who, in frigid contrast, barely touched his helmet with one finger. Seeing that the latter's escort, unlike his own, was unarmed, Pizarro said, " I see you are out on a little pleasure ride." To this piquant remark he received the suave reply, " Yes, sir, to be of service to you." The two rivals and the priest then entered the house where a heated conversation ensued. Pizarro asked his former friend why he had taken Cuzco from him, and why he had imprisoned his two brothers. To this Almagro replied that, according to the royal warrant, the city came under his jurisdiction, and that, in defending it, Hernando and Gonzalo had rebelled against his authority, and, incidentally, against the Crown. As might be expected, the argument about the border line became more and more heated, and in the circumstances there was little the priest could do to calm tempers.

It has been said that Gonzalo Pizarro (who had recently escaped from Cuzco) had prepared an ambush for Almagro, and that, having got wind of it, one of the latter's captains approached a window of the room in which the parley was being held, and repeatedly hummed two lines of an old Spanish ballad :

> *Tiempo es, el caballero,*
> *Tiempo es ya andar de aqui.*

which might be translated as :

> Time it is, oh caballero,
> High time to get out of here.

Taking the hint, Almagro hurriedly left the house, mounted his horse, and, together with his escort of twelve, galloped back to Chincha.

After this sudden and dramatic collapse of direct negotiations, the priest continued to make efforts to find a solution to the difficult problem. As time dragged on, Almagro's supporters became impatient, and rumours began to spread among them that they were about to be robbed of everything. Soon discontent gave way to bitterness, and during demonstrations officers and men shouted, " We have arms, and are ready to use them against Pizarro," and when Almagro still refused to act, they accused him of senility and cowardice, and in loud voices demanded that Hernando Pizarro—who was still held as a prisoner—be beheaded at once. Wishing to avoid bloodshed, Almagro remained silent.

In Lima, Pizarro was greatly worried about his brother's safety, and to protect his life he proposed to let Almagro have Cuzco, until the king's verdict regarding the boundary line should become known, provided Hernando was set free. Despite his captains' warnings not to listen to this proposal, Almagro personally released the prisoner who promised that he would return to Spain within a few weeks, taking with him the royal fifth.

No sooner was Hernando back in Lima than he pressed his brother with regard to the wrongs he had suffered, and said that it was a matter of honour to avenge them. Pizarro listened, but refused to act. " I fear the king's anger," he explained, to which Hernando hotly replied, " and did Almagro fear it when he took Cuzco by force, and threw me into prison." Pizarro began to waver.

The arrival of a new warrant, signed a few months previously in Madrid by the king, brought things to a head, for, according to this document, Cuzco fell within Pizarro's jurisdiction. On the strength of this, Pizarro ordered Almagro to proceed into his own territory in the south, and once and for ever to give up the idea of governing Cuzco ; but Almagro, who suspected his rival of underhand play, flatly refused to hand over what he firmly believed to be his. Words having failed, Pizarro decided to try deeds. Calling together his captains, he denounced Almagro as a rebel, and at the same time informed the assembly that, in view of the situation, Hernando was not to leave for Spain until peace and order had been restored.

The stage was set for another stormy scene in the intense drama of Peru, but this time the tempest was to rage among the Spaniards.

XIII

THE arrival from Panama of new soldiers in search of fortune and fame, had gradually increased the strength of Pizarro's army which now numbered almost twice as many men as that of Almagro, who was getting so old and infirm that he had to appoint his most experienced captain to take command of his troops. Lack of unity, and disagreements among the officers so interfered with plans that when hostilities began, the Pizarros were able to take advantage of this circumstance. After having committed some serious blunders, Almagro's officers decided to retreat into the mountains, and entrench themselves in Cuzco, though a few, including the leader himself, were in favour of making another attempt to settle the dispute by compromise. When an envoy was sent to sound Pizarro, he vaunted that from now on his jurisdiction extended down to the Strait of Magellan. This arrogant reply left no one in doubt that Pizarro was determined to ruin his adversary and to take possession of all his territory, and therefore everyone realized that only a battle now could settle the bitter controversy. By this time Almagro was so ill that he had to be carried in a hammock, and in one place along the difficult march over the tremendous mountains, he had to rest for three weeks.

Holding to his intention, Pizarro only accompanied his troops until the main Andean ranges were reached. There he handed over the command to his brother, Fernando, who, by a devious route, led his troops in the direction of Cuzco.

The captain who was in command of Almagro's army, decided to meet the enemy on a small plain situated about a mile and a half from the city. There he placed his men—about five hundred in number, more than half of them horse, and six cannon—and awaited Hernando's force which, though numerically about twice as strong as his, was inferior in the matter of cavalry. In due time the Pizarristas approached with banners unfurled, and armour glittering in the evening sun. Preferring to defer the attack until next day, Hernando pitched for the night.

News of the impending battle spreading through the region, masses of Indians hurried from far and near to witness what promised to be a glorious spectacle, as far as they were concerned. When the sun rose, all the hills and other points of vantage nearby, from where a good view of the plain could be obtained, were thronged with Indians who stolidly looked on, whilst their white oppressors made final preparations for the fray.

Mass having been said, Hernando Pizarro—who was conspicuously dressed in an armour over-vest of light orange colour, and with a white plume in his helmet—gave orders to attack. His army's inferiority, as far as cavalry was concerned, was more than counter-balanced by a strong body of arquebusiers who had a novel pattern of fire-arm which threw two bullets linked together by a short chain. This new weapon had only recently been introduced to Peru from Flanders where it had been used with great success.

At the first clash, when cannon and fire-arms thundered, belching out fire and clouds of sulphurous smoke, and Spaniards threw themselves at each other with terrible fury, the mass of Indian spectators cheered with fiendish delight. The desperate struggle went on for some time, and then Hernando's arquebusiers came into action with such deadly effect that with the first volley they put some fifty horsemen out of action. Officers and men fought with great gallantry, though with such hatred that no quarter was given. In the midst of this bloody *mêlée*, captains occasionally managed to single out one another, and to meet in single combat.

After about two hours, so many of Almagro's soldiers had been killed or wounded that the others were fighting utterly at bay. By degrees the Pizarrista's devastating fire threw them into a confusion which ended in a wild flight towards Cuzco. From a hill, lying in his hammock, Almagro had watched the battle in which he would have given much to have fought. When he realized that defeat was inevitable, with a painful effort he managed to mount a mule on which he fled towards the old Indian fortress of Cuzco, where he took refuge in one of the underground passages.

The wild stampede having left the bloody battle-field deserted, the Indian spectators came down from the hills to strip the dead and dying, and to take possession of whatever had been left behind.

When compared with European military actions, this battle—in which about only one hundred and fifty men were killed—may appear to be insignificant, but it must be borne in mind that it is not the number of soldiers involved that makes a battle important, but the prize at stake. In this case it was the control of a vast and rich empire.

Almagro was soon discovered in his hiding place in the old Indian fortress, and, having been captured and put in irons, he was imprisoned in the same building in which, not long before, he had detained the two Pizarros. Among others who were incarcerated, was his illegitimate son, Diego, a very promising youth, to whom his father was devoted.

After a few days, Hernando sent Diego to Lima to be placed in charge of Pizarro. This greatly distressed the father, who only realized the sinister reason for this step, when he was informed that during a secret trial the judges had found him guilty of conspiracy and rebellion against the Crown. When told that he had been sentenced to death, he pleaded with Hernando who coldly replied that he was astonished to see an old, emaciated and gouty man fear death, when, in any case, the few remaining days of his life would have to be miserably spent in prison.

The death sentence caused a great sensation in Cuzco, where many Spaniards realized that Hernando was not in a position to execute a man of Almagro's standing, both in the eye of the law and of the king.

Resigned to his fate, the condemned prisoner calmly made his will. As his successor he appointed his son, but as he was still in his minority, he named his most trusted friend provisionally to assume the governorship of his jurisdiction. All his personal property and possessions he left to be divided between the king and his son, and in connection with this he pointed out that a large sum of money was owed to him by Pizarro. No doubt, this clause was cunningly put into the will to serve a double purpose. First of all, it was likely to secure royal protection for Diego, and it might also bring about an investigation of Pizarro's affairs, with concomitant trouble. His affairs thus put in order, Almagro was garrotted in his prison whereafter, in accordance with the sentence of alleged treason and conspiracy against the Crown, the head was severed from the body, in the main square of Cuzco. The victim's remains were then taken to the house of friends, later to be interred in the Church of Our Lady of Mercy, where Hernando and his staff and officials assembled to take part in this solemn ceremony.

Shortly after this rash execution, Pizarro arrived in Cuzco from Lima. Although he rode into the city with pomp and ceremony, and many of his followers lined the streets to greet him, he was visibly ill at ease, for not a few of his own partisans were so indignant on account of Almagro's execution that in loud voices they denounced Hernando as a tyrant, and some even threatened to avenge the crime he had committed.

Despite the defeat recently suffered by the " Men of Chile ", as Almagro's followers were called, the situation in Cuzco was far from satisfactory. Dons who had been promised heaven and earth by Hernando, now demanded many favours he was not in a position to grant. This naturally caused dissatisfaction, and the only way to be rid of those who clamoured most insistently was to equip expeditions for them to explore unknown parts of the continent. The late Almagro's supporters had to endure many injuries and insults, for besides having had their houses plundered, these and their estates were confiscated and transferred to Pizarro's supporters. This reduced a number of victims to such poverty that they sought refuge in isolated valleys where they lived like Indians.

When the Don whom Almagro had nominated as temporary governor of his jurisdiction (until Diego should become of age) spoke to Pizarro on the subject, he hotly answered that in having rebelled against the Crown, Almagro had forfeited all claims to governorship, and that the southern territories were now under his governorship. " From now on," he haughtily exclaimed, " my jurisdiction extends from the Straits of Magellan to Flanders."

Realizing that nothing could be done with a Pizarro as proud and inflexible as ever, the Don retired to Spain, where he appealed to the king.

Several months having passed since Almagro's execution, Hernando—who in the meantime had acquired mines and much land—considered the time ripe to return to Spain with the royal fifth. Trusting that treasure would be the best means to justify his actions at Court, he collected as much gold, silver and precious stones as could be found, and then made final preparations to leave. He strongly advised Pizarro to send Almagro's young son to Spain with him, and in so doing be rid of one around whom the " Men of Chile " might yet rally to give serious trouble. However, his brother merely laughed at these suggestions and warnings.

When Hernando sailed from Peru, he felt so guilty about Almagro's execution, and some of his actions against certain " Men of Chile ", that he dare not land in Panama where, according to a well-founded rumour which had reached him prior to his departure, the authorities had received orders from Spain to arrest him. But he was not the type of man to turn back. Relying on the rich treasure he had with him, and possibly also on his faculty of verbal persuasion, he was confident that he would be able to convince the Court that, in executing Almagro, he had acted in the interest of the Crown.

By-passing Panama, Hernando sailed north, and eventually reached the Isthmus of Tehuantepec in Mexico, or " New Spain," as the country was called at the time. On his way across the narrow strip of land which divides the Atlantic from the Pacific Ocean, he was arrested and taken to the capital. However, as the Governor had received no orders or instructions from Spain regarding the prisoner, he allowed him to proceed on his voyage, for at home the authorities could bring him to trial, if this was their desire.

Embarking at Vera Cruz, Hernando thought it wise only to proceed as far as the Azores, and there to enquire if it would be safe for him to land in Spain. In due time, influential friends advised him that he had nothing to fear, and that he should present himself before the king without further delay.

Back in his homeland, Hernando soon found out that he had lost favour in every quarter, high and low, for the Don whom Almagro had appointed to act as his executor and provisional governor of his jurisdiction, had informed the Court as to the state of affairs in Peru, and he had blamed the Pizarros for most of the trouble there. Even the treasure Hernando brought with him, failed to sway opinion in his favour, though in a few isolated cases handsome presents of gold purchased him a few doubtful friends.

Although, shortly after his arrival, his accuser died, the seeds sown by him soon bore fruit, for Hernando was brought to trial, and, having been found guilty of various charges brought against him, he was sentenced to imprisonment in the castle of La Mota, near Medina del Campo. The king was so lenient that the word " detention " is more appropriate than " imprisonment " in the case of Hernando, as we shall see later.

With Almagro dead, and his supporters crushed and disbanded, Pizarro was master of Peru; in fact, not only within his own jurisdiction, but from the neighbourhood of Panama down to Chile.

Although more or less regular contact was being kept up between the motherland and the colonies in the New World, Peru was too far away to be controlled by a council sitting in Spain. By the time the authorities realized this, it was too late ; strife and civil war had split up the *conquistadores* into two camps which Pizarro hoped to weld into one—naturally to the advantage of his own supporters and friends, and to the detriment of the " Men of Chile " whom he hated more than ever after having heard of Hernando's imprisonment in Spain, brought about by Almagro's executor.

What with the new share-out of land, and quarrels between the Spaniards, the unfortunate Indians had a bad time, and in the confusion knew not who was their master. Taking advantage of the situation, the *Inca*, Manco—who had been hiding in a remote valley ever since his last defeat —once more came on the scene with hordes of Indians who rallied round him. Descending from the mountains, they sacked various Spanish settlements, and killed or tortured any white men who were unfortunate enough to fall into their hands. Soon these guerrilla attacks became so serious that Pizarro sent his brother, Gonzalo, with a strong force to put an end to Manco's activities. The Indians held all the principal mountain passes, and although during encounters with Gonzalo's men they were invariably defeated, or forced to retire into the *cordilleras*, they always rallied and renewed their surprise attacks.

Finding Manco impossible to defeat with arms, Pizarro next made attempts to come to an agreement with him. A young negro was sent to deliver a handsome present to the *Inca*, but the messenger was slain by the Indians, whereupon, to avenge his death and to intimidate Manco, Pizarro cruelly executed one of the *Inca's* favourite wives. However, this despicable deed failed to have the desired effect, and the Indians continued to harrass Spanish settlers, and to interrupt communications with the interior of the country. Pizarro then decided to build fortifications at various important points, and thanks to these the situation was greatly eased, which enabled him to devote most of his time to his pet scheme ; the building of Lima. Besides this, mines were opened in different parts of the country, and agricultural enterprises were extended. At intervals, many new colonists and adventurers arrived from Panama, and so many men were now available that various expeditions were organized to explore unknown regions.

As soon as Manco's activities were crushed, Pizarro sent his brother Gonzalo to govern Quito, and at the same time urged him to explore the unknown regions to the east of that city, where, among other riches, cinnamon* and spices were rumoured to abound. This request made to the courageous and adventurous Gonzalo, led to an expedition which has no parallel in history.

XIV

OVER two years passed, and the *Inca* Manco still occasionally attacked Spanish settlements or convoys on the way to the interior ; but thanks to the fortifications constructed at different points, the Indians' hostile activities were confined to worrying surprise attacks, followed by quick retreats into the Andes, where Manco had established his headquarters. Otherwise things were progressing most satisfactorily for the Spaniards in Peru. Livestock, seeds and plants arrived at regular intervals in ships which also brought new colonists, soldiers and other enthusiasts. Mines, worked by Indian slaves, yielded considerable quantities of precious metals, and agricultural enterprises flourished, promising well for the future.

The news of Hernando's imprisonment had already come as a great shock to Pizarro who was even more seriously disturbed when he was informed that, dissatisfied with the disorderly state of Peru, the Council of the Indies had decided to intervene, and were sending out a man to act in the capacity of royal judge. This meant that this representative of the king would investigate the grievances of the " Men of Chile ", and that measures would be taken to prevent the unfortunate Indians from being abused.

The man who was reported to have been selected for this delicate mission, was Vaca de Castro, an experienced and highly respected judge and man of the world.

---

* Cinnamon is prepared from the bark of small trees. After having been dried, the bark is soaked in salt water, and then distilled. In Pizarro's time it was extensively used as a flavouring in cooking, and fetched high prices in European markets.

The news of the appointment of a royal judge gave the "Men of Chile" new hopes, and they joyfully looked forward to his arrival, trusting that the wrongs and humiliations they had suffered at the hands of Pizarro's adherents would be righted.

Left without means of support, and in many cases in extreme poverty, they now regarded Almagro's son, Diego, as their leader. The youth was allowed to live in Lima where his house became the meeting place of many who had good reason to hate Pizarro. Friends constantly warned the latter never to go out without an armed escort ; but he merely laughed at these suggestions, and went about his business as usual. One day, when he was in his orchard, proudly surveying orange trees which bore their first fruit of this kind to be grown in Peru, one of the "Men of Chile" happened to halt near him. When Pizarro—who by this time had become rather short-sighted—recognized the bystander, he exclaimed, "Well, well, Juan de Rada ; they tell me that you are busy acquiring weapons wherewith to kill me." To this the Don replied, "They speak truly, I have just purchased two breast plates and a coat of mail for my protection, for it is being said that, not satisfied with having executed Almagro, you are intending to kill all his former supporters, as well as the judge who is on his way here from Spain, sent by the king. Spare young Diego. I beg you banish him from the country in a ship. If you will permit, I will accompany him, no matter where."

Moved by the Don's loyalty to Almagro's son, and at the same time incensed at the mentioning of his sinister intentions, Pizarro exclaimed with some heat that there was not a shred of truth in these malicious rumours. He then presented Rada with several oranges, whereafter the two men parted on such friendly terms that Pizarro felt surer than ever before that he had nothing to fear from the "Men of Chile".

At this critical stage, those who hoped to have their wrongs redressed on the arrival of the royal judge, had a rude shock when a rumour circulated that the ship in which he travelled had been wrecked in a storm, and that everybody on board had perished. The " Men of Chile " now became desperate, and decided to take the law into their own hands, and that, regardless of consequences, Pizarro must be assassinated. How and when this was to be done, was, however, not decided.

Again and again friends warned him that an attempt against his life was being plotted, and even when a priest interrupted one of his meals in coming with the information as to a conspiracy, Pizarro replied that there was no foundation in such a rumour, and jokingly added that this was merely a yarn invented by Indians, or by one who hoped to be rewarded with a horse for his warning. The priest having departed, Pizarro calmly resumed his seat at the table, and with a wink remarked to his friends who dined with him, " I wonder if this good priest hopes to be made a bishop ? "

That night, a page brought the news that everywhere in Lima it was being openly said that on the morrow the " Men of Chile " would kill his master. " You know nothing about such things ; begone, young rascal ! " was all Pizarro said. Early next morning, friends came to corroborate this alarming report, but he was so confident that he refused to take even the slightest precautions.

When confronted with such situations, brave men often fall victims to their excess of self-reliance, much in the same manner as the faint-hearted precipitate their undoing by excessive fear.

Early in the morning, on Sunday, June 26th, 1541, several of the conspirators were still fast asleep in young Diego's house, when an agitated nobleman knocked at the door. Upon being recognized by the servants, the caller was permitted to enter, whereupon he rushed into the room where Rada was resting. " Rise quickly," he shouted, shaking the sleeper, " our plot has been discovered, and we shall all be hanged, drawn and quartered ! "

Everybody immediately jumped out of bed, buckled on their armour, and made ready to defend themselves to the last ; but when, upon investigation, it was found that the main *plaza* and the streets leading into it, were deserted of human beings, and that everything in the city was serene, the alarmed plotters somewhat calmed down and took council.

Convinced that they must act quickly, or be lost, they decided to assault Pizarro upon coming out of the cathedral where he never failed to attend mass. Peeping through windows, the conspirators watched worshippers enter and leave the cathedral ; but saw no sign of their intended victim. His non-appearance filled the would-be assassins with grave fears, but a certain relief was felt when a confederate came with the news that a slight indisposition had detained him in his house. Again a council was held, and as all those present suspected that news of the plot had leaked out, and all were of the opinion that it would be fatal to delay longer in putting their plan into execution, it was agreed that the time had come to act.

It was about noon when a piece of white cloth—which was to be the signal to accomplices outside the house—was hung out of one of the windows, whereupon, led by Rada, the conspirators rushed out into the *plaza*, brandishing their weapons and shouting, " Long live the King ! Death to tyrants ! "

Upon reaching a puddle where a little canal had overflowed, one of the plotters was about to make a *détour*, when Rada angrily shouted at him, " What ? Here we are, about to stain ourselves with human blood, and you are afraid of wetting your feet with water. You're not fit to assist us in our task ; go back ! "

Still demonstrating loudly, the " Men of Chile " crossed the square, whilst many people who had assembled there after divine service, looked on with indifference. Pizarro's house was situated directly opposite the cathedral, and when one of his pages saw what was happening, he ran to inform his master who was in the reception room on the second floor, in the company of friends.

" To arms ! To arms ! " the page shouted as he rushed

in, " the ' Men of Chile' are coming to kill the Marquis, my master ! "

Immediately, all who were present jumped to their feet, and some, anxious to save their skins, hurried down the stairs, hoping to make their escape before it would be too late. However, the conspirators had already entered the house, and were coming up the stairs, loudly clamouring for Pizarro's blood. His chicken-hearted hangers-on— about fifteen in number, among them a " learned " judge— who now were frantic to escape, managed to do so by letting themselves down into the orchard from first-floor windows at the back of the house.

Meanwhile, upstairs, Pizarro with only three loyal friends and his half-brother, Alcantara, and four faithful servants, two of them young pages, made hurried preparations to fight off the intruders who came up the stairs, shouting in a frenzy. " Where is the tyrant ? Death to him, and to his satellites ! " Accompanied by his half-brother, Pizarro hastened into an adjoining room to buckle on his cuirass, and to fetch his sword. A strong door which was situated at the top of the staircase had been securely bolted, and it looked as if the handful of defenders would be able to fend off the attackers until aid should arrive.

Intending to parley with the conspirators, one of Pizarro's friends foolishly opened the door, but he had only spoken a few words when he and the two servants at his side were killed with thrusts of several swords. Pizarro, assisted by Alcantara, was still making desperate efforts to buckle on his armour, but when the latter realized that the murderous intruders had reached a passage leading towards the reception room, he sprang up to impede the assailants' further progress. Two of these he instantly killed, and although in the ensuing struggle he, a Don, and the two pages were seriously wounded in several places, they fought on with great bravery. Unable to adjust his cuirass without assistance, Pizarro threw it aside, and flung himself into the fray with such fury that, before the intruders had time to stagger back, two of their number fell under his terrible sword. After a brief pause during which he cursed and defied his enemies, he returned to the attack with such effect that soon his assailants found themselves so hard-pressed that they called to accomplices, who were on the stairs below, to bring lances.

Despite the defenders' valour, so uneven a fight could not last long. Soon Alcantara, weakened by loss of blood, fell, as well as the two pages who had fought on bravely despite being severely wounded. Left with only one friend to assist him, Pizarro renewed the attack in an effort unsurpassed in even his best fighting days, and when his only remaining companion was struck down, he still continued the now utterly hopeless struggle. During another brief lull to take breath, Rada exclaimed, " Time is passing ; death to him ! " and with this gave a hard push to one of his accomplices, thrusting him against Pizarro. Whilst the two men were locked in a death struggle, several of the assassins rushed forward, and Pizarro received a severe wound in the throat, and a number of sword thrusts in the body. Despite this, however, with one mighty last effort, he managed to kill the man with whom he grappled, whereupon, completely exhausted and weakened by loss of blood, he sank on the floor. Breathing and speaking with difficulty, he asked for a confessor, and when he realized that the end was near, he half raised himself on an elbow, and with his own blood shakily traced a cross on the floor, and kissed it. Whilst the killers stood near, silently watching this final act, one of their number boldly stepped forward, and gave the dying man the *coup de grâce*.

Leaving the bloody scene, the assassins rushed out into the *plaza*, shouting jubilantly, " The tyrant is dead ! The tyrant is dead ! Long live the king ! Up Diego Almagro ! " As if by magic, supporters came flocking to the main square, brandishing weapons which hitherto had been kept carefully hidden. Things had happened so quickly and unexpectedly that Pizarro's utterly bewildered partisans shut themselves up in their houses, some of which were plundered by the more revengeful among the " Men of Chile." In the *plaza*, Rada proclaimed young Diego Almagro as the new Governor of Peru, and during the ensuing scenes of enthusiasm, someone suggested that Pizarro's head be severed from the body, to be exhibited on a pole. Had it not been for the timely intervention of the bishop, this outrage would probably have been committed at once.

After nightfall, whilst some of the leading *Pizarristas* were being arrested (fortunately without violence), a faithful negro servant and his wife who had attended to Pizarro for a number of years, stole into the house where lay their master and those who had been slain with him. Assisted by three men the bishop had sent along, they wrapped up the body in a white cotton sheet, and smuggled it into the cathedral. In a corner, a stone slab of the floor was lifted, and when a grave had been hastily dug, the corpse was lowered into it. All this was done so quickly that there was not even time for a simple burial ceremony. The grave having been filled in, and the stone slab replaced, the few who were present silently disappeared into the darkness of the night.*

Although messengers were sent to all the towns and settlements throughout Peru, to proclaim young Diego as the new Governor, the chief conspiritor, Rada, and his closest associates, now ruled over the land. Many *Pizarristas* in Cuzco, and others in the north, soon rose up in arms against those whom they considered to be rebels against the Crown, and it looked as though they would join forces and make things most unpleasant for Rada, among whose

* At the time of his death, Pizarro was between sixty-four and sixty-seven years of age. Before being executed, Atahualpa had asked Pizarro to look after his favourite children, a son and two daughters. When baptized by Friar Valverde, the son was given the name of Juan (John), and the daughters were named Beatrice and Angelina. Some years later Pizarro had a son by this Angelina, as well as a daughter by her aunt. After his assassination, friends took charge of his two children. The boy died before reaching manhood, but the girl was later taken to Spain where she became the wife of her imprisoned uncle, Hernando Pizarro, by whom she had three sons and a daughter. Later the oldest of these sons was given the title of *Marques de la Conquista*, together with a pension from the Government in recognition of the services rendered to Spain by his father and uncles. The title was handed down from generation to generation of Pizarros, a number of whom to this day are to be found in the town of Trujillo.

associates many jockeyed for position and power, whilst the more careful and calculating members of either faction thought it wiser to sit on the fence and await developments. The already intricate and critical situation became even more involved when the sensational news shook the whole land that the royal judge, Vaca de Castro—who had previously been reported to have lost his life in a shipwreck—had landed at the port of Buenaventura in Colombia, and was on his way to Lima. Even more breath-taking was the well-founded rumour that before Vaca de Castro had left Spain, he had been given the power, in the event of Pizarro's death, to take over the control of Peru.

Young Diego's supporters, especially those who had taken a hand in the assassination, now fully realized that in having taken control of the government, they had outlawed themselves, for whatever had been their quarrels with their victim, he had represented the Crown in Peru. A few hot-heads now suggested that the best way out was in marching against the royal judge, but eventually it was agreed that it would be wiser to retreat to Cuzco, which young Diego considered to be his by virtue of his father's will. At this critical time Rada fell ill with fever and died, whereafter rivalry broke out between the two leading rebel captains, which led, first to the assassination of one, and then to that of the other. This left the youthful and inexperienced Diego master of the situation in Cuzco, and under the evil influence of advisers who were determined to fight Vaca de Castro, should he demand control of the town. Soon intelligence reached them that the new Governor was slowly marching south from Quito, and that everywhere he was received with great enthusiasm. More alarming still was the fact that two *Pizarrista* armies had joined him.

Diego immediately tried to negotiate, but without success. Accordingly, in Cuzco feverish preparations were made to fight the combined armies which steadily advanced from the north.

At about this time Gonzalo Pizarro returned to Quito

from what had turned out to be a disastrous expedition in search of regions where spices and other riches had been rumoured to abound. Two and a half years had passed since (towards the end of 1539) he had set out on his quest with three hundred and fifty soldiers, four thousand Indian porters, and, among other provisions, with a herd numbering five thousand swine. Only eighty naked Spaniards, including Gonzalo, looking more like apes than human beings, returned to Quito from the green hell where most of their companions and half the Indian porters had lost their lives. (For details about this expedition, see Appendix II). Upon learning of his brother's assassination, and prevailing conditions in Peru, Gonzalo immediately sent a messenger to Vaca de Castro, offering him his services, only to be refused.

As Vaca de Castro advanced, Diego made another effort to negotiate ; but with the same result as before. All this time the rebels in Cuzco armed themselves to the teeth. In this they were greatly assisted by the *Inca*, Manco, who had good reason to hate the *Pizarristas*, under whom he had suffered much. He had always had a special regard for the late Almagro, and he now transferred his allegiance to his son Diego, in whom he saw a possible liberator of the oppressed Indians.

On the 16th of September, 1542, on a narrow plain in the mountains near Ayacucho, the inevitable battle was fought. With varying fortunes the fight lasted throughout the afternoon until nightfall, when Diego's ranks began to crumple. Many were the acts of valour on both sides, but when the situation became hopeless for the rebels, many of them threw down their arms, and fled in every direction into the night, leaving a battle-field strewn with hundreds of dead and wounded. Young Diego tried to escape, but was caught and taken to Cuzco, and handed over to Vaca de Castro when he entered the city with his victorious army.

After a well conducted trial, Diego and a number of his chief accomplices were declared guilty of treason, and sentenced to death. In the *plaza* of the old *Inca* capital where, only a few years previously, Almagro had been executed by Hernando Pizarro, the same fate befell his son, who met his death calmly and with the stoicism he must have inherited from his Indian mother. According to his last request, his body was interred alongside the grave of his father, in the monastery of La Merced.

Until the great and bloody battle had been fought, the *Inca*, Manco, had hovered in the neighbourhood of Cuzco, but immediately after Diego's defeat, he once more sought refuge in the fastness of the *cordilleras*. On this occasion he was accompanied by a number of Spanish soldiers who had managed to make good their escape after the encounter with Vaca de Castro's forces.

Shortly after these events, Gonzalo Pizarro arrived in Lima from Quito, and when the new Governor summoned him to appear before him in Cuzco, he promptly obeyed the order. Gonzalo was very dissatisfied with the general state of affairs in Peru, and Vaca de Castro was relieved when he departed to supervise the working of the mines near Potosi. A number of Dons who loudly demanded rewards for services rendered during the recent campaign, were dispatched on different expeditions, this being the easiest and safest way in which to get rid of them, and to satisfy their lust for gold.

.   .   .   .

Civil wars among the Spaniards were invariably followed by a general new division of land and Indian labourers. This involved a great deal of suffering among the unfortunate natives who often were ill-treated by a succession of new masters, whilst thousands were forced to work in mines, many perishing miserably.

Ever since Spaniards had settled in numbers in Peru, llamas had been killed off recklessly, without a thought being given to the future. To worsen the situation in this respect, scab—a hitherto unknown disease in Peru, but in all probability brought into the country by imported Spanish sheep—reduced the existing flocks of llamas by

M   177

two thirds. In consequence, the number of these animals decreased to such an extent that a shortage of meat threatened to cause a famine.

Ever since the early years after the discovery of the Americas, a saintly Dominican friar, Bartolomé de las Casas,* had fought a ceaseless and vigorous battle to

* When Columbus returned to Spain from his voyages of discovery, he brought with him a number of Indians, some of whom he presented to friends to act as slaves. When Queen Isabel, " The Catholic," heard about this, she was indignant, and exclaimed : " Who has given Columbus the right thus to distribute my vassals ? " Then, immediately she made a public proclamation, commanding that all these slaves be set free, and sent back to their homeland. The costs of repatriation were to be paid by the slaves' new masters, and any who failed to obey this royal command were warned that in doing so they faced the penalty of death.

A young man who was studying law at the university of Salamanca had received an Indian boy slave from his father who had accompanied Columbus on his second voyage of discovery. This young student was Bartolomé de las Casas, whose father had originally come to Spain from France. Before settling down in Seville he had distinguished himself in the wars against the Moors, and his name had been Causas which later he had changed for Casas.

In making her proclamation ordering the release and repatriation of the Indian slaves, Queen Isabel had sown a seed that was to bear fruit a thousand-fold, for when young Casas finished his studies he decided to go to the West Indies in order to investigate the Indian problem. Eight years later he gave up his profession, and became a priest. Though still very young, he had become known for his learning and prudence, and soon rose to become the man without whose counsel and approbation the Governor-in-chief of the West Indies made no decisions. One day, having witnessed a massacre of Indians by Spanish soldiers, Casas decided to become the protector of the natives. As such, despite violent opposition on the part of the Spanish settlers, soldiers, and even a number of the clergy, he worked ceaselessly and untiringly throughout his long and eventful life. Thanks to his efforts, the Queen gave orders that all Indians should be free of servitude, that they should not be molested or ill-treated, and that they should be governed with the justice due to all vassals of the crown of Castile. She also recommended that through good works and kindness the Indians should be guided towards the Christian religion, and she had it proclaimed that any Spaniard who disobeyed her orders would be severely punished.

Neither the good Queen, nor saintly Casas appeared to realize what difficulties beset the path of the reformation of abuses, especially so when these have reached a point to be almost out of control, and more so when distances are great and communications slow, as was the case between Spain and her colonies.

Very soon Casas became the object of hate among many of the conquistadores and settlers who faced ruin without the help of slaves. Abuses and even massacres of Indians occurred with frequency, for by this time the natives had good reason to fear the Spaniards, and to attack them when opportunities to do this successfully presented themselves.

Queen Isabel's death left Casas and his followers with only the lukewarm support of the king and of the Church. The Pope and a number of bishops still held the Indians to be *gente sin razon*, that is, people without reasoning power, beings without souls, and therefore of the devil, and lost to eternal protect the Indians against their white oppressors. Although he himself had only been in the West Indies, in Central America and Mexico, he included Peru in the sphere of his dynamic activities which were far from popular with the majority of his compatriots in the colonies.

At about the time when Vaca de Castro made his successful campaign against young Diego Almagro and his partisans, Friar las Casas was back in Spain where, at long last, his labours of more than twenty years were beginning to bear fruit. On his relentless insistence, a council was called at Valladolid, and despite vigorous opposition by interested parties, the uncompromising " Protector of the Indians ", as he was called, valiantly argued and fought until he won the day. Supported by many clergymen, officials and lawyers, the opposition was over-ridden, and all Indians were declared free men, and vassals of the king. Land owners who in any way abused or ill-treated natives, would have their land confiscated. Among many other laws and regulations which were sufficient to upset the whole system of colonization, was one to the effect that anyone who had been prominently implicated in the quarrels between *Pizarristas* and the *Almagristas*, was forthwith to lose any land he possessed. Thus, by the strokes of official quills, millions of Indians were made free men, and many Spanish Dons and colonists faced ruin when this remarkable document received the final sanction of the king. At the same time it was resolved that a Viceroy, together with four special judges, should be sent to Peru to take over the government from Vaca de Castros, and to see that the new laws and regulations were enforced.

The man, selected by the king to act as Viceroy, was Nuñez Vela, a Don of ancient noble lineage. Why this important and difficult position was not given to Vaca de

damnation. Still, despite the countless obstacles and vigorous opposition placed in his way, Casas, the Protector of the Indians, continued his saintly labours until advancing years and ill-health obliged him to retire to Spain, where he died at the age of ninety-two, to be buried in the Chapel of the Holy Virgin, in the convent of Atocha, where he had spent the last years of his long and active life.

Castro, who had done such excellent work, and who had the necessary experience, is not known. As it turned out, the newly appointed Viceroy proved to be totally unsuited for the high office entrusted to him.

After young Diego's execution, thanks to Vaca de Castro's wisdom and untiring efforts, affairs appeared to be settling in Peru ; the government was strengthened, schools were established, and the Indians' hard lot somewhat alleviated. When intelligence of the new colonial laws, and concerning the appointment of a Viceroy arrived from Spain, there was consternation, everybody realizing that the new regulations spelt ruin to land and mine owners.

Early in 1544, Nuñez Vela landed in the north of Peru in great state. To transport his enormous entourage of judges, their servants, and several hundred impoverished noblemen with their wives and families, some fifty vessels had been employed.

Already during the sea voyage, the conscientious though intolerant and officious newcomer had made himself unpopular, and although upon landing he was well received by the settlers, their attitude towards him soon changed. Determined to see the new laws brought into effect, the Viceroy immediately freed all Indian slaves, leaving the settlers without labourers to work the plantations.

Though his intentions were good, the situation was intolerable, as far as the Spanish colonists were concerned, and they protested, or attempted to explain this, he merely replied that he had not come to discuss laws, but to execute them.

Assisted by an army of Indian porters who were liberally paid for their services, the Viceroy and his vast retinue slowly travelled towards Lima where, despite a theatrical entry, he was given a very chilly reception. The settlers' discontent soon began to give way to anger and indignation, and when government officials joined in the colonists' demands that the new laws be amended, the haughty and unapproachable Viceroy at last began to suspect that serious trouble was brewing.

CORICANCHA

XV

TAKING advantage of the Spaniards' quarrels among themselves, the *Inca*, Manco—who had been hiding in the mountains ever since young Diego's defeat by Vaca de Castro's combined armies—once more became active. With him were a number of Spanish soldiers who had taken refuge in his camp after the disastrous battle which led to their young leader's capture and execution in Cuzco. Sallying forth from the fastness of the *cordilleras*, he attacked settlements and convoys, and soon his name became a terror once more among the Spaniards who never knew when or where they would be pounced upon by the *Inca* and his savage warriors.

Throughout Peru unrest rapidly grew among the white settlers and soldiers who looked for a leader to oppose the Viceroy.

The indicated man was Gonzalo Pizarro, who, at that time, was supervising the working of his mines near Potosi, in what is now Bolivia. When urged by the malcontents to become their leader, he at first refused, but after further pleadings he somewhat reluctantly gave in, and returned to Cuzco, where the population received him with jubilation.

To organize an army without the sanction of the Viceroy was a serious proceeding which, in all probability, would be regarded as being the first step in an attempt with armed forces to oppose the rightful representative of the Crown. Therefore Gonzalo looked for a good excuse, and found it in pretending to be arming an expedition to rid the country of Manco, whose guerrilla tactics made communication between the coast and the interior extremely hazardous.

When the Viceroy heard of these warlike preparations on the part of Gonzalo, he immediately ordered him to disband his forces, a command which was flatly refused.

At about this time news reached Cuzco of Manco's death. According to reports, he was playing a game of bowls with some of the Spanish soldiers who had sought refuge in his camp, when a heated dispute arose among the players. During the fight which ensued, Manco boxed one of the Spaniards' ears, and in retaliation had a bowl thrown at him, fracturing his skull and causing his death, with which disappeared the last pure-blooded member of his race to make a stand against the conquerors.* Immediately after this incident, the infuriated Indians tore the Spanish soldiers to pieces.

Suspecting Gonzalo's real intentions in raising an army which he refused to disband, Nuñez Vela made preparations for war. With so many malcontents to deal with, this was no easy matter, as he soon found out when a number of the officers and men on whom he relied, passed over to Gonzalo's camp. Not knowing where to look for support, the Viceroy became suspicious of everyone around him, and in this state of mind he even imprisoned a number of innocent Dons, among them Vaca de Castro, whom he detained in a ship which was lying at anchor off Lima. Accusations and arrests became almost daily occurrences, and when it was discovered that during a private interview the Viceroy had killed, and subsequently secretly buried, a highly respected government official whom he suspected of plotting against him, public indignation was great.

In the meantime, Gonzalo and his army marched towards Lima from Cuzco. He had been joined by a very remarkable captain, who, despite the fact that he was nearing his eightieth year, was still regarded as one of the most redoubtable fighters in Peru. This old warrior, Francisco Carvajal, had previously fought with great distinction in Italy and Mexico, and later with Pizarro. Very tall, powerfully built, possessed of both physical and moral courage, and a peculiar caustic wit, Carvajal was an outstanding personality among his countrymen in Peru, where he had become an almost legendary figure. During Vaca de Castro's recent campaign against Diego Almagro, his valour and experience in military tactics had greatly contributed to the winning of

---

* He left a very young son, Sayri Tupac, who, when he grew up, gave a certain amount of trouble to the Spaniards.

the decisive battle, after which he made preparations to retire to Spain. He was about to sail when news reached him about Gonzalo's determination to fight for what he and the majority of his countrymen in Peru considered to be a righteous cause. When asked to join Gonzalo, Carvajal explained that he had done enough fighting during his long life ; but eventually he gave in, and promised to remain in the land until it was rid of the Viceroy and the hated new laws.

In Lima affairs fared ill with the representative of the Crown, and things came to a head when, one night, together with the populace, his judiciary whisked him out of the palace and placed him under arrest, whereafter a prominent opportunist lawyer who was declared head of a provisional government, immediately suspended the dangerous new laws. At the same time it was decided to return the Viceroy to Spain, together with a judge who was to make a full report to the Court. In due time, the ship with its two important passengers set sail for Panama on the first stage of its voyage.

New recruits flocked to Gonzalo's banner in every town and settlement he passed through on his march towards Lima, and soon his army numbered twelve hundred well-armed officers and men, as well as several thousand Indian porters. Members of the newly constituted provisional government grew very nervous, for it was evident that he was determined to take the reins of government in his own hands, and recognize no authority, other than that of the King of Castile.

As a last hope, therefore, they sent a message informing him that a revolution had taken place, that the Viceroy was on his way back to Spain, and that, the new laws having been suspended, his forces might be disbanded. Gonzalo, having quite different ideas on these counts, sent back a reply saying that the people had called him to take over the government, and that, if it was not handed over to him, he would take it by force. Upon nearing Lima, as a gesture to show that he meant business, sent ahead the redoubtable Carvajal who, with a small detachment of soldiers, entered the city at night, dragged several officials from their beds, and hanged them without ceremony. This drastic measure had the desired effect, for the now terrified members of the provisional government forthwith sent word to Gonzalo, inviting him to enter the city on his own terms.

During a stately march into Lima, on which the royal standard and the banner of Cuzco were carried side by side, masses of spectators deliriously acclaimed Gonzalo as a saviour, and in a solemn ceremony the judges proclaimed him Governor and Captain-General of Peru, until such a time as the king's decisions should be known regarding the government of the country.

. . . . .

Gonzalo, whose influence now extended from Chile to Ecuador, brought to trial a number of the leaders who had opposed him. Old Carvajal was all for executing those who were found guilty, but Gonzalo who was not so adamant, contented himself in banishing them from the country. In order to protect sea communications, an edict was issued for the building of several ships. A number which happened to be lying in different ports, were immediately dispatched in charge of a reliable captain and a strong force, to occupy the port of Nombre de Dios, on the Atlantic side of the Isthmus of Panama. Thus, Gonzalo made certain that he would be in a position to dictate terms to any expedition which might be sent out from Spain to interfere with him in Peru.

Everything went smoothly and according to plan when, one morning, it was discovered that Vaca de Castro—who had been kept under detention in a ship ever since the Viceroy had sent him there—had disappeared, together with the vessel. This surely meant that Castro had fled in an attempt to reach Spain, where he would report the state of Peruvian affairs to the king. Soon after this escape, it was reported that Nuñez Vela—who was thought to be on his way back to Spain—had landed at Tumbez in the north, and was raising an army.

When this disquieting report reached Lima, Gonzalo, accompanied by Carvajal and a well-equipped force, set out to nip the Viceroy's activities in the bud. As soon as Nuñez Vela heard of the approach of this army, he and his followers beat a hasty retreat into the mountains, in the direction of Quito, where he hoped to find reinforcements. Chased by Gonzalo and Carvajal, the Viceroy's retreat over frozen mountains and through densely wooded valleys, was an epic of endurance, but upon reaching Quito he was sadly disappointed with the cold reception accorded him there. With Gonzalo still hot on his heels, Vela was forced to retreat far into what is now Colombia, where he finally halted with only one-fifth of his original troops.

After a long and much needed rest, during which he was joined by local troops, the Viceroy stupidly walked into a trap set for him by Gonzalo, who had given up the chase in the neighbourhood of Quito.

A fierce battle was fought, and shortly before the Viceroy's inferior force was overwhelmed, its leader was recognized and singled out by one of Pizarro's captains. Soon Vela fell mortally wounded, almost at the same instant to be decapitated with one stroke of a negro slave's sword.

The news of Vela's defeat and death was greeted throughout Peru with jubilation, and when Gonzalo and his victorious troops triumphantly returned to Lima, he was greeted with delirious enthusiasm. During festivities which lasted for several days, it was suggested that Gonzalo renounce his allegiance to the King of Castile, and that he make himself King of Peru. With Spain so far away, Panama in his hands, and his strong garrisons and ships firmly established all along the Pacific coast, Gonzalo was in an almost unassailable position. However, being still loyal to the king, he declined the opportunity which, though it may appear ridiculous at first sight, had great and far-reaching potentialities for the future, and might have proved highly beneficial to the masses in South

America, Spaniards and Indians alike. It was proposed that Gonzalo marry an *Inca* princess, and set up a kind of feudal nobility. Such a bi-racial marriage might easily have made it possible to re-create a species of *Incaic* empire, with the two races, their institutions, customs and laws, fused into one.

Gonzalo, now the supreme and undisputed master of Peru, and lord of the Pacific, from Chile to Panama, was treated by everybody as if he were the very king of Castile. Despite living in royal style, however, he busied himself improving conditions in the land ; agricultural enterprises were extended, mines were exploited with great success, schools were opened, and although the law regarding slavery had been rejected, efforts were made to better the hard lot of the Indians.

. . . .

Distances being enormous, and communications difficult and slow, months passed before reports about events in Peru reached Spain. Gradually these became so alarming that an extraordinary council was called together to discuss the serious situation in the colony. Certain members of the council insisted on sending a strong expeditionary force to South America, but, eventually, in view of Gonzalo's strategic advantages, it was decided that a kind of peaceful penetration was the only possible way in which to solve the knotty problem.

After much deliberation, an ecclesiastic named Pedro de Gasca was unanimously chosen to be recommended for the king's approbation. Gasca, a man of outstanding genius, was of ancient noble lineage, and possessed of many remarkable qualities. During his brilliant career he had distinguished himself, not only in the fields of theology and scholarship, but also in active warfare, jurisprudence and administration, besides being renowned as a convincing orator. This saintly man of humble appearance, was possessed of unlimited courage. In accepting the nomination, he made it quite clear to the council that he would accept neither salary nor compensation of any kind for his services, and before he sailed from Spain with a small squadron, King Charles went to the extent of giving him absolute and unlimited Viceregal powers.

After an uneventful sea voyage, Gasca landed at the port of Santa Marta, in what is now the republic of Colombia, and there he learned of the Viceroy Vela's death and of Gonzalo's supreme rule over all the lands along the Pacific, as far as Panama.

With neither an army nor a navy at his disposal, the lone emissary's chances of success seemed to be hopeless, but instead of feeling disheartened and returning home, he set sail for Panama, and calmly walked into the lion's den. His modest and humble appearance caused much mirth among the soldiery who had expected to see a new Viceroy arrive in great pomp, escorted by a strong fleet and a formidable army.

Unheedful of the soldiers' gibes, Gasca first of all explained to Gonzalo Pirazzo's captain (who had been sent to hold the isthmus) that he had come on an errand of peace, and that, in virtue of the fact that the king had given him full and unlimited power to act as he thought best, he proposed to pardon all those who had taken part in the rebellion against the late Viceroy. He also assured Gonzalo's captain that he intended to revoke the new and troublesome laws, and that he would make many necessary reforms to improve conditions in the colony. The captain, who was loyal to both the king and Gonzalo, now found himself between the devil and the deep blue sea, so he merely listened, and as Gasca had no troops at his disposal, allowed him to settle down to a game of patient waiting and scheming.

Meanwhile Gonzalo had firmly made up his mind to keep the new Viceroy out of his domain. In order to inform the Court in Spain of the state of affairs in Peru, and at the same time to vindicate his actions, he sent off a commission, headed by one of his most trusted partisans and the Bishop of Lima. When the members of this commission arrived in Panama, and Gasca unostentatiously informed them of the unlimited powers the king had given him, they began to waver ; for to act against a person with such hitherto unheard-of powers seemed to them to amount to practically direct rebellion against the Crown.

Noticing the effect his words had on the members of Gonzalo's delegation, Gasca again made it clear that he had come on an errand of peace, and that it was his intention to pardon all those who had taken a hand in the rebellion which led to Nuñez Vela's death. Thus, with guile, Gasca won his first bloodless victory, for all his listeners, as well as the captain who commanded Gonzalo's troops in Panama, solemnly took the oath of allegiance to the king, and at the same time some twenty of Gonzalo's vessels were handed over to Gasca who, during an impressive ceremony, hoisted the royal standard on board the squadron. This done, he sent four ships to cruise along the coast, as far as Lima, in order to make it known to the people there what were the powers entrusted to him by the king, and to assure settlers that they had nothing to fear, and much to gain, if they remained loyal to the Crown. A Dominican friar was sent along with this small fleet, with orders to stir up the priests, and numerous letters were dispatched to the same end, including one to Gonzalo, who was promised a full pardon, provided he handed over the government to the king's representative.

When these letters reached their destinations, even the old warrior Carvajal was in favour of accepting the offer, but Gonzalo and some of his more ambitious advisers thought differently. So, with a jest implying that life is short, and that he was old, anyway, and therefore might just as well be hung for a sheep as for a lamb, Carvajal promised to remain with his leader, no matter what might happen.

The news of the fleet's desertion came as a staggering blow to Gonzalo, who now made hasty preparations for battle. Wealthy Dons and settlers, and the populace in general, were heavily taxed, or forced to make loans to defray the cost of the impending campaign, and against their inclination, men and women were made to take an oath of fidelity to Gonzalo's cause. Evidently he and his leaders overlooked the fact that in civil wars fidelity and loyalty are frequently sold or promised on loan.

Meanwhile, Gasca's astute propaganda was taking effect. Settlers whose only desire was to live and work in peace, and rich men whose chief ambition was to keep their possessions, shrunk from taking part in a war against the Crown. In order to avoid trouble, many sought refuge on board Gasca's vessels which were still cruising along the coast, while others escaped to the mountains, taking with them their gold and other valuables. A few of Gonzalo's captains and officers took advantage of the promised royal pardon, and hurriedly made for Trujillo where, thanks to the Dominican friar's exhortations, the entire garrison had passed over to the royal cause. In the south, also, troubles were brewing for Gonzalo. Old Carvajal made a joke of all these serious setbacks, and every time news of the desertion of more partisans was received, he hummed an old Spanish ditty, which might be translated as :

> " Oh mother, dear, my thinning hair,
> In locks is blown off, pair by pair."*

Upon being informed that Gasca was about to sail from Panama with the entire fleet, Gonzalo left Lima and led his army towards the south, where, for the time being, he hoped to make his headquarters in Arequipa, before proceeding to Chile to make a campaign against the feared Araucanian Indians. Soon, however, Gonzalo came to the conclusion that in order to gain favour with Gasca, an incursion into the Anti Indians' country, situated in eastern Peru, was more promising, but the presence of a strong royalist army, which barred his way near Lake Titicaca, presented a very serious obstacle. A messenger was dispatched to negotiate for a free passage through to the east ; but when overtures were turned down, Gonzalo, stung to the quick, made up his mind to fight, despite the

* " Estos mis cabellicos, madre ;
   Dos á dos me los lleva el aire."

fact that the opposing forces were almost twice as strong as his. However, thanks to Carvajal's military skill and courage, Gonzalo won a hard-fought battle during which the enemy lost some three hundred and fifty men to his one hundred and fifty, besides a great number of wounded. Elated by this victory, Gonzalo abandoned the idea of conquering the Antis, but instead marched into Cuzco, where his supporters gave him a rousing reception.

In the meantime, despite having encountered terrific storms, Gasca's fleet made a safe landing in Peru, where the new Viceroy was received with joy. Belalcazar, the conqueror of Quito, and a very able captain, Valdivia, who had recently returned from a campaign in Chile, joined the royalist cause with considerable reinforcements. (For details about the expedition to Chile, see Appendix III).

The news of Gonzalo's victory near Lake Titicaca, and his taking of Cuzco, were severe blows to Gasca, but instead of being disheartened by these set-backs, he redoubled his efforts to equip and train his army which now numbered some two thousand men, half of them with fire-arms, and a large proportion of the others well mounted. A number of heavy guns were taken off ships, stores and ammunition were procured, and when all was ready the march towards Cuzco was commenced.

In the old *Inca* capital, Carvajal was busy organizing and equipping for the decisive fight, but Gonzalo, who rested on his laurels after his recent victory, took things easily, apparently convinced that for him another triumph was a foregone conclusion. Had he acted more quickly, and in accordance with Carvajal's suggestions, he might have annihilated the royalists' greatly superior forces from points of vantage among the mountains. When, after much dallying, he at last decided to do this, it was too late. Still confident in ultimate victory, he marched his troops some fifteen miles out of the town, and in a valley prepared to meet his foe. Though remarkably well equipped, his force was only about half the size of Gasca's, but thanks to Carvajal's military skill, this numerical inferiority was counterbalanced by choosing an advantageous position where the arrival of the royalists was awaited. When these drew near, and took up their position with remarkable skill, Carvajal—who did not know that Valdivia had returned from Chile, and was directing operations for Gasca—exclaimed in admiration, " Surely the devil or Valdivia is responsible for this ! "

Gonzalo, superbly mounted, and wearing his finest armour, was galloping along his lines, encouraging the men, and giving final instructions to officers, when the unexpected happened. A lawyer, supposedly one of his staunchest supporters, slipped away, and although his intentions were suspected, and he was chased and slightly wounded by one of Gonzalo's men, managed to reach the enemy's lines where he surrendered. His example was soon followed by others, and before Gonzalo and Carvajal fully realized what was happening, and had time to do anything to prevent it, a whole column deserted, whereupon, demoralized and in a panic, the bulk of the army threw down their arms, and fled in the direction of Cuzco.

All the while, Gonzalo sat his horse as if petrified, but Carvajal merely hummed his favourite little ditty :

> " Oh mother, dear, my thinning hair,
> In locks is blown off, pair by pair."

Having recovered the faculty of speech, Gonzalo turned to the few Dons who had remained at his side, and in utter dismay asked, " What shall we do ? "

" Attack, and die like Romans ! " one of his few brave and faithful followers stoutly exclaimed. Sadly shaking his head, and at the same time turning his horse towards the enemy, Gonzalo replied, " No, better die like Christians," and with this he slowly rode towards the royalists' lines, and in token of surrender handed over his sword to an officer. When brought before Gasca, Gonzalo attempted to justify his actions, but his arguments were cut short, and he was put under close confinement in a tent.

Immediately after the rebel army's *débâcle*, Carvajal attempted to escape, but his horse stumbled and fell, and in so doing threw the rider, who was seized by some of his own soldiers who would have killed him, had it not been that one of them had the idea of exchanging the old man for a pardon from Gasca. Throughout this critical episode, and even when brought before the captains in the enemy camp, Carvajal made caustic jests at the expense of his captors. Many soldiers who had a great admiration for the redoubtable old warrior, crowded round to gaze upon the famous prisoner. Valdivia conducted him before Gasca who angrily accused him of many evil deeds, but all this time Carvajal stood in silence, looking at the various faces near him, until, infuriated by this indifference, Gasca ordered him to be taken away, and put under a strong guard.

After a short trial, Gonzalo and Carvajal were declared guilty of treason and rebellion against the king. Accordingly, both were sentenced to death, and on the day after their capture and trial, on the 10th of April, 1548, the sentences were carried out.

Unrepentant to the end, eighty-four year old Carvajal joked even as, in a crate with only his head sticking out, two mules dragged him towards the place of execution. As he was being bumped and jolted he exclaimed, " Cradles for babes, and a cradle for the old man," and when he jokingly complained that the violent rocking he was being subjected to was too much even for a white man, many of his former enemies—who had a secret admiration for him—picked up the crate, and carried it, together with its occupant, who died as he had lived : bravely, and with a smile of contempt.

Gonzalo was magnificently dressed when he emerged from his tent, to be led to the place of execution. Previously he had spent several hours with a confessor who, now joined by a number of other priests and friars, escorted the prisoner towards the scaffold. In his brief last speech, Gonzalo asked the soldiers assembled there to pray for his soul, whereafter he knelt down before a crucifix and silently prayed for a few minutes. Rising, he beseeched the executioner to do his work with a steady hand, and then, having refused to be blindfolded, he calmly submitted his neck to the sword which severed the head from the body with one stroke. Gonzalo's body was taken to Cuzco where it was buried alongside the graves of the two Almagros, in the chapel of the convent of Our Lady of Mercy.

Many difficult tasks lay ahead of Gasca ; the entire administration of Peru had to be reorganized, and masses of reforms had to be made, among them the freeing of all Indian slaves. With great determination he toiled incessantly, and when his work was completed, and he had appointed a committee of judges to act as Provisional Governors until a new Viceroy should arrive, he made preparations for his return to Spain. People, including the Indians, hailed him as saviour of Peru, for it looked as if a new era of peace and prosperity had begun in the colony.

With the execution of Gonzalo and Carvajal, the only one of the early leaders among the *conquistadores* to survive those turbulent days was the former's brother, Hernando Pizarro, who was still in Prison in Spain. His detention was shared by his niece whom he had married, and when, after twenty years, during which he followed all news regarding Peru with interest, he was released, law suits and confiscations gradually reduced his fortunes. Though an old and practically forgotten man, his brothers, friends and enemies all having passed on in the meantime, Hernando survived his imprisonment by several years, and only died, it is said, in 1578, when he had reached the astonishing age of a hundred.

Coricancha, the *Incas'* Garden of Gold, by this time had become a legend ; its trees, flowers and animals made of the precious metal, had vanished like glittering dew drops before the morning sun ; but yet another *Coricancha* : spreading from the Caribbean Sea down to Cape Horn, a vast continent, five thousand miles in length, and in places three thousand miles in width, waited to be cultivated and developed into something infinitely finer and more beneficial to mankind than was Cuzco's Garden of Gold. The flowering of South America ended with the Pizarro period, and the ripening fruit fell intermittently after Gonzalo's execution to the war of emancipation. Since that time, and the stormy period which followed it, many quaint Spanish and Portuguese colonial towns have grown into huge Babylons. Immense pampas and plains which formerly were the haunts of fierce nomadic Indians, now are some of the world's most important granaries and larders. The snorting of railroad engines and of motor vehicles make enormous herds of thorough-bred cattle look up from their grazing, and even interrupts the concerts of brightly-plumaged birds and howling monkeys in some of the dense tropical forests. Ocean going liners and ships ply far up rivers to deliver their cargo from the four corners of the world, to return to their respective home-ports with their holds filled with South American produce. Aeroplanes streak through the skies, carrying passengers and mail as far as down to Tierra del Fuego, whilst in rapidly growing cities the wheels of industry hum to the rhapsody of material progress. Students, thirsting for knowledge, flock to schools and universities, and theatres and concert halls are filled with discriminating audiences.

All these, and innumerable other changes have taken place since, in 1532, Francisco Pizarro and his handful of daring *conquistadores* delivered their fateful blow to Atahualpa and his army in Cajamarca. Fortunately, perhaps, nature and time have obliterated most of the trails the Spaniards trod or blazed, and thus the fearless men who died during some of those almost incredible exploits, lie in peace, undisturbed by human voices and footsteps. In the depth of jungles, steaming malarial swamps and shimmering deserts, on frozen Andean heights, in vast awe-inspiring valleys, gorges and canyons, the birds of the air, wild beasts, thunder and wind, sing odes to those forgotten sleepers who, whatever were their human failings, knew how to die like men, as did those who in vain attempted to defend their land against the white invaders. But despite the passing of centuries, Indian shepherds can occasionally be seen to-day, sitting on the ruins of old temples and palaces, situated here and there in high regions among the Andes. As they watch their little flocks of sheep, or proud-looking llamas, they play melancholy tunes on pipes, or dreamily sing songs their remote ancestors used to sing in the days of the *Incas*. At night, whilst their animals are huddled together in small corrals, and the icy blasts come down from the white *cordilleras*, whistling and moaning through cracks in the low stone-built huts, the shepherds and their families draw closely together around tiny fires made with a few handfuls of llama dung, placed in holes in the centre of the mud floors in their primitive abodes, and listen intently as an old legend of their *Incaic* forefathers is being repeated.

According to this legend, it was prophesied that white men would come across the seas to conquer the Indians' land ; but that, centuries later, a white man would appear, once more to set them free.

The gold out of temples and palaces has vanished together with the pomp and vainglory of two empires ; but the solid things achieved by *Incas* and *conquistadores* alike, will remain an everlasting testimony to their real greatness. And meanwhile Indians continue to sit in their huts, listening intently, hoping and praying that the second part of their forefathers' prophecy as to ultimate deliverance from white men will be fulfilled.

APPENDIX I

About the *Incaic* civilization, its history, legends and traditions.

ACCORDING to the Peruvians' belief, the Sun was the creator of the world, and everything in it, including mankind. One day, feeling sorry for the miserable and savage state in which men lived, the Sun sent two of his children to guide them to better ways. These two " Children of the Sun " were Manco Capac and his sister, Mama Ocllo. Descending from their celestial home, the pair came to earth near Lake Titicaca, high up among the Andes. Before they left their home, Pachacamac, the Creator and Ruler of the Universe, had given them a sacred golden rod, with the instructions that when they came to a place on earth where the rod sank into the ground with ease, there they should found a city where they should instruct men how to lead good and useful lives. In due time, Manco Capac and his sister tested the ground, here and there, but without success. Wandering along the banks of the lake, the pair then directed their steps towards the north, soon to enter a valley where, upon making the test with the rod, it rapidly sank into the ground, and disappeared.

The town that was founded there, soon became the centre, or *cuzco* (navel) of a mighty empire which was called *Tavantinsuyu*, meaning " Four Corners of the World." Manco Capac taught men how to cultivate the land and work mines, and his sister—who was his wife, for in the Sun all beings were considered to be brothers and sisters—instructed the women in the art of weaving, embroidery, and spinning. People flocked to be taught by the two " Children of the Sun," and from that time on, happiness spread through the land. Manco Capac and his wife-sister produced children who, thanks to the celestial origin of their parents, were firmly believed to be divine beings. The oldest son was called *Inca*, signifying lord or ruler, and the oldest of his sisters—who was to become his wife—was given the name of *Coya* or Queen. Thus the sceptre of Manco Capac and Mama Ocllo was handed down from generation to generation of *Incas* and *Coyas*, all of whom, being brothers and sisters of pure divine descent, were not considered to be beings of this world, but ambassadors of the Sun. Therefore, in addition to being all-powerful rulers in a worldly sense, *Incas* and *Coyas* enjoyed their subjects' adoration as divinities. Among the Peruvians incest was a serious crime, but in the case of the *Incas*, their wives always had to be sisters, in order to preserve the purity of their celestial blood. However, besides his obligatory sister-wife, the *Inca* could keep as many others as he wished, though children by such only qualified to become members of the nobility.

Dismissing from mind the old Peruvian legend and belief that the first *Inca* and his sister-wife came down from the Sun, and like marine gods rose out of the waters of Lake Titicaca* to found the city of Cuzco and to civilize the savages in the neighbourhood, and abiding by facts, as far as such can be traced, or surmised, the city of Cuzco was founded in the eleventh century by Manco Capac and Mama Ocllo who probably also were the founders of the *Incaic* dynasty which, according to Peruvian tradition, comprised thirteen *Incas* whose reigns embraced a period of close on five hundred years.

Long before the *Incaic* civilization came into being, others had existed in the Americas, particularly in Mexico, Guatemala, and in the Andes. Near Lake Titicaca are to be seen the remarkable ruins of Tiahuanacu, asserted by some scientists to date back to pre-historic days. Curiously, these gigantic ruins show a much

* This name is derived from an Aymara word, Inti Karka, the name of a rock adored by the ancient inhabitants of those regions. When the *Incas* first appeared in Peru, the Aymara nation possessed the country situated on the high plateaux in the regions of Lake Titicaca. Temples, palaces, and a number of monuments, some to this day intact, but most of them in ruins, are believed to have been built in the remote past, long before the Aymara nation came into being, by the Collahuas, whose descendants the Aymaras boast to be. With the formation of the *Incaic* monarchy, the Aymaras were displaced from most of their country which originally had been over two hundred miles in length, and about ninety in width. Some Aymaras remained in the regions of Lake Titicaca, but others were driven as far as the Pacific Ocean, whilst the rest were exterminated during subsequent wars against different *Incas*.

The Aymaras were, and still are, rather more primitive than the Quichuas, who formed the majority in the *Incaic* empire. They deformed skulls at birth, giving them conical forms by means of boards tied to the heads, so as to compress them to the desired shape. The dead were buried in tombs which had the shape of trunkated pyramids, twenty to thirty feet high, and constructed of adobe. Bodies were embalmed and clothed in a kind of sack, only the face showing. In these tombs, called *chulpas*, the dead were seated in a circle, a little opening in the eastern wall allowing the rising sun to shine on the circle of mummies. Titicaca, the Aymaras' sacred alpine sea, nearly 12,800 feet above sea level, is dotted with a number of islands which in the past were held as holy. To this day many Aymaras refuse to step on the sacred islands of their forefathers.

more advanced skill in building than is to be found in any construction, including the fortress of Cuzco, attributed to the *Incaic* period. This leads to the conclusion that, as far as architecture is concerned, the civilization of Tiahuanacu was much more advanced than the more recent one of the *Incas*.

The controversy as to whether or not ancient civilizations north of Panama have any connection with those to the south of it, or what course migration between North and South America took, is still a matter of debate. But taking into account unmistakable guiding points, such as racial characteristics, architecture, religious beliefs and legends, it can immediately be seen that a close relationship exists between American and certain Asiatic peoples, past and present. This leads to the conclusion that once upon a time connection between Asia and America had taken place, either by sea, or more probably via the Behring Straits which in that period may have been an isthmus with a milder climate than those regions have to-day.

Considering that American Indians grow neither beards nor moustaches, it is noteworthy that some Mexican and Andean sculptures represent bearded men with flowing robes, and very interesting is the fact that in parts of America, types of men, certain monuments, institutions, and even hieroglyphic paintings closely resemble some of the ancient people of Asia and Egypt. It is known that in the early ages of the world migrations the Misraites (Children of the Sun) wandered from the heart of Asia into the Valley of the Nile ; but how Egyptian influence came to parts of the Americas, remains an unsolved riddle. In the woods of Guina and Venezuela, on the *plateaux* of Bogotá, and in different remote regions in northern South America, are to be found traces of civilizations that are much older than that of the *Incas*. The *teocalli*, as Mexican pyramids are called, and similar constructions in Peru, closely resemble those of Egypt. There is no doubt that at various times, for long periods, American civilizations were arrested, or even disappeared, to be followed by new civilizing impulses.

Some historians and writers, who have never seen the South American ruins described in their books, have greatly exaggerated them, and mysteries have been made out of quite simple things. In this way, assisted by easily impressed travellers, the snowball of romance has grown to such an extent that many of those descriptions give a very wrong impression. For instance, a great mystery has been made out of the Peruvians' method of quarrying stones. True, no tools for cutting such have been found; but it appears probable that the Indians hid their treasured implements when they heard of the arrival of the Spaniards, and their greed for metals. As for the method of fixing the blocks together without the use of a binding substance, this was probably done by rubbing them together until they fitted. Labour was never a problem in Peru, and as time was not considered, some such slow and painstaking method must have been devised to deal with even the largest stones.

To pass on to the *Incaic* period, if the old Peruvian legend is accepted, Manco Capac was the first *Inca*, and he reigned for some fifty years during which he civilized different tribes in the neighbourhood of Cuzco. Until he appeared, the Peruvian savages had lived in caves, and worshipped various animals and objects. Succeeding *Incas* rapidly expanded the borders of their empire, and by degrees education became public, *amautas* teaching poetry, philosophy, music and the sciences of astronomy and medicine. Medical science was limited to the use of herbs, bleeding and purges, and poetry was chiefly confined to songs of victory, odes and dithyrambs in celebration of the *Inca's* power and personal qualities; but love, nature, flowers, stars, the turtle dove and the butterfly came in for their fair share. The *varavicus* (poets) were usually accompanied by a musician, who, as in Greek and Latin times, gave the note to the declaimer on a reed flute, sustaining the modulations. The mysteries of the heavens and of religion were not for the people, the teaching and study of these being exclusively reserved for certain members of the nobility and of the priesthood.

Although various languages and dialects were spoken, the official tongue was Quichua. Without the mastery of this, no person could hold a government position. Teachers were sent throughout the land, and even the humblest peasants in remote valleys could attend classes to learn the official language of the empire.

Agriculture was expanded, aqueducts and irrigation canals were constructed, and even *guano* was used to fertilize the soil. This manure of sea birds was brought from islands along the Pacific coast, and the Peruvian authorities showed great sense and foresight in protecting the useful birds during the period or laying and hatching eggs. Primitive arts flourished; towns, palaces, temples, bridges, and storehouses were built throughout the rapidly growing empire.

During times of war, the usual reed instruments and Pandean pipes were reinforced with drums, cymbals and horns. In open-air theatres, tragedies, comedies, and what might be described as morality plays, were performed. Only men acted, the *Inca* himself usually playing the leading part. The Peruvians' knowledge of astronomy was poor, though the revolution of the world round the sun, and the moon round the earth, was known to them, and they had a calendar. Many were the legends told by the *amautas*, and the Peruvians had numerous superstitions, many of which were based on the mysteries of the heavens, stars and lightning ; but one of their greatest fears were eclipses which invariably caused a nation-wide consternation, and, on occasions, even panics.

As the *Inca* and his sister-wife were believed to be of divine origin, they were venerated almost as gods by their subjects, including the most important noblemen of royal blood. The *Inca* was the Church, the State and dignity in one. His nobility consisted to two distinct classes : those of royal descent, and of chieftains of conquered nations. Only the former qualified to hold positions in the Church, to command the armies, to sit in councils, or to hold key positions in the administration of the empire. The *Curacas* of conquered nations held inferior positions, being mainly responsible for the order and discipline in their respective regions. Before being raised to the status of *Curaca* they had to spend some time in Cuzco, in order to learn Quichua, the official language of the empire, and they were only appointed after having given ample proof of their loyalty to the *Inca*.

The High Priest—who came next to the *Inca* in importance— had to be of royal blood, and usually was one of the monarch's brothers. Of these there were many, the *Inca* having numerous wives besides his sister, the *Coya*, for this sister-wife was frequently only a " blind " to deceive subjects into believing that the *Incaic* blood had remained as pure as the legend of the first *Inca* and his sister demanded. The whole governing system of Peru was cunningly devised to suit the ruling class, and to keep all subjects outside the royal pale in subjection, and in a state of servility. Primarily, this system was based on religious beliefs, or, in other words, Peru was a theocracy, and the *Inca* an undisputed despot.

CORICANCHA

In his early youth the royal child was taken away from his parents, and entrusted to the care of *amautas*, as the Peruvians called their "wise men". Up to the age of sixteen, the boy's education was chiefly of a religious nature, but having attained that age, he mixed with the sons of nobles, in a kind of military academy. Life there was very Spartan, candidates for graduation having to endure many hardships. Besides army training, aspirants had to study State administration, and when the course came to an end they were examined. Those who graduated had to appear before the *Inca* who, after an address, pierced the lobes of their ears with a pointed reed as thick as a finger. Later these holes were gradually enlarged until heavy golden disks could be inserted into them. In time the weight of these gradually extended the lobes until they reached down to the shoulders, or even further. On account of these long ears, the Spaniards called Peruvian noblemen *orejones*, meaning "big ears." Special sandals, robes and sashes were presented to the graduates, but if an heir apparent to the throne was among them, his head was ornamented with a tassled yellow fringe, made of fine material. This ceremony was followed by public festivities during which there was much dancing, singing, and general merry-making. The heir apparent was now qualified to sit in council beside his father, but during campaigns he accompanied different generals in order to gain experience in the field of military action.

When an *Inca* died, the Peruvians believed that he was called back to his father, the Sun. His body was embalmed and taken to the Temple of the Sun in Cuzco. There, dressed in the finest regal robes, and wearing the imperial *llautu*, the deceased was seated on a golden throne, in a row with all the previous *Incas*, the *Coyas* (queens) being placed on the opposite side, facing their respective husbands.

After a Peruvian monarch's death, a number of his attendants and favourite concubines were put to death by the High Priests of the Sun. This was done because it was believed that they would accompany their Lord, and attend to his comforts and pleasures in the mansions of his father, the Sun. The Peruvians were such firm believers that it often happened that servants or concubines who were not chosen for this great honour, committed suicide in order to follow the *Inca*.

During certain festivals, mummies of different monarchs were taken out of the Temple of the Sun, and carried through Cuzco in great state. In the main square a banquet was given, presided over by the phantom *Inca*, whose gold and silver plate and enormous treasures were used or displayed.

The Peruvian nobility consisted of two classes ; those of *Incaic* descent, and chieftains and noblemen, conquered and subdued during wars. Only those of royal Peruvian descent could attend meetings of the imperial council or qualify for priesthood.

The Peruvians believed in the survival of the soul, and in the resurrection of the body. The good people who in this world toiled incessantly, and who never disobeyed the *Inca's* laws, were believed in after-life to be rewarded with a life of ease and plenty, whereas the lazy and wicked were condemned to eternal labour and suffering.

The numerous priests, and the nobility in general, were exempted from all manual labour, though all had certain duties to perform. The priests had to attend to religious matters, ceremonies and feasts. During certain festivals, animals, flowers and different objects were offered as sacrifices in temples, but on special occasions, such as coronations, severe droughts, floods, or the death of an *Inca*, young girls were sacrificed to the Sun.

The Virgins of the Sun were chosen when they were mere infants. They were taken away from their parents—not necessarily nobles—to be educated and trained by *mamaconas**
who had grown up within the walls of the cloisters. If a girl was taken away from her parents to be made a Virgin of the Sun, this was considered a great honour, for in being chosen she officially became one of the *Inca's* wives. When the girls attained a certain age, the *Inca* selected from their ranks those he wished to join his concubines. If, for some reason or other, he dismissed any of them, they returned home where they were held in great honour. Virgins of the Sun were taught to weave and spin the fine materials used by the *Inca* and the royal household, and they embroidered the cloaks used on ceremonial occasions. It was also their duty to assist during banquets, and to attend to the sacred fires in temples. Certain chroniclers assure us that although any attempt to make love to a Virgin of the Sun involved the penalty of death, this danger was frequently braved by Peruvian Don Juans.

* By some chroniclers also spelt *mamacunas*.

Religious feasts served as a kind of safety valve to the enslaved masses whose lot in life was toil, with little or no opportunity of bettering their position. During festivals there was much eating, drinking, dancing, and singing. If certain eye-witnesses' accounts are to be believed, these celebrations not infrequently ended in disgusting orgies.

Polygamy was only permitted among the nobility. The rank and file of the Peruvians were obliged to marry at a certain age, though it was necessary to obtain the consent of both parties and their parents. Marriage ceremonies were always held *en masse*, the *Inca*, some nobleman, or local chief declaring candidates to be united. All marriages were at once recorded by *quipucamayas** and sent to the capital for statistical purposes. Married couples were provided with a house and sufficient land for their requirements, and for every child born they received a further grant of land. Thus, every man, woman or child, whether able-bodied or not, was allowed sufficient arable soil for his or her needs. No Peruvian was a landowner, being merely a tenant with a lease that lasted for only one year, whereafter a new division of land was made, though usually people retained their previous allotments, and remained permanently in the same town, village or hamlet. Prostitution was tolerated, but *pampayrunas*, as prostitutes were called, had to live on the plains (pampas) outside towns and villages.

Of the land granted to any subject, only one-third part benefited him or her directly, for out of the produce gained in crops, the second third had to be given to the *Inca*, and yet another third to the " Sun ". The tributes paid to the *Inca* supported the vast royal household, and those paid to the " Sun " maintained the numerous priests and temples with their many attendants. As these two tributes were usually far in excess of requirements, surplus was stored in granaries and warehouses throughout the empire, and during lean years these stores were rationed out to the people. Thus, although tributes paid to the *Inca* and to the priesthood were high, in one respect they were not unlike an insurance premium.

In tilling the land, and reaping harvests, priority had to be given to the " Sun ", in other words to the priesthood. Next came the interests of the old, the sick, cripples, orphans, the

* Peruvian scribes who were familiar with the intricacies of the Quipus, described on page 206.

infirm and widows, and when these had been attended to, came those of the workers, and lastly the *Inca's*. Land was ploughed by means of wooden spikes, dragged by a number of men, or tilled with spades resembling wooden oars. On such occasions, as well as during harvests, the whole community joined together, and with much chanting and general merriment worked the fields in rotation. Inspectors supervised the task, and saw to it that the various divisions of the produce were made fairly and accurately, and to everybody's satisfaction. Thus it will be seen that in Peru there were neither rich nor poor, though the masses fed and clothed the privileged class. However, even the " upper crust " had to fulfil some duties and obligations, though manual labour was not among these.

Gold, silver, and precious stones were of no commercial value, and money did not exist. Markets and fairs were regularly held locally, and people exchanged certain commodities by bartering. Therefore, in old Peru there were no speculators or middle-men, and no one could enrich himself by the labour of another, though certain people such as shepherds, miners, craftsmen and artists constituted a class apart. All llamas belonged to the *Inca*, and the animals were looked after by officially appointed shepherds. Wool was distributed among the people who had to spin and weave it into cloth, some of which had to be delivered to store houses within a specified period of time. All mines belonged to the *Inca*, and for the working of them men with special aptitude were selected. Any unhealthy work, such as mining or the draining of bogs and swamps, was temporary, and care was taken not to send labourers to regions with climatic conditions to which they were unaccustomed. Metals were smelted down in crude furnaces, later to be shaped by craftsmen whose art and skill was handed down in families, all of which were exempted from agricultural labour, but provided for by the State.

There being no need for the ordinary Peruvian to travel, people, excepting officials, were not allowed to go far from their homes, or to change their residence without permission from the authorities. As will be seen, under the *Incaic* system personal liberty did not exist. Nevertheless, if a man or woman kept within the law and worked, he or she had no more responsibility than a modern soldier. With a minimum of labour, the maximum protection against any eventuality was equally enjoyed by everybody alike.

Local chieftains—who were trained for their positions—settled minor disputes among their people, but more important differences or crimes were dealt with by visiting judges of varying importance. Since land and house property did not exist, and all precious metals belonged to the State or the Church, theft was limited to articles and commodities which in normal times sufficed individuals' needs everywhere. Therefore, Peruvian laws chiefly dealt with criminal matters, such as murder, offences against religion, adultery, rebellion, or wilful damage to public works. Though most of these offences were punishable by death, the judges usually showed leniency in dealing with such cases.

The population was divided into groups, beginning with four provinces which, in their turn, were split up into divisions of ten thousand inhabitants. Over the provinces, and these large groups of people, were placed governors, or officers who belonged to the *Inca* nobility. In ever smaller sections, the population was divided until there were groups of ten, over which were placed supervisors who were responsible for their charges' welfare, and whose duty it was to keep them in order.

Every able-bodied man was liable to be called up for military service, and even during times of peace, local drills were regularly held under instructors who were trained in military matters. The Peruvians' weapons consisted of lances, bows and arrows, a kind of short sword, and slings which, to this day, their shepherd descendants handle with great dexterity. For protective purposes, shields and bucklers were used, and the different units of the army wore distinctive costumes, chiefly close-fitting tunics made of cotton or llama wool. Banners and standards were carried by the different units who took great pride in them. An army on the march caused no inconvenience to the population, for at regular distances granaries, store houses and *tambos* provided the troops with everything they needed.

Newly conquered tribes or nations were treated as potential assets to the *Incaic* empire, and the Peruvian priesthood showed great cunning and foresight in dealing with such people's religious beliefs. The Peruvians were crusaders whose ambition it was to spread their religion ; but unlike most white men, they were compromising in religious matters.* Although newly conquered nations were converted to the adoration of the Sun, they were

* A striking example of this is mentioned in the footnote on page 103.

allowed to continue worshipping their idols, some of which, together with the chieftains, were taken to Cuzco to be incorporated—for the satisfaction of the newly conquered people—into the *Incaic* religion. As soon as the captive chieftains had acquired a good knowledge of the *Quichua* language, and had proved that they were loyal to the *Inca*, they were sent back home as *Curacas*. Thus, in time, the official *Quichua* language spread all along the Andes.

Sometimes, truculent nations were forced to migrate from their regions, and were made to settle in parts where they were surrounded by loyal subjects of the *Inca*, so that, in time, the rebels were won over without the necessity of shedding blood.

One of the most remarkable things about Peru was the system of registering official information such as births, marriages, deaths and revenues, and it is astonishing with what exactness general statistics were kept in Cuzco. All news and such official information were conveyed to and from the capital by means of a curious system of communication known as the *quipus,** a primitive though intricate and efficient method which enabled scribes to do their work with minute accuracy. The *quipus* consisted of a short wooden rod to which was attached a number of coloured ribbons or strings which, when tied into different combinations of knots, served as a kind of writing, an art that has unfortunately been lost.

Chasquis who had to run in relays from *posta* to *posta*, separated at distances varying between three to five miles, were especially chosen from the fastest runners in the country. They wore distinctive clothes and carried messages to the remotest parts of the land, being everywhere respected. This service was so fast that fish, wrapped in seaweed was often still alive when delivered at the royal palaces in Cuzco, although the distance from the coast, as the crow flies, is about two hundred and fifty miles. Correspondence travelled at such a speed that the capital was in constant contact with even the remotest frontier. This is all the more remarkable when one considers that in those days communications were very poor in Europe—despite the relatively short distances there, when compared with Peru.

As already pointed out, the Peruvians' knowledge of science

* The quipus, in different forms was used by the Canadian Indians, and was also known to the Chinese in a very remote period. The Mexicans also had a similar system for recording events. Among the last the quipus was known by the tongue-twisting name of *repohualtzitzin*.

was very primitive.* Possibly this was due to the fact that only the nobility was allowed to take an active interest in the sciences, it having been considered unwise to instruct those of humble birth, probably for fear that they surpass their noble instructors in the knowledge of certain mysteries, and thus lose respect for the ruling class. Be this as it may, what the Peruvians lacked in the knowledge of science, they amply made up for in agriculture. Their canals, terraces, irrigation systems, and similar works, were far in advance of any to be found in Europe at the time. Their numerous flocks of llamas were well looked after by expert shepherds. At regular intervals male llamas were killed, and their meat salted and dried in the sun. The royal household having been provided, the vast bulk of this meat was distributed among the population. Occasionally, also, big hunts were organized, and skins of wild animals and feathers of birds were collected to be made into different articles of clothing, or to serve as ornaments. The fine wool of the vicuña was woven into cloth, to be used by the *Inca* and the nobility.

Some rather fanciful modern writers have pictured life under the *Incaic* system as Paradisian ; but although much is to be said in its favour, it had many serious disadvantages. The masses of the *Inca's* subjects were mere slaves, prevented from bettering their position in life, materially and intellectually, and liberty of action and thought was so restricted that national progress was severely retarded.

If one compares the stone work of the different *Incaic* periods, one forcibly comes to the conclusion that with the passing of time the art of building did not progress, but became retrogade in Peru. If there is some foundation in the legend of the first *Inca*, and in the stories told about his immediate successors' architectural activities, a certain decadence must be noticed in later epochs. Heaviness took the place of elegance, the size of stones evidently becoming considered of more importance than the finish of the work. The beautiful rustic surfaces, exclusively employed in the early Peruvian edifices, disappeared,

* Undoubtedly at one time the Peruvian " wise men " had known a great deal about astronomy and navigation. In connection with this it is of great interest to note that, in 1567, Pedro Sarmiento de Gamboa, on the strength of information he had collected in Peru, sailed to re-discover " two large islands " Tupac Yupanqui, the wisest of all Incas, had visited during an extensive voyage which had lasted over a year. There is but little doubt that during this voyage Tupac Yupanqui discovered Australia, for in due time Sarmiento found that the Peruvian records of bearings were correct.

and were replaced by cyclopean blocks which, though impressive, constitute a phase of decay, and a tendency to barbarism. Perhaps it may be guessed with a fair degree of accuracy that with the rapid growth of the *Incaic* empire, later rulers became somewhat bombastic and vulgar, hence those unmistakable signs of architectural decadence and degeneration, beauty having been sacrificed for the sake of size.

A vast community in which the masses of the people were kept in servitude amounting to slavery, under a social system in which only a hereditary ruling class enjoyed the privilege of learning, had the seeds of its own destruction within it. When the Spaniards took the upper hand, the structure collapsed like a card house. In fact, disintegration had already commenced before the Spaniards came on the Peruvian scene, when the two brothers, Atahualpa and Huascar, took up arms against one another in disputing the absolute rule over the vast empire. Had the Peruvians been a free people, in all probability Pizarro would have been faced with a very different proposition upon invading their land.

APPENDIX II

TOWARDS the end of 1539, Gonzalo Pizarro set out from Quito in search of the fabled El Dorado. When he marched from the city he was accompanied by three hundred and fifty soldiers, nearly half of whom were well mounted. Four thousand Indians acted as porters, or as drivers to a herd numbering five thousand swine. The very fact that so enormous a walking larder was taken along, proves that it was fully anticipated that the exploration would be long and difficult.

(Pigs were not indigenous to the New World, and it is remarkable that, although only thirteen years had passed since Pizarro had presented the Indian Chief at Tumbez with two specimens of the species, his brother Gonzalo could get together a herd numbering five thousand. Evidently during the intervening years the Spaniards had imported many more pigs which bred prolifically.)

In addition to this enormous herd of swine, ammunition, general stores and provisions, Gonzalo took with him a thousand fighting dogs. With such an expedition, progress had necessarily to be slow, but time mattered little when the prize was expected to surpass even the wealth previously found in Cuzco.

A few days after friendly Quito had been left behind, Gonzalo and his men interned themselves in the high mountains where snow, ice, sleet and terrific winds added to the obstacles placed there permanently by nature. Not to improve things, volcanic eruptions, accompanied by ear-shattering thunder and blinding flashes of lightning, seemed to warn the daring travellers to venture no further. Undaunted, the white men pushed on, and after weeks of forcing their way through this imposing wilderness of high, snow-clad mountains and deep valleys broiling in the equatorial sun, they descended into the jungle regions situated to the east of the mighty Andean barrier. In the regions Gonzalo had now reached, the heat was clammy and oppressive, and torrential rains and swarms of insects made life intolerable. Many turbulent rivers and treacherous streams were crossed, and frequently the expedition had to make vast *détours* to avoid swamps. Occasionally, roaming Indians who were captured for interrogation, reported that the rich land the white men sought, lay farther to the east.

Slowly the Spaniards pressed on, though fever and sickness began to claim victims among them and their unfortunate Indian porters. The soldiers' armour, and weapons which had formerly been the owners' pride, had long since rusted in the humid tropical atmosphere, and garments had rotted on sweating bodies.

After several months, the River Coca* was reached, and there gold was found in the possession of the primitive inhabitants. This river, which is a tributary of the Napo, flows through a veritable green labyrinth, of which the only denizens are a few primitive savages, reptiles and prowling beasts. For some time the expedition followed the Coca downstream by hacking their way through the dense vegetation along one bank, but eventually it was decided to build a boat. With great ingenuity and much hard labour, a crude craft—made of green timber, without the use of nails, the seams being caulked with resin of trees and tattered shirts and cloaks—was constructed, and half the soldiers, among them all the sick, embarked under the command of Francisco de Orellana, who also took with him his 100,000 *pesos* of gold and emeralds which had been collected during the march. It was agreed that this captain should proceed downstream for some distance, and collect provisions for the rest of the expedition

* It is also said that the expedition followed the river Marañon. If so, in all probability this was done during the return journey.

which was to follow overland as fast as possible. This decision was reached because Indians had informed the white men that further downstream they would come to regions where food was to be found in abundance.

By this time the provisions were exhausted, and the men were obliged to eat tender inner leaves of palms, roots, berries, grubs, and even snakes and other reptiles. Occasionally, hostile dwellers of the dark forests attacked the intruders of their domain, and whenever the Spaniards captured savages, they invariably pointed in an easterly direction, and spoke of a wonderful land there situated. Encouraged by such reports, Gonzalo and his men pushed along the bank of the Coca, every day hoping to catch sight of Orellana's craft. Two months passed, but not a sign of him was vouchsafed, and Gonzalo feared that the frail boat must have been dashed to pieces in the swift waters whose rapids and cataracts he noted with awe on the march downstream.

At last the junction of the Coca and the Napo was reached ; but still there was no trace of Orellana and his ship. Little did Gonzalo and his half-naked starvelings dream that if they followed the Napo a few hundred miles downstream, they would reach the upper reaches of the Amazon which flows towards the east, for hundreds of miles, growing more and more immense as many other tributaries join it on its majestic course to the Atlantic Ocean.

One day Gonzalo's men, while prosecuting their search, came upon two practically naked white men wandering through the forest. Upon approaching these grotesque figures, it was found that they were of Orellana's party. The story these veritable " Wild Men of Borneo " had to tell, left their listeners dejected and bewildered. Apparently, after many narrow escapes, Orellana had safely reached the junction of the Amazon, but as it was impossible to navigate the strong current, and Gonzalo's party failing to arrive, it was thought that he and all its members must have perished. Accordingly, Orellana decided to sail down the Amazon. Considering this plan to be impossible and dishonourable, the half-naked wanderers of the wilds related how they had left the ship in order to look for Gonzalo's party. Should he and his companions have perished, as Orellana had feared, the lone wanderers had made up their minds to retrace their steps to Quito to give an account of the disaster which had befallen the expedition.

Having listened to this recital, Gonzalo realized that the only hope of salvation lay in attempting to return to Quito. When this was decided, the expedition had been on the way over a year, during which time over a thousand weary miles had been travelled.

Without delay the return march was commenced, the sick dragging themselves along as best they could, assisted by compassionate comrades. Hoping to shorten the distance, a new route was taken, but, as it turned out, this was an even more difficult one than that followed on the outward journey. Armour and weapons, long since rusted, had been discarded, and the last remaining shreds of clothing had fallen off the travellers' emaciated bodies, leaving them naked, like those of the Indians who occasionally harassed them with their silent and deadly blow pipes and poisoned arrows.

Two and a half years after having set out from Quito, eighty men out of the three hundred and fifty approached the city whence they had set out. Two hundred and seventy of their companions had either died or disappeared with Orellana, and more than half of the four thousand Indian porters had miserably perished. With tears streaming from their sunken eyes, Gonzalo and the other survivors staggered into the church to offer thanks for the fortune of their deliverance.

. . . . .

Meanwhile, Orellana and his party had drifted down the Napo and the mighty Amazon in their frail craft. Escaping shipwreck and death at the hands of many hostile Indians who frequently attacked the ship in their swift canoes, those of the white men who had not died on the 5,000 mile voyage, after eight months reached the mouth of the river. Then, without instruments of any kind to guide them, they miraculously managed to reach Trinidad, whence Orellana proceeded to Spain, where his arrival caused a tremendous sensation.

When summoned to appear before the Court to give an account of his sensational voyage, Orellana told many fanciful tales which were readily believed. He informed his credulous listeners that, judging by many reports made to him by Indians, there could be no doubt that an El Dorado existed in the vicinity of the Amazon. Among many other hair-raising stories, he told of a tribe of fierce women warriors who inhabited a region near the river.

Honours were showered upon Orellana who was given every assistance to prepare an expedition to conquer and colonize the regions he had discovered. Accompanied by many followers, who had visions of wealth and fame, he sailed from Spain, but died on the way.

It is, of course, not impossible that at one time a tribe of warrior women existed in a region near the Amazon,* and therefore it would be rash to accuse Orellana of having been deliberately untruthful, though undoubtedly his imagination matched that of Baron Munchausen. Old Brazilian Indian legends speak of the existence of such a community which greatly resembles those Herodotus and Homer, alleged to have lived in Asia and Africa ; while among the Tapuya Indians of the Amazon region it was usual for women to fight alongside their men.

APPENDIX III

ANOTHER memorable Spanish expedition was also made at the time when Gonzalo Pizarro and the survivors of his party wandered through the forests and jungles in eastern Ecuador, and Orellana fought his way down the Amazon.

The hero of this other epic was Pedro de Valdivia, a Don who had formerly distinguished himself in Venezuela where he had gained much experience in Indian warfare.

Guided by a priest—who had been with Almagro on his expedition to northern Chile a few years previously—Valdivia, accompanied by one hundred and fifty soldiers and a number of Indian porters, set out from Cuzco in January, 1540. Having reached the northern shore of Lake Titicaca (12,600 feet above

* Forty years before Orellana's amazing voyage, a famous Spanish seaman, named Vicente Pinzon, had discovered the mouth of the Amazon. He sailed only about fifty miles upstream before returning to the sea, and named the river : *Rio Santa Maria de la Mar Dulce*. Later this was changed to *Mar Dulce* (Sweet Sea), on account of the fresh water, called *dulce* (sweet) in Spanish. Subsequently the Amazon became merely known as *Rio Grande* (Great River), which name it retained until it was changed to Amazon.

Some of the natives called the river *Amassona*, meaning " boat destroyer," for during certain seasons it is very dangerous in many places. The various tribes along the river had different names for their sectors of it, but it is possible that the name *Amazon* was derived from *Amassona*, and not, as generally thought, from Herodotus' alleged female warriors.

sea level), the expedition struck out in a westerly direction, and by way of Arequipa reached the Pacific coast. The dreaded Atacama desert having been crossed successfully, Valdivia pushed on towards the south for several hundred miles. Here and there, the natives offered stubborn resistance, but Spanish arms and courage prevailed. On the 12th of February, 1541, the city of Santiago was founded, and the newly conquered land was named *Nueva Estremadura.**

A certain quantity of gold and silver having been found, Indian captives were forced to work in mines, but at the same time Valdivia did not neglect the development of the fertile land. Seeds of wheat, different fruit trees, and even of flowers, were successfully planted, and the chickens, pigs and horses brought by the expedition, thrived wonderfully in their new surroundings.

Whilst busy settling Chile, Valdivia sent a small body of men to make a report in Lima. After untold hardships and much fighting against Indians, this party almost miraculously succeeded in reaching its destination. From Lima, a ship and seventy horses were immediately dispatched, and in due time arrived at Valparaiso, then only a tiny fortified settlement.

Whilst exploring regions towards the south, in an effort to reach the Straits of Magellan, the Spaniards ran into serious trouble when they clashed with the terrible Moluches† whom they named *Aucas*, this appellation being synonymous with " rebels ", " savages " or " bandits ". The Araucanians, as these warlike Indians later became known, were South America's greatest and fiercest fighters, and successfully resisted white men's advances into their territory for three and a half centuries.

About twelve years after his first expedition into Chile, Valdivia was captured during an Indian uprising. Both his arms were cut off with sharp sea shells, and eaten in his presence, death releasing him from torture three days later.‡

* The country's new name, Chile, is of uncertain origin. Some say it is an old Indian word for " snow ", others believe it to be the name of a tribe, and some think it expresses the call of a certain bird.

† Molu : war ; ches : men.

‡ About a year later, Ercilla, the great Spanish soldier-poet, who had only recently been in England with Philip II, arrived in Chile to help in the attempt to crush the Araucanians. Later in life, when back in Spain, the widely travelled Ercilla wrote his immortal poem, *La Araucana ;* a partly true history, though embellished with romantic episodes. Published in three parts in 1569, 1578, and 1590, it was highly praised by Cervantes (1547-1616) and later by Voltaire (1694-1778).

CORICANCHA

AT the time of the conquest, Cuzco is estimated to have had a population of between two and three hundred thousand inhabitants. Palaces, temples, and many of the houses were solidly built of stone, hewn in different irregular shapes, and ingeniously fitted together with the use of mortar. Most of the streets were narrow, but the squares were spacious, and well-kept. The fortress, called Sacsahuaman, situated on a high hill overlooking the city, excited the admiration of the Spaniards especially. Its walls consisted of gigantic blocks of stone, and were arranged in three tiers, forming ramparts and terraces. At the summit of the cyclopean fort, were two high towers from which a magnificent view of the surrounding country could be obtained.

The exteriors of even the finest palaces and temples in Peru were unattractive to the eye. The solid stone walls, though constructed with great precision and admirable skill, gave such buildings a somewhat cold and austere aspect. The thatched roofs were supported by wooden frameworks, and many of the doors with their inclined jambs had a touch of old Egypt about them. A stream divided the town into two parts ; the higher, and the lower. The former was under the protection of the *Inca*, and in it lived the poorer section of the community, whereas the latter was presided over by his wife, the *Coya*, and there resided the nobility and dignitaries of State and Church. In the lower city were to be found most of the principal buildings, temples and palaces, and therefore that part of Cuzco had a more pleasing aspect than the other which consisted of an agglomeration of mud-built huts. It seems strange that the *Inca* should have chosen to live in the poor part of the city, separated from the nobility and other dignitaries, though by doing so he avoided seeing too much of irksome hangers-on to the Court ; a plague not uncommon in our modern times. Not unlike Hindoos, natives from different parts of the *Inca* empire, and even inhabitants of the various quarters of Cuzco, wore distinctive head dresses, made of cloth dyed in variegated colours.

Near the Temple of the Sun and its several annexes—dedicated to the moon, the stars, thunder and the rainbow—were several minor palaces, as well as a number of residences to house priests and some three thousand attendants. Yupanqui, a former *Inca*, who had a special taste for animals, had ordered menageries to be built in different parts of the capital. In one, an aviary contained birds of every species, and in others were kept reptiles and many wild beasts, some of which were brought from remote parts of the empire. One building near the fortress served as a kind of museum, and among the weird things displayed there was a gruesome collection of stuffed and painted skins of Indians who had once revolted against an *Inca*. These stuffed skins, about a hundred in number, were suspended from the ceiling, and made to represent dancers and musicians holding drums and flutes. Before the Spaniards arrived, a kind of garden, at the disposal of the Virgins of the Sun, had been adorned with plants, flowers, even trees, snakes, lizards, butterflies, birds and wild beasts made in gold, some studded with precious stones of various colours. This garden was known as *Coricancha*: Garden of Gold. In the outskirts of the city, dwellers of humble abodes had small plantations of maize, beans, sweet potatoes and quinoa.

On the site occupied by the Temple of the Sun and its dependencies, four Dominican monks who were among the ecclesiastics who accompanied the Spanish expedition, founded the convent of Santo Domingo. Some of the walls of the original edifice were included in the new construction. A Father Olivera was made the first Bishop of Cuzco, soon to be succeeded by Valverde. By a bull of Paul III the thatched building which formerly had been a heathen temple, was elevated to the rank of episcopal church.* Valverde only enjoyed his bishopric for some three years, being killed by Indians whilst on tour in one of the provinces.

* About forty years after Pizarro's entry into Cuzco, Viceroy Toledo pulled down the first church used by the *conquistadores*, and ordered a cathedral to be built. It took eighty-two years to complete this very indifferent construction which stands to this day. Owing to graft it cost nearly £3,000,000. Impatient people, including the King of Spain—who followed events in Peru with great interest—used to ask if this cathedral was to be built of solid gold and silver.

CORICANCHA

A SHORT QUICHUA VOCABULARY.

God	Pachacamac	head	uma
World, universe	Pacha	potato	papa
Giver of life,	} Camac	sweet potato	camote
Animator		pea nut	inchic
devil	cupay	bird	pichi
man	runa	vulture	cuntur
woman	huarmi	turtle dove	urpi
child, baby	huahua	river	mayu
father	tayta	sea, lake	cocha
mother	mama	forest	satcha
sun	churi	flower	sisac
moon	quilla	house	huasi
star	coyllur	meat	aycha
day	punchao	tobacco	sayri
night	tuta	maize	sara
rain	paray	white	yura
thunder	illapa	black	yana
water	unu	red	puca
fire	nina	yellow	keellu
cold	chiri	blue	ancas
hot	rupay	green	komer

one	huc	seven	cchanchis
two	iscay	eight	puzac
three	quisma	nine	isccon
four	tahua	ten	chunca
five	pichcca	eleven	chunca-huc
six	zocta	twelve	chunca-iscay

and so on as far as twenty, the ten being placed before the unity.

Twenty is " twice ten " :	iscay-chunca
twenty-one	iscay-chunca-huc
twenty-two	iscay-chunca-iscay
	and so on.
thirty	quisma-chunca (three times ten)
thirty-one	quisma-chunca-huc
	and so on.
forty	tahua-chunca
a hundred	pachac
a thousand	huaranca
ten thousand	chunca-huaranca
a hundred thousand	pachac-huaranca
a million	chunca-pachac-huaranca

Anything beyond a million : panta china (innumerable sum).

INDEX

217

INDEX

INDEX

INDEX